The Year's Best Sports Writing 2026

The Year's Best Sports Writing 2026

Edited and with an introduction by
Mirin Fader

TRIUMPH
BOOKS

Library of Congress Cataloging-in-Publication Data available upon request

This book is available in quantity at special discounts for your group or organization. For further information, contact:

Triumph Books LLC
814 North Franklin Street
Chicago, Illinois 60610
(312) 337-0747
www.triumphbooks.com

Printed in U.S.A.

ISBN: 978-1-63727-816-1

Design by Sue Knopf
Page production by Patricia Frey

Contents

Introduction

"I can't believe it." My sports writing friends and I kept exchanging the same text messages to each other, over and over again.

I can't believe it.

I can't believe it.

The Washington Post had announced it was getting rid of its sports section earlier this year.

Then I started getting text messages from family members—people who don't necessarily follow sports. Even they were concerned. This was starting to feel like a cultural moment; one that you remember where you were when the news broke. And then, it became a funeral. A public mourning.

Journalist Ashley Parker, a stellar former *Post* reporter, memorialized the loss in her column for *The Atlantic*, aptly titled, "The Murder of *The Washington Post*": "The power of the *Post* has always been its pulsing humanity, the zippy teamwork that has allowed each individual to produce something so much greater than they could have achieved on their own."

Its pulsing humanity. It felt like this, the live, human heartbeat of sports reporting—especially with the rise of AI and ChatGPT and Google Gemini—felt like it was being lost. The real reason I got into sports writing was to cover the human stories behind the box scores. And now those human stories seemed harder and harder to find.

Seeing the *Post* sports section disappear felt surreal, but it was the same kind of feeling I had felt since the pandemic—that many of our oldest institutions were falling away, one by one.

And all of this was on the heels of *The New York Times*' decision the previous fall that it, *too*, was repositioning its sports section.

I couldn't believe that either. I sent those same text messages then. Where else was I going to find a heartwarming story on MIT basketball? Or an incredible investigation into the wrongdoings of an NFL franchise? Something deeply important was being lost—and my fellow journalists and I were scrambling to figure out how we could do something—*anything*—to save our profession.

Out of all the unraveling threads of the fabric of America that we have witnessed over the last decade—the rise of autocracy, the crises of homelessness and opioids, the violence against Black and Brown people—what in the world did sports writing do to deserve such a fate? Why should this *too* unravel?

I promise I'm getting somewhere with this—somewhere more hopeful. I promise you're reading this book for a reason.

Again, the crumbling: We've seen our sports writing industry shrink and contort itself to fit the times; to adapt, to grow, to evolve, just as other genres of journalism have. *Twitter! (X!) Video! Back to long form! Now only short form! Essays on TV! Podcasts! Too many podcasts! Back to video!* And so on and so on and so on. We tell our younger students in journalism schools to keep going. To persevere, like the athletes we cover. I remember telling myself the same mantras, when I graduated college in 2013. Even back *then*, my sports writing heroes told me the industry was looking bleak, and advised me to look elsewhere.

I'm so glad I didn't. I'm so glad I kept going. Somehow, we kept going. We kept writing. We kept showing up to games, to locker rooms, to press boxes. We unionized, we organized. We fought. We kept saying: Human stories are sports stories. Sports stories are human stories. Sports is a microcosm for society. Read us. Don't forget us.

But seeing two of our oldest, most esteemed outlets, in the *Post* and the *Times*, basically say sports writing isn't valuable anymore was a gut-punch that felt too visceral to me to bear.

And we have shouldered a lot of grief over the years. Layoffs. Complete shuttering of sections. Some of our favorite writers discarded after decades of fantastic work, as if age meant they were somehow less poised and not more.

In my own private ways to keep going, I always used humor. I'd joke that sports writing felt like *The Hunger Games* movie franchise. I'd pull out my other favorite joke (coping mechanism): as a long form sports writer, I'm basically paddling a canoe, and sometimes there are more turbulent waters, and less turbulent waters, but I'm still gripping the paddle—white knuckled—to be ready for anything.

But we shouldn't have to live like this. Write like this. Sports writing matters more than ever, and shuttering the *Post,* the *Times,* and any other sports section across dozens of local papers in the country is shortsighted—and wrong. Sports writing has never been more valuable than it is today. Athletes are using their power in ways they never have before. Women have been empowered in ways they never have before. And as we all try to navigate these uncertain times, both at home and watching wars abroad on our screens, I know this to be true: sports is a microcosm of society, a kaleidoscope of who we are in all of our complexities. We are both fractured and unified; despairing and hopeful. Fearless and terrified. Welcoming and isolated. If you want to understand the full human experience—the grit, the joy, the sadness, the frustration and excitement in all of us, sports writing is that place. In a world that is telling us that this writing isn't as important as other writing, we know better.

When we read great sports writing, we feel more resilient. More inspired. More admiring of the people we watch. We are less judgmental, less likely to say horrific things online, because we know the athletes wearing those jerseys are just simply...people.

Writing these stories isn't easy. We've lost many great writers along the way. It is not possible for everyone to keep going. Many have kept going for hardly any money. Hardly any opportunity. Exposure doesn't pay grocery bills.

I wanted this edition of The Year's Best Sports Writing to be a love letter to sports writing. I want people to fall back in love with sports writing. I want reading this to feel like we used to feel when our favorite sports writer put out a piece, and everyone would comment on Twitter, "Appointment reading." Or "Blind retweet."

Trust that the pages in this book will comfort you, transport you to other worlds, and remind you why you subscribed to *Sports Illustrated* as a child; remind you of the excitement of tacking a poster from *SLAM* magazine on your bedroom wall. I want this book to remind you of the thrill of the ESPN cover story or when a sports story makes A1 of the local paper. This is for the copy writers, the editors, the people who stayed up until 2:00 AM to make sure the sports intern's copy spelled everyone's name right. This is for the sports writers who collect their press passes as badges of honor—and of joy.

Each pass holds a memory. A friend. A story. We are so lucky to do this. We are so lucky to be read. Especially in a time where access to athletes to write these critical stories is diminished. Some professional sports team PR staffs or sports information directors at universities would have you believe that all you want are canned quotes from a press conference. But we know that isn't true. We want the little gems of details found in sports stories. An athlete's favorite cereal. A quote from the athlete's mother. An anecdote of when someone was cut from a team. The enemies a player made up in his mind—imagined or real—that motivated him to keep pushing, keep going.

Because that's what all of this is really about: continuing to write, continuing to show people that our work matters. And our work will continue to matter. Sports fans and non-sports fans alike need the moments behind the scenes—the failures that we don't see from curated Instagram posts or sponsored ads for sports drinks. We need the moments when an athlete almost quit, when they shined a flashlight inside themselves and said when no one was watching: "Who am I? Am I good enough? Do I have it in me?"

We need the moments a team lost its identity and found a new one. Questioned itself on the road, on a brutal back-to-back. We need the moments when a captain called a team meeting and vowed to turn things around. That can only come from the beat reporter who travels with them, game after game, showing up at the bus, the loading dock, asking question after question. Staying later. Flying their own redeyes to get back to their own children, while filling out a story after the game, long after all their readers have gone to sleep, because they knows these nuggets are important. And while those in power like to think anyone can write these stories, they are wrong. There is something about writing a sports story at 3:00 AM in an airport Dunkin' Donuts that just hits different.

We cannot rely on AI to know how to walk up to a player in a locker room and ask if you can ask a couple of questions. We aren't just asking about a final play, a fantastic pass; we're asking about how you felt being traded, how your family coped with the move while juggling a new baby and having just finished your home at your last place. We're asking about what music you listen to and why it brings you joy. We're asking about the last time you really had fun with a team.

Sports writers, sports readers, sports lovers: I see you.

I don't care what anyone says; this kind of writing will never go out of style. Somehow, after every change, after every devastating round of layoffs, the word keeps going. It shows up in different forms, yes, with many multimedia forms around it, but it does all stem from telling a story. Sharing a story. And like oral traditions having survived for decades, I believe sports storytelling will too.

We look for ourselves in movies and books and podcasts. We want to see how we can relate to the characters on screen. It is the same with the athletes we write about. We shouldn't really think we can relate to millionaires who are on TV, who can't go outside without people flocking to them for their autograph. But we relate to them because we understand what failure is. What disappointment is. What joy is. What hard work and discipline is.

And we find those things in sports writing. Their stories are our stories.

I speak to a lot of university journalism classes, filled with students full of enthusiasm. They are working on their first features, and they have so many questions. *How do you get someone to open up about their lives? How do you get them to feel safe to speak about their lives? How do you organize your story? How do you ask someone if they want to talk to you?*

Their hope gives me hope. I don't know the answers. I don't know how we keep going. Only that we must. I won't let go of my paddle, and I hope you won't either.

The stories in this book remind me why holding on is necessary. These stories are sports writing at its finest. These stories are both comforting and devastating, joyful and painful, and optimistic and heartbreaking. They make me feel as if I'm on a quest with the athlete, and by the end, I'm hungry to know what happens. These stories remind us why we need community—and why we must resist isolation. They remind us that at our core, we are motivated by different things. Winning? Power? Fame? Money? Family? What is it that burns in someone? That is what the sports writer tries to find out. That is what the sports writer brings: the inner life to the outer world.

Good sports writing reminds us of the universal; the binding force we need when tribalism has taken over our politics and our streets. It reminds us that there are things to look forward to. Games to watch. People to root for.

Read these stories. I guarantee they will renew your spirit.

The Year's Best Sports Writing 2026

Victor Wembanyama Is Preaching Ethical Basketball. There's a Larger Truth to It All

MARCUS THOMPSON II

FROM *The Athletic* • DECEMBER 25, 2025

Victor Wembanyama, it seemed, issued a decree. One veiled in gratitude and sealed with sarcasm.

"I'm just glad to be part of something that's growing to be so beautiful," he said.

"Pure and ethical basketball."

This rang as from a herald, with the panache of a proposed law. Especially because it came after a win over the Oklahoma City Thunder—the NBA's new face of manipulation, given their position as dominant defending champs—Wembanyama seemed to revel in a sweet victory of a hero over a villain. As if the future face of basketball threw down a challenge to the next generation of superstars.

Cut the shenanigans.

See, the San Antonio Spurs' big man didn't invent the term. Ethical basketball as a talking point was born in an ideological battle waged online for years now. Conceived by the flopping era and the NBA's freedom of movement edict. What was once niche—Reggie Miller extending his leg on 3-pointers, and Michael Jordan getting phantom whistles—seemed to grow into an epidemic of players falling like touch fouls were sniper fire. So the concept of ethical basketball praised players such as Steph Curry and Kevin Durant for not intentionally feasting at the free-throw line. And, simultaneously, it chided players such as James Harden and Joel Embiid for unabashedly manipulating the rules as a steady diet.

Ethical basketball is an ode to a straight-up version of the game most people grew up playing. When it wasn't about milking loopholes. Or banking on coercion. Or hoping for help from ambiguous rules. It's shooting to make instead of aiming to draw a foul. It's playing defense instead of hoping for a pass-and-crash charge. It's finding honor in not needing any of that.

For some, finding an edge is part of the game and its own version of genius. Even Curry acknowledged the skill of drawing fouls. He sees it with Jimmy Butler now. He played with Corey Maggette as a rookie. Curry's career is bookended by professional foul-drawers.

The rip-through. The subtle leg kick. The ability to exaggerate contact on the fly. The expertise at manipulating leverage, getting defenders off balance and punishing them for being out of position. It's as meticulous and crafty as dribbling through traffic. The way Harden negotiated the NBA's gather-step rules could be considered artistic or unbecoming.

It sounded as if Wemby planted his flag on the side of the latter. As if he chose the era when footwork didn't require expertise at Twister because traveling was an easy call. As if he grew up in France playing the no-blood-no-foul rules of blacktop, and calling a charge provoked a flagrant reaction.

Curry, fresh off a weight-lifting session after a home win against the Phoenix Suns, took a moment to process the idea of Wembanyama potentially leading the new era into a basketball purity vow. Then he gave a succinct reaction: "I love it."

Wembanyama, when asked to explain further ahead of last week's NBA Cup final, clarified his meaning.

"In modern basketball," he said, "we see a lot of brands of basketball that don't offer much variety in the dangers they pose to the opponents. Lots of isolation ball and, sometimes, kind of forced basketball. And we try to propose a brand of basketball that can be described as more old-school sometimes—the Spurs way as well. So it's tactically more correct basketball, in my opinion."

Admittedly, his explanation didn't scream revolutionary. His follow-up sounded much more like a mid-major coach throwing shade at AAU hoops than a beret-ed activist of ethical basketball.

But if he didn't mean to pick a side, he should have. It's the one he's already on.

Wembanyama, through Sunday, has averaged 5.0 free throws per game for his career. That ranks 35th among all players from the start of the 2023–24 season until now—just six spots ahead of Curry.

Only eight players have averaged seven or more free throws in that span: Giannis Antetokounmpo, Embiid, Luka Dončić, Shai Gilgeous-Alexander, Paolo Banchero, Zion Williamson, Butler and Trae Young.

But the problem isn't players getting free throws. Throughout the history of the NBA, getting to the free-throw line has been a central part of being a great scorer.

Of the top 30 scorers in NBA history, by total points, only two average at least four shots for every free throw: Curry (4.13) and Alex English (4.09). Only six others average at least three shots per free throw: Ray Allen (3.9), John Havlicek (3.6), Vince Carter (3.5), Kevin Garnett (3.4), Kareem Abdul-Jabbar (3.0) and Elvin Hayes (3.0).

Most of the league's best scorers fall somewhere near 2.5 shots per free throw. The best scorers will get to the free-throw line. That's basketball.

The issue is bigger than drawing fouls. It's the aesthetic. It's the popularization of the underhandedness. Some of the largest men in the world, and some of the best athletes, snapping their heads back after the slightest graze to the chin, as if they routinely skip neck day. It's the same player being allowed to push off but getting the whistle when he's pushed. It's the flailing and flopping—and the constant complaining when neither yields returns—while some real contact gets deemed as marginal. It's this great league having games morph into legal proceedings, with officials approaching the scorer's table like a lawyer approaches the bench.

Even Los Angeles Lakers coach JJ Redick voiced his concerns about the inconsistency of officiating. And free throws to the Lakers are like potatoes to Idaho.

Judging by the number of coaches losing it lately, this reeks of something bigger. Perhaps even something coming to a head. Something without a doubt connected to watchability. It certainly doesn't help to have the gambling connection photobombing the scene either.

Minnesota Timberwolves coach Chris Finch's crash out against the Thunder last week brought to light his comments about OKC from earlier this year.

It's discussed behind the scenes, more as a reality to deal with than a complaint. Oklahoma City's suffocating defense is athletic, long, physical and aggressive. It seems to operate with the understanding that the refs can't call every foul. They don't intentionally foul as much as they simply don't mind fouling. That's the nature of swarms.

Finch, like an increasing number of non–Oklahoma City fans, finds it unpleasantly ironic for a squad with that defensive bent to also feature one of the NBA leaders in free-throw attempts.

To be clear, the criticism aimed at OKC is just a natural part of its dominance. The Thunder don't win because of the margins, even if they play them well. They win because of excellence. They play with championship confidence, which has produced another level that makes them seem invincible. Thus, they've become prime targets. It happens to all great teams.

But it also points to a larger truth about ethical basketball. It's required to win big.

People often refer to basketball gods and playing the right way. It purports this idea that the karma of basketball catches up with the people who hustle their way through. The truth: Winning at the championship level is so hard; gimmicks aren't enough. Living by those schemes only works to a certain point.

When the game's on the line, when the stakes reach higher levels, victory demands purity. The best in the world won't be thwarted by tricks. Shots must be made. Fouls must be earned. Defense must be stingy. Pressure must be handled. Teams must be worthy.

Wembanyama is just shy of 22 years old, but remember what he went through last summer in the Paris Olympics. What he witnessed and experienced. Ethical basketball is what beat him in the gold-medal game, what added fuel to his fire to be the best in the world.

That's what Wemby stands on, even if he won't say it blatantly. Yet.

MARCUS THOMPSON II is a lead columnist at The Athletic. He is a prominent voice in the Bay Area sports scene after 18 years with Bay Area News Group, including 10 seasons covering the Golden State Warriors and four as a columnist. Marcus is also the author of the bestselling biography *Golden: The Miraculous Rise of Steph Curry*.

Why the Spirit of WWE Legend Eddie Guerrero Lives On

ROBERTO JOSÉ ANDRADE FRANCO

FROM ESPN • NOVEMBER 12, 2025

When he was five years old, legendary wrestler Eddie Guerrero would climb the ropes of a ring his father had built in their backyard in El Paso, Texas. He would watch his older brothers fighting on the mat. The slaps across the chest, the staggering as if they were hurt, the echoes of their bodies getting slammed.

"You're doing it wrong," his father Gory would yell out. Eddie was captivated. Even before he knew what he wanted, he wanted to be in the ring. He wanted to live the life his brothers were living. He wanted Gory yelling out at him. He wanted to be a wrestler.

"We lived on Huerta Street," his sister Maria says. She takes a sip of coffee inside a restaurant a 10-minute drive north of the U.S.-Mexico border. As she tells me about her family's past, she searches inside a manila folder. Depending on what memory she pulls from her mind or from the folder, her expression changes between smiling eyes and a straight face.

She's the last of the Guerreros in the city synonymous with their name, talking of where they all once lived. That single-story brick house in the Buena Vista neighborhood was a God-fearing home. It was three blocks from the border separating El Paso,

Texas, and Juárez, Mexico, and a five-minute drive from the El Paso County Coliseum where the family spent most of their time. "We came to El Paso in 1962," Maria explains. Her father Gory, the patriarch of her legendary family, started wrestling at 16. When the fighting part of his career declined with age, he brought his family here. "My father liked that it was both Mexican and American," she says.

Wrestling had been a staple of El Paso entertainment since the 1920s. Those shows with masked men would eventually birth the Mexican style of wrestling called *lucha libre*. Then a growing city, El Paso relied on the so-called five C's—copper, cotton, cattle, climate and clothing—to power its economy. Gory had always focused on the business side of wrestling. Monday night shows at the county coliseum, other nights in surrounding areas that would have them. From making sure wrestlers had whatever they needed—like sports tape to hide razor blades affixed to their wrists—to making popcorn for concessions, everyone in the Guerrero family had a job. Never far from being inside the ring, Gory also passed what he knew to his sons. "We had a wrestling ring in the backyard," Maria says. "That's where my father trained my brothers."

The choreographed violence inside the ring is a delicate mix. When a single inch makes all the difference, every step and hold must be as close to perfect as possible. Too much distance between fiction and reality and it's not believable. "This is Chavo Sr. and Mando," Maria says of a black-and-white photo from some time in the 1960s. Her younger brothers are in the backyard, practicing leg locks while her father watches and points.

They were the first two Guerrero boys. After them came Hector, Eddie, and even Gory's grandson, Chavo Jr. All of them learned to wrestle inside that ring. Another colorless photo and Maria points to its top right corner. "This is Eddie as a baby," she says. It's a family photo with Gory, his wife, Herlinda—who knew the business as well as anyone since her three brothers wrestled in Mexico—and their four sons and two daughters. Gory is carrying

Eddie. He was by far his youngest child, so it looks more like a grandfather holding his grandson.

"My aunts in Mexico thought he was mine, and that my family was covering it up," Maria laughs as she remembers the brother nearly 21 years younger than her. Those memories brighten her eyes. She can still see him as a young boy—Ewis, they called him—playing inside the ring in the backyard of their home.

Her voice fills with pride when talking of how Eddie carried the Guerrero name as high as it could go and how people still remember him though he has been gone for 20 years this month. "He would have been 58 right now," Maria says of Eddie. On the morning of a show in Minneapolis, Eddie died of a heart attack while brushing his teeth in a hotel bathroom. "He was about to retire," Maria continues.

A moment of quiet as we sit across from each other with pieces of the past in front of us. "He's still very present," Maria says. A sip of coffee and another search. She then slides Eddie's funeral program halfway across the table.

"THAT'S GORY'S SON," my grandmother told me the first time I saw Eddie.

I was around 7, the age when a stranger's presence can bury itself into a malleable mind. Until then, I didn't know who Eddie was. But I knew Gory because during my summers spent with my grandmother in Juárez, she'd tell me stories about him.

She'd talk about lucha libre, explaining how its characters could be good or bad, the babyfaces or heels. That some of the masked men carried on the names of those long before them. How Gory helped popularize lucha libre across Mexico as its most famous non-masked wrestler. That, when she was a little girl, he was the tag team partner of El Santo, one of the most famous grapplers of them all. She told me Gory was so great as a heel he needed a police escort to protect him from fans who wanted to hurt him.

Her love of wrestling made her scream obscenities at the heels inside Gimnasio Municipal Josué Neri Santos. The gym with faulty plumbing and bad lighting was in downtown Juárez, a half mile south of the border. Years later, Konnan, Eddie's former tag team partner, remembers the gym also lacked security. "I turned heel, against Eddie of all people, and the fans were super pissed," he says. "They threw everything from dirty diapers to battery acid at me," he adds. "It was just a very rabid fan base, which is what you want."

Inside that gym is where I spent a lot of my time during the summers, when my parents were working an eight-hour drive north in Colorado. I still remember how my mother cried the first time we moved there. She tried to console us, but especially herself, by telling us to enjoy the state's natural beauty. Green and cold, it was the opposite of the desert we came from.

From the moment I saw him, I knew Eddie was different. Some of the other wrestlers were older with receding hairlines that couldn't hide the scars on their foreheads from having been sliced by razor blades. They carried the hurt from the countless times they got body-slammed. They looked unbalanced whenever they limped to the ring's top rope. Unlike them, Eddie's body and skin weren't scarred. At 19 years old, he moved with the confidence of youth. Athletic and acrobatic, whenever he climbed to the top rope, he'd stand there gracefully for everyone to see.

When he jumped and his long black hair flowed in the air, it looked as if Eddie could fly. It also looked like what evolved into the Frog Splash. That was Eddie's signature move where he'd jump from the top rope, tuck his knees to his chest, then uncoil as he landed on an opponent.

With that move he would become the Eddie Guerrero the wrestling world would remember. The wrestler who once gave The Rock among the best matches he has ever had. The one who John Cena called a genius.

Every time he'd land the move that would later be known as the Frog Splash, I'd jump out of my seat, cheering along with everyone else.

"He visits me three, four times a year," Sherilyn Guerrero says about the dreams she has of her father. She is Eddie's middle daughter. Just 10 years old when she last saw him walking into Phoenix Sky Harbor International Airport.

Sherilyn liked to playfully wrestle with Eddie. They'd wrestle in their living room and sometimes in the ring before his matches. He'd tell her stories of his own father, who died before she was born, and the family they came from. Wrestling felt natural to her, so innate that Sherilyn is now training to be a wrestler, too.

"They've never been sad," she says of her dreams.

Family members have told her they've also dreamed of Eddie. Sometimes they wake up confused, trying to understand why they can't see his face. But with Sherilyn, each of those dreams feels like a blessing. If they come during difficult times, she is convinced it's him telling her everything will be all right. "He was a great father," Sherilyn says.

Some kids called in sick to school for legit reasons. Sherilyn's sick days were often excuses to travel with dad. Most kids spent spring break at home, but Sherilyn and her older sister, Shaul, along with their mother, Vickie, spent that time at WrestleMania. "Your dad is so cool," classmates would tell her when she returned.

A genuine connection between a wrestler and fans is one thing the business can't script, and Eddie had it. Her father could make the crowd love or hate him, sometimes in the middle of matches as he switched between babyface and heel. The "Latino Heat" character he created from the people and places he came from was impossible to ignore. He'd yell "Viva La Raza!" as a catchphrase, speaking in Chicano slang, and drive lowriders up to the ring. Bordering on slapstick comedy, he was even funny in how he'd frame opponents when the referee wasn't looking.

It felt good to hear classmates talk of her father, but that also made Sherilyn shy and guarded. She wondered if people wanted to be her friend only because she was Eddie's daughter. To this day, when she meets someone around Houston, where she lives, she doesn't mention his name. But Eddie lives an immortal existence online, so they eventually find out.

"Every day someone's sending me something on my dad," Sherilyn says. Something as simple as tagging her social media with a clip of Eddie's wrestling highlights. Other times it's messages from those who've made art inspired by him.

"His spirit is so alive," Sherilyn says. She admits that everything has made it difficult to process that he's gone. He was home for just a couple of days each week, so part of Sherilyn feels as if her father has still been on the road. That eventually he'll call with the time his flight arrives at the airport. While she waits, a part of Sherilyn has yet to fully mourn.

"What happens the day I do?" she asks herself, wondering how she'll feel when that moment comes. It has been difficult to get there when she sees him every day, even if it's the fictional part of who he was. That's why those three or four dreams a year feel like a blessing. In those dreams where the two of them play, she's with a side of Eddie most didn't know. She tells me about those dreams, and I feel guilty for asking if she can tell me more. Like I've opened a door to a visiting room where I don't belong. But rather than leave, I stand there and watch with that familiar feeling of being a stranger.

THE FIRST DREAM I ever chased was being a wrestler. I was 7 and spending the summer in Juárez designing a mask and a matching cape. I'm certain I also made up a name. I don't remember it so it must have been bad.

What I do remember is how I'd slap myself across the chest, throw myself against a wall, fighting someone who wasn't there. I'd jump on beds in my grandmother's home, pretending I was flying off the top rope, stopping only after breaking one of them. I was trying to replicate the moves I saw during the Thursday and Sunday shows I attended. I'd try to memorize what I saw in the ring, then a day or two after, I'd pick fights with uncles just to have someone to practice against.

They were much older and stronger, but they'd go along with my game until they got annoyed and the play wrestling turned real. Once I'd get body-slammed and struggled to breathe, it was time to leave them alone.

Years later, I'd pursue other dreams, each of them an empty search. But long before then, I imagined myself as a wrestler in Juárez, and the reason was Eddie. I wanted to wear a mask and cape and be anyone who didn't have to feel the summer end. I didn't want to return to feeling like a stranger; the boy who spoke with an accent in that green and cold of Colorado.

THERE'S A TRAILER parked on the plot of land Mando Guerrero owns. Since it's the middle of July and that land is in a small Texas town between San Antonio and the Gulf of Mexico, it feels like breathing inside a sauna.

"It's not set up," Mando says of the pieces of metal resting atop the trailer. "It's our ring."

He can't remember the last time it was fully built, so he has been thinking of assembling it. But at 75 years old it's not as easy as it once was for Eddie's oldest living brother. Not when he feels the toll of a physical life, first as a wrestler around the world, then as a stuntman and coordinator in Hollywood. It's hard enough to walk with prosthetic knees without having to carry heavy pieces of metal.

"I want to see what's left," Mando says, curious about what remains of the ring that was once in their backyard and traveled wherever they promoted a show. "We were like a circus," he remembers. "We would come in, set it up, and break it down," he says. "That's what we were, a circus. And the 'Wrestling Guerreros' was our name.

Family was the most important thing, so Gory took them on the road with him. He'd tell his children everything was all right when they watched him bleed. Other times he'd tell them to sit in the stands but never mention they were his children, worried they'd be hurt by those who refused to distinguish what's real from what's staged.

"It has sentimental value, but there's really nothing I can do with it," Mando says of the ring. It's where all the Guerreros learned to wrestle and its canvas—parts of which he's sure rats have eaten away—is stained with the blood and sweat of his father and brothers.

Mando has a stepdaughter who lives in Minneapolis. He loves her but laments not having children of his own. Maybe they'd be here to help rebuild the ring. Maybe they'd be here to learn all the things he got from his father.

"We represent something that was a phenomenon in the game of professional wrestling," Mando says with a prideful tone. He's protective of the family name especially when talking of his baby brother. He isn't alone. Some who knew Eddie the best would rather let what remains of the family legacy speak for itself.

"Eddie was a natural," Mando says of his brother, who was inducted into the WWE Hall of Fame in 2006. He explains how Eddie took everything he learned from his father and three older brothers, mixed it with the high-flying acrobatics of Mexican lucha libre as well as the wrestling style north of the border that relied on storylines and brute strength, and from that he created something of his own. In that way, Eddie benefitted from being the youngest of them all, but Mando says that also had its negatives. Because when family saw Eddie struggling with painkillers and alcohol, the baby of the family refused to even listen when they tried to help.

"He just wanted to be left alone," Mando says of Eddie during those years when he navigated his own personal desert. That all came after a nearly fatal car crash during the early hours of New Year's Day, 1999. Driving impaired, the crash left Eddie with a fractured collarbone, broken hip socket, lacerated liver, a shredded calf and compressed discs in his spine. Painkillers and alcohol eased the hurt. Add to that the pain that came inside the ring—the broken fingers and toes, blown-out knees, and backs that never recover once they go bad—and Eddie was soon taking any pill he could get along with drinking more.

"Do you remember the last time you spoke with Eddie?" I ask. Mando makes a deep sigh and thinks. Though they sometimes spoke on the phone, he struggles to remember the last time he saw him. Eddie was on television so often, it mixes with the moments of seeing him in person. "I don't recall," he says.

On Nov. 13, 2005, the phone rang and my mother answered. "Roberto," she said after the short call. "Your grandmother said Eddie Guerrero's dead." That memory is clear. And likely because I was dealing with my own struggles, I don't remember feeling much.

On the day Eddie died, I was a 25-year-old who had barely graduated high school and was bouncing around between a series of construction jobs. I slept on a broken futon with a thin mattress that left my back sore. Whatever dreams I had then felt as broken as where I slept.

Back living with my parents, I was depressed and ashamed from feeling like I'd wasted the opportunities they'd struggled to give me. I was lost, living between Phoenix, Tucson and El Paso. And on each of those long, quiet drives through the lonesome deserts connecting those cities, I wondered why I was in the middle of losing an entire decade of my life, searching for what I couldn't find.

I stopped watching wrestling long before Eddie died. But in between the time I first saw him and when he died, I kept an eye on him as he won tag team, European, United States, Intercontinental and WWE championships. On the occasions I'd see him on television it always felt like reconnecting with an old friend even if he looked different. With about 220 pounds of muscle on his 5-foot-8 frame, Eddie had a larger presence than he ever had in Juárez. Not just physically but also as a character since his confidence and charisma had also grown. But he was still the same Eddie who made me feel that warm sense of pride whenever he got introduced as being from home.

"I was very proud of Eddie, too," Hector Rincon would tell me years later. Best friends since they were teenagers, their wrestling photos are next to each other in the 1985 Thomas Jefferson High School yearbook. Fighting as Hurricane Hector, Rincon also pursued dreams of professional wrestling until the time away from his family became too much. In some ways, he lived his dreams through Eddie. When Eddie won the WWE Championship in February 2004, Eddie called Rincon from the locker room and they cried together. "Nov. 13 is a bittersweet day," Rincon says. "He passed on the same day as my daughter's birthday."

I almost feel ashamed to admit it, but there was no overwhelming sadness when I heard Eddie died. There was no sense of disbelief, no contemplation of my own mortality. No proper understanding that Eddie was one of the few to make it out of here, then, at his peak, he was gone. It was as if he had climbed to the top rope, jumped and flew away before I could fully understand why he meant so much to me.

All of that took years to find.

"I FELT EVERYTHING was OK," Dean Malenko says. His gruff voice can't hide the pain when talking of how unexpected Eddie's death felt. They were close friends even if they wrestled as bitter rivals inside the ring dozens of times.

Practically inseparable since they met in 1993 while wrestling in Japan, they had an instant connection as the youngest sons of heels. Dean's father was Boris Malenko. He played the role of Soviet agent so well that Malenko's friends were afraid to visit their home. Malenko and Eddie also bonded over their lifelong love of professional wrestling, both knowing from an early age that it would be the dream they'd pursue.

Across different promotions—ECW, WCW and WWE, among them—their careers grew together. They were travel partners navigating the unseen world of their profession. "The easiest part of our business is the wrestling," Malenko says. "The difficult parts are the politics born out of something that relies on emotion. But more than that, it's the loneliness of being on the road and how quickly it can spiral out of control."

The wrestling life is being in one city then on to the next as soon as a match ends. That life continues over and over, year after year.

"There's horror stories of the guys that passed away in their hotel rooms," Malenko says of the life that's violent, grueling and often short. On the road, traveling the unseen parts of the profession is also where Malenko began to worry about his friend.

"Eddie wasn't one to hide stuff," Malenko says. By his own admission, Guerrero was an angry drunk who'd fight anyone. At first, those occasions were a funny story to tell. But when those instances went from once or twice every few months, to every week, to every day, Malenko recognized that his friend needed help. They were in the WWE in 2001 when Malenko told management that Eddie had a problem. "The worst thing to do is rat on a friend," Malenko says, "but I was trying to save the guy."

Years later, Jim Ross, the legendary commentator, then the senior vice president of WWE talent relations, recalled that moment on his podcast, *Grilling JR*.

"I saw one of the greatest pro wrestlers in the world that we were about to lose if we didn't get our arms around his problem," Ross said of Eddie. "But in order for us to get our arms around his problem, he's got to cooperate with us. He's got to allow us to hug him."

Because of Malenko, the WWE ultimately sent Guerrero to rehab for four months. But it also fractured their friendship. "Eddie didn't want anything to do with me," Malenko says, still certain he did the right thing because by November 2005, things had changed. By then, Eddie was past the days of relapsing and getting fired by the WWE. Eddie had reconnected with his faith, apologized to friends and family, and renewed his marriage vows to Vickie. Things were going so well he even met the conditions for a return to the WWE, "clean and sober through testing," Ross said, and he even started to forgive his friend.

"I felt like we didn't have to worry anymore," Malenko says. "Which made his death even harder."

The Hennepin County medical examiner said Eddie died of heart disease. Past use of painkillers, alcohol and steroids hardened and narrowed his arteries. In the days before he passed, Eddie would close his eyes and nod away during conversations. It looked like he was sleeping, so friends and family thought he was just tired from the road. They later understood that was his heart slowing down, until it stopped inside Room 3015 of the Minneapolis Marriott City Center.

Three months after he passed, with the shock of one of its biggest stars gone at 38, the WWE implemented a random drug-testing policy.

"I miss him," Malenko says. "Eddie was like my little brother." He still watches their old matches even if it hurts. "They remind me of how much he meant to me as a person," Malenko says of those fights.

A FEW YEARS after I dreamed of being like Eddie, I watched Julio César Chávez knock out Meldrick Taylor in the last seconds of a fight. The way my father—a strong, stoic man—hugged me as it happened, you would have thought we'd just seen a miracle. That's when I wanted to box. That lasted until I got punched in the face a little too hard.

In my early teenage years, I was sure I'd play college football. I even taped a photo of the Heisman Trophy to the ceiling directly above my bench press for motivation. Then I stopped growing early in high school.

In my early-to-mid 20s, I sought more realistic things. They weren't dreams but ways to survive and get out of working construction. I wanted to be a mechanic like my father or sell bootleg CDs and DVDs at the swap meet like my uncle. I wanted to work at the copper mine or as a city maintenance worker since that provided medical insurance.

I was 28 years old when I wanted to be a high school teacher since that was the profession of my future wife. I took the El Paso Community College placement exam and almost didn't return after scoring a zero on the writing section. I enrolled and have rarely felt the self-doubt I had on that first day of class. I sat close to the door in case I wanted to leave since I was afraid that I was too old. Afraid I was wasting my time. Afraid of what came next if this also didn't work.

I forced myself to stay in that uncomfortable space of being a stranger again. Around books and between a struggling life, I was surprised to find I wanted to be a writer. That took me years to pursue, afraid I'd fail at that too. But I chased that dream. I wanted to tell stories, like the ones my grandmother had told me, of people in places important to me.

That's why I wanted to write about Eddie. I tried to for years but I didn't know how. Until one day it hit me like a moment of clarity. The realization that if I was going to write about someone who isn't here, it had to be a story of how they exist in the space between reality and fiction. And what those memories mean to those who still love him.

MOST OF WHAT Kaylie Mahoney Guerrero knows of her father comes from the memories of others. From her mother, Tara, who tells her stories about the man she loved, from the friends who used to wrestle with him, and from aunts and uncles who tell her about their little brother.

"I'm the youngest daughter," Kaylie says. "I was only 3 when he passed."

Since she was a toddler, Kaylie has a couple of memories of her own but not much more. There's the one of Eddie singing and playing "The Name Game" where Eddie would say her name and alter it as he sang. And the one where she and her two half sisters were at a store with him.

"I was in a shopping cart," Kaylie says. Eddie was at the height of his fame, trying to avoid attention. "He's telling my sisters, 'Don't mess around with the cart, you're going to flip her over,'" Kaylie says. She remembers falling to the cold floor. She wasn't hurt but cried from being startled. And because others stared, she remembers the look of shock and embarrassment on her father's and half sisters' faces.

"For some reason, that memory makes me laugh," Kaylie says. "He's just being an average dad going to the store. He's just trying to get what he needs, and his daughters are causing a scene." As she shares the memory with me in the same way others have shared theirs with her, she can't help but laugh some more.

In search of memories and connections, she finds comfort in their similarities. Things like their October birthdays being only three days apart. Or the gold and diamond necklace Eddie gave to her mother that she wears when she wants to feel close to him. Earlier this year, Kaylie attended a wrestling show at the El Paso County Coliseum. She got to be inside the place where her father spent most of his childhood. Back in his hometown, which will soon proclaim Nov. 18 as Eddie Guerrero Day, she even visited the murals dedicated to him.

"It was beautiful," she says of the fading mural under the bridge connecting the border between El Paso and Juárez. It has become a place of pilgrimage where people pull off the road to stop and pay their respects. Next to Eddie's mural is another one of the Wrestling Guerreros.

"There's this interview," Kaylie says of the video she found on YouTube as part of her search. It's an hour and 48 minutes long and it's just Eddie. Not the man who looked larger than life on television. It's just Kaylie's father speaking honestly about his struggles, his family and wrestling. "It's like he left it as a time capsule for me," Kaylie says of the interview she'll watch as often as needed.

She'll watch to see his mannerisms and similarities between their faces. To see his smile and hear him say, "Follow your heart" when asked to give advice.

Every time she sees it, Kaylie feels as if her father is talking directly to her.

When your first sports hero dies at an early age, it alters your perception of time. Because no matter how old you get, some part of you returns to childhood whenever you think of them. Until one day you're as old as they were when they took their last breath. That's when you feel that relationship change.

What began as a childhood wonder with masked men who looked like they could fly around the ring, evolved into a focus on Eddie. During a time when I lived in what felt like different worlds, he reminded me of home.

I don't remember when I started to wonder more about Eddie as a person and less about him as a wrestler, but it was long after then. Probably when I outgrew making heroes out of athletes.

Searching for the Eddie that wasn't on television, I looked in old yearbooks with broken spines inside his old high school and in the scraps of things once important. I walked into the memories and dreams of those who loved him. I searched where everything began. Driving down Huerta Street with the car windows down and radio off, I listened to see if the echoes of the Wrestling Guerreros were still there.

And what I found, as someone now seven years older than when Eddie died, was the realization of how young he was and how fast it goes. When yesterday I was a 7-year-old in an unfamiliar world, today I'm a father, trying to instill a confidence I lost when arriving in this strange place north of the border. And because Eddie represented much more than a wrestler, I now introduce him to my daughter.

We watch videos of Eddie wrestling in front of what feels like the entire world chanting his name. I show her videos of him talking in English and Spanish so she can hear that familiar accent of someone who lives between two places. We watch so my daughter can see how someone from here, a place that isn't growing anymore, made it there.

"Eddie was one of us," I tell her.

"This is his place," Linda Guerrero Rodriguez says as we stand where Eddie rests.

It's a cemetery in Scottsdale, Arizona, not too far from where she lives and where Eddie spent some of his final years. The dry heat eased the chronic pain he felt from an 18-year career and nearly 1,500 matches.

"How often do you visit?" I ask.

"At least three times a year; his birthday, Christmas and usually in the spring," Linda says. "And there's always something here."

Today, around a marker that reads Eduardo Gory Guerrero, there's a replica of a WWE Universal Championship belt, a small sombrero, a toy lowrider car and a Mexican decorative skull left by those who remember the dead. Sometimes there are cards and letters where people write of how much Eddie meant to them. When he first passed, Linda and her mom would visit and read those letters.

Out of all the siblings, Linda and Eddie were especially close. They were the youngest, and when the oldest Guerreros moved out—Chavo Sr., Mando and Hector to pursue their wrestling careers and Maria to become a teacher—only Eddie and Linda were left.

With that bond, Linda could tell Eddie the painful truths. That he was like a different person when he drank and abused painkillers. When he once stopped breathing and had to be rushed to the hospital, Linda was the one who yelled at Eddie from his bedside even when she was unsure if he could hear. The one who wanted to talk about his problems even when he didn't. In the grip of addiction he overdosed three times, went bankrupt, but more than anything, lost a decade's worth of time.

Conversely, Eddie talked with Linda about things he couldn't tell others. The pressure he felt carrying the Guerrero name. How he wondered if their father would be proud of who he had become. When his 12th attempt at rehab worked, Eddie told Linda he wanted to be open with fans about his problems.

"He had just gotten his four-year sobriety chip when he passed a month later," Linda says with a look of hurt in her eyes that turns to love. "His last four years were beautiful. He transformed back to my little brother."

"Our family was never the same," Linda says of Eddie's passing.

Linda holds a quilt as she speaks. Her friend made it from Linda's old wrestling shirts with Eddie's face on them that she just couldn't wear. She works as a flight attendant, and every few months someone at the airport or on a plane will wear a similar shirt. Sometimes she'll tell them Eddie was her brother, and then they'll ask if she can take a picture with them.

"Why do you think so many fans still remember Eddie?" I ask.

"Because he was so honest with his crowd," she says.

From a lifetime around wrestling, she knows that has always been the most important thing. That none of this works if it's too removed from reality. It just looks foolish if you can't feel what's inside the ring. And that ability to honestly portray what isn't real is what Eddie did better than anyone else.

Linda goes quiet, staring at what's left—even if Eddie's presence remains in photos, dreams and memories. She's the one who tries to keep his daughters close to her family even when it's complicated.

The one who apologizes as she cries when two decades ago still feels like yesterday.

ROBERTO JOSÉ ANDRADE FRANCO is a feature writer at ESPN. He's been a finalist for the National Magazine Award and the Dan Jenkins Medal for Excellence in Sportswriting. He lives in the El Paso–Juárez borderland.

Becoming El Jefe

SIMON LEWSEN

FROM *Toronto Life* • JULY 28, 2025

From the moment he was born, Ryan Wedding was the family darling. He belonged to a sporty, tightly knit clan with a shared love of the outdoors. In the 1960s, his grandparents, Laurence and Marlyn Spiess, had purchased the Mount Baldy Ski Area, a ski club near Thunder Bay. Their ambitions were modest. Marlyn sat behind the ticketing desk, and Laurence, who carried a key ring befitting a prison warden, did triple duty as manager, landscaper and handyman. Mount Baldy wasn't a ritzy destination resort but a scrappy hub for local families. It had an old rope lift, a T-bar pulley, and a chalet that sold hot dogs and Molson Canadian. Skiing was the family religion. The Spiess's son, Craig, coached the women's national alpine ski team in the early '90s; their daughter, Karen, married an engineer named Rene Wedding who'd skied competitively in university. Ryan Wedding was born on September 14, 1981, the first son of the third generation. Laurence had him on skis almost as soon as he could walk.

As a child, Ryan was daring and adventurous, with a capacity for intense focus. He'd sit behind his father's drafting table for hours, drawing perfectly scaled buildings, then go out on his bike, alone, to explore the logging trails that wended through the surrounding boreal forest. When Ryan was still young, his grandfather put him behind the wheel of the family car and showed him how to work the transmission. He learned how to use the pedals before his feet could even reach them. But his appetite for risk went beyond family-sanctioned activities. Occasionally, he'd disappear, and his parents would find that he'd snuck into a neighbour's garage to rummage through their tools.

Wedding started snowboarding at age 12, shortly after he moved with his parents and two younger sisters to Coquitlam, BC, for his dad's work. He won the first race he entered and caught the attention of Bob Allison, a former professional skier, windsurfer and rock climber, who was building a team of elite snowboarders to represent Canada. Wedding was the baby of Allison's team, the cherubic blue-eyed kid. At national competitions, he'd head to bed early with his teddy bear while his teammates, a band of roofers and roughnecks, hit the bars and tried to get laid. Come morning, though, Wedding was as bold as any of them. He was fearless on the slopes, barrelling headlong down steep mountain faces over icy terrain and carving perilously close to the snow. At home with his dad, he occupied himself with mini experiments, testing out boots and bindings to see which would enable him to glide just a bit faster.

At 15 years old, Wedding made the Canadian national team. Soon, he was competing internationally in the Alps and the Andes. Success fed his rapidly growing ego—he became obsessed with winning. He took home bronze at the junior world championships in 1999 and silver at the same competition two years later. People started mentioning him as a potential challenger to Ross Rebagliati, who'd won gold at Nagano in 1998. And then Wedding was chosen to represent Canada at the 2002 Winter Olympics in Salt Lake City.

For a 20-year-old athlete who wanted to become a household name, Salt Lake City could have been a dream come true. But, for Wedding, it was the end of a dream. At the giant slalom event on Valentine's Day, he came out of the gate aggressively, carving deep into the slope. It was a poor choice for the conditions of the day: the sun had melted the snow from powder into slush, which makes carving risky. Wedding managed to stay upright, but the initial jolt threw him off his rhythm. He placed 24th, his time a second too long to qualify for the next round. That day, Wedding learned a crushing lesson: you can be extraordinarily, even freakishly talented—you can dedicate your life to a single pursuit, pushing your body far beyond what most people consider possible—and, statistically speaking, your efforts probably won't be enough. Not everyone gets to win.

Snowboarding was never a reliable route to fame anyway. Even the most successful athletes can chase adrenalin for only a handful of seasons before their bodies give out. Of the first-generation Olympic boarders who represented Canada at Nagano, Salt Lake City, Turin and Vancouver, only Rebagliati transcended his sport, partly because of his athleticism and partly because of the controversy after he tested positive for cannabis. The overwhelming majority of Olympic athletes live and die in obscurity. Wedding gave up on the Olympics, but he didn't give up on his ambitions. Instead, he learned something that eludes many of his athlete peers: if adventure, glory and status are your goals, there are other ways to get them.

AFTER SALT LAKE City, Wedding moved to Vancouver to study at Simon Fraser University, but instead of applying his competitive streak to academics, he hit the weight room. According to a profile in *Rolling Stone*, he transformed his body from the lithe, athletic build of an alpine racer to the muscular, thickset physique of an action-movie star. He told a friend that he resented the men at the gym who were bigger than he was, and he set out to surpass them. For work, he picked up shifts as a bouncer at Vancouver-area clubs, many frequented by gang members in designer streetwear and Swiss watches. Soon, Wedding was dressing like them.

After two years, he dropped out of school. With a $250,000 loan from his father, he bought and quickly flipped a house in Maple Ridge, an affluent garden suburb of Vancouver. He then set himself up in a condo with 30-foot ceilings in Vancouver's ritzy Westwood Plateau neighbourhood, outfitting the space with a pinball machine and a video game station with race car seating. In his building's garage, he stored snowmobiles, a Ducati and a BMW M5.

If his lifestyle seemed too lavish for a bouncer with a bit of real estate cash, that's because it was. To finance the designer clothes and luxury vehicles, Wedding started a business on a rural property in Maple Ridge. It was owned by a friend of his who called it Eighteen Carrot Farms, but the real crop was cannabis—and Wedding was mass-producing it in a warehouse on-site. Twice a month, he drove out to the property to harvest some of its 6,800 plants and deliver his yields to a supplier.

In the summer of 2006, the authorities received a tip about Wedding's operation. When the RCMP searched their database, they learned that Wedding had been named in a 2004 investigation into marijuana grow-ops. Eighteen Carrot Farms was consuming 2,000 kilowatt hours of electricity per month, far beyond the average for a warehouse of that size. In a non-residential building, there are only a few practical uses for such an enormous amount of energy. Powering grow lamps is one of them.

On September 22, 2006, the RCMP raided the property and discovered a mix of dried cannabis and live plants worth an estimated $10 million, plus a shotgun and numerous rounds of ammunition. But they didn't find Wedding at the site, and they were unable to make a strong enough case against him to justify pressing charges.

Looked at one way, Wedding's early forays into criminality were unremarkable. BC was the epicentre of the North American cannabis industry, which had grown precipitously over the late 1990s and early aughts, aided by the proliferation of organized crime syndicates. Between 1997 and 2003, law enforcement investigated 25,000 grow-ops in the province, likely a tiny proportion of the overall number. Police couldn't keep up, so they focused their limited resources on shutting down facilities rather than prosecuting suspects. Out of every 100 people charged with growing cannabis in BC, maybe eight or nine would see prison time.

Arguably, Wedding wasn't doing anything outlandish: he was just getting in on the local industry, and he happened to be good at it. But the scale of his operation set him apart. To turn a grow-op the size of Eighteen Carrot Farms into a profitable business, one would need to rub shoulders with experienced criminals. All that product had to go somewhere, after all, and in the early 2000s, much of it was going to points south. The work of moving plants in bulk across international borders was done almost entirely by criminal organizations: the Hells Angels, the largest biker gang in the world; the United Nations, whose members practise Thai kickboxing and swear fealty to an ancient samurai honour code; the Independent Soldiers, who, in 2003, got into a deadly shootout with the Hells Angels on the dance floor of a Gastown nightclub; and the Red Scorpions, who massacred six people in a Surrey apartment complex in 2007, leaving them face down in a pool of blood. By the time Wedding's grow-op was busted, he had sinister people in his orbit.

ONE OF WEDDING'S new associates was Hassan Shirani, a Persian Canadian who had been implicated in a police investigation into a Vancouver-area murder, though he wasn't ultimately charged with the crime. Shirani was useful to Wedding because of his connections to a niche corner of the underground economy: a money-transfer system known as hawala that dates back to eighth-century India and still has networks around the world.

Hawala runs on trust. If you live in Toronto and are seeking to send, say, $10,000 to your brother in Tehran, you might give the cash to a hawala broker (or hawaladar) operating out of a dry-cleaner's or car dealership or convenience store. The broker will put the money in his safe. For a fee, he'll instruct a fellow hawaladar in Tehran to make the same amount available to the intended recipient, who will identify himself by an agreed-upon code word. Hawaladars keep track of inflows and outflows, and every once in a while they coordinate with colleagues to settle up outstanding balances, perhaps through cash transfers, exchanges of goods or professional favours. Because the network is informal, it's ideal for law-abiding Canadians who distrust the banking systems in their countries of origin. Because it leaves no digital record, it's ideal, too, for criminals looking to discreetly move money across international borders.

In 2008, Wedding turned to Shirani to help him in a new venture, one with the potential to be much more lucrative than cultivating cannabis. Together, the duo hatched a plan to smuggle 24 kilograms of cocaine into Canada via San Diego. That spring, Shirani met with a hawaladar in Vancouver and deposited $300,000 that he would then be able to draw on in California. Wedding and Shirani flew to Los Angeles on June 10. At LAX, they met up with a Russian Canadian named Michael Krapchan, whom Shirani had hired to set up the purchase. Krapchan had also brought along the seller, a menacing-looking heavyset ex-KGB agent named Yuri.

The situation was tense. Yuri was under the impression that the four men would drive directly from the airport to San Diego to do the deal, and he became agitated when Shirani and Wedding explained that they needed a few days to retrieve the funds. Shirani and Wedding were mystified: did Yuri really think they'd flown in from Canada with hundreds of thousands of dollars in their suitcases? Yuri asked, angrily, why he'd even been brought to the meeting.

Everyone was suspicious of everyone else. Nevertheless, they agreed to move forward. Over the next 72 hours in LA, Shirani and Wedding visited malls, restaurants and hookah bars, and they stopped by a Persian rug store that was also a hawala brokerage. There, they retrieved a portion of their cash: $120,000 in American bills, bundled up in newspapers. They hid the package in a drawer below the TV in their hotel room.

On June 12, Shirani and Wedding met with Krapchan in Anaheim and gave him $17,000 (US), enough to procure the first kilo of cocaine. The next day, to inspect the sample, they drove to a San Diego hotel room that Krapchan had rented. Krapchan headed off in a rental car to buy the drugs from Yuri while Shirani and Wedding holed up in the room—they believed, erroneously, that if the cops showed up at the buy and they weren't present, they couldn't be prosecuted. As lunchtime drew near, the guys grew hungry and impatient. After an hour and a half, they ventured out to get food—only to be quickly apprehended by the FBI, which had arrest warrants for both of them.

The whole thing had been a set-up. Yuri, the ex–KGB agent, was really a confidential police informant who'd been wearing a wire at the LAX meeting. The cocaine he'd sold Krapchan in San Diego had been given to him by the feds. As soon as Krapchan had completed the deal, agents arrested him, then headed to the hotel to round up Shirani and Wedding.

Both Krapchan and Shirani pleaded guilty for participating in the plot. Wedding pleaded not guilty and stood trial in San Diego in November of 2009. His mother and two younger sisters attended the trial, dismayed but supportive, firm in their conviction that Wedding was, at worst, a bit player in the scheme.

In the courtroom, Wedding's lawyer made this exact argument, claiming that Shirani had brought Wedding along as a fall guy. To create the impression that Wedding was bankrolling the entire operation, the lawyer said, Shirani had told Wedding that his credit card was maxed out, tricking him into shelling out for daily expenses. When the conspirators discussed business, by phone and in person, they frequently spoke Farsi or Russian, languages Wedding didn't understand. Even when speaking English, the men used code words, referring to the drugs as "cars." Perhaps, the lawyer argued, Wedding really believed that he was in LA to buy automobiles.

In his testimony for the prosecution, Shirani told a different story. He conceded that he'd managed the hawala transfer to the LA rug store and that he'd arranged for the drugs to be smuggled into Canada, but he insisted he was just the logistics guy. Wedding was the ringleader—the man who'd instigated the scheme and put up most of the money.

Which version of the story was true? Brett Kalina, one of the FBI officers who arrested Wedding in San Diego, says he suspects the latter. If Wedding was a bit player in the plot, Kalina argues, he didn't present like one. At the San Diego hotel, Wedding was dressed head to toe in Ed Hardy gear, with a Breitling watch as heavy as a paperweight. He was physically imposing, having reached a level of bulk that can be achieved only through steroid use.

Wedding said almost nothing to Kalina during his arrest. He was eerily silent—until the strip search at the detention facility, during which he saw Kalina watching him and called him a "faggot." The slur was shocking because it was so unusual. "Typically, when people are arrested, they try to make nice," says Kalina. "They're vulnerable. They know who has power at the moment and who doesn't." Kalina remembers Wedding as the most hostile suspect he's ever arrested.

During the 17 months Wedding spent awaiting trial, he was held at the Metropolitan Correctional Center in San Diego, where the FBI monitored his calls. These phone conversations revealed that Wedding was a callous and calculating operator. He had as many as five girlfriends back in BC, all of whom believed themselves to be dating him exclusively. At Wedding's behest, they would wash his cars, clean his condo, or pick up money from his associates and use it to pay off creditors. Wedding spoke to male colleagues on the phone too, bragging about the "good connections" he was making in prison.

This was likely true. Because of its proximity to Tijuana, southern California is one of the hottest spots in the US-Mexican drug trade. For anyone looking to meet well-connected drug traffickers, there may be no better place on earth than a San Diego jail. And Wedding was exactly the kind of person Mexican cartels are known to seek out: a white Canadian with an English name, someone who doesn't fit the stereotype of a cartel associate and can therefore do business abroad without arousing suspicion. "We knew we were giving Wedding all the contacts he needed to return to a life of crime," Kalina says ruefully, "but there was nothing we could do about it."

On November 30, the jury found Wedding guilty of conspiracy to distribute cocaine. At his sentencing hearing on May 6, 2010, Wedding finally struck a note of contrition. "What I did was completely out of character for me, and it is a personal mission of mine to rebuild my reputation," he said. "As an athlete, I was always taught that there are no second chances, and, well, I'm here asking for exactly that." The judge imposed a lower sentence than he'd initially intended. At the time, 80 to 100 months was standard for such crimes. Wedding got 48 months, minus time served.

He was sent to the Reeves County Detention Complex in Texas, a private prison populated mainly by migrants awaiting deportation. On Valentine's Day in 2011, exactly nine years after he'd competed at Salt Lake City, Wedding, then 29 years old, got married in prison to a Persian Canadian entrepreneur and caterer from BC. Later that year, his new wife would become a person of interest in a police investigation into a Vancouver-area kidnapping, in which a man was held captive for 20 hours, at times with a gun to his head. In 2020, her name would come up again in relation to a police raid on a grow-op in Abbotsford, BC, during which the cops seized two and a half tons of cannabis. The woman was never charged in connection with either crime. When contacted by phone, she said, "These cases have nothing to do with me." When asked about her marriage to Wedding, she added, "It was a long time ago. I live a normal life. I have kids, and I'm remarried."

Was the union a love match? Maybe, but it's more likely that it was a strategic business move. A source close to the San Diego investigation pointed out that, if you're married and imprisoned, you can sometimes get permission to talk to your spouse on the phone without anyone listening in. One thing is certain: despite what Wedding told the judge at his sentencing hearing, he had no intention of going clean.

WEDDING WAS RELEASED from prison and deported to Canada in December of 2011. If he'd left the country a few years earlier as a mid-level drug smuggler, ambitious but green, he was now returning a new man—well connected and hardened by prison. He settled in a luxury condo in downtown Montreal, despite having no legal source of income, and soon established himself as a drug kingpin. Drawing on his newfound understanding of drug-trade logistics, he organized far more sophisticated schemes than the ones he'd tried on the West Coast. One of his associates was Philipos Kollaros, who had once been arrested in Toronto with millions of dollars' worth of cocaine. With Wedding's help, Kollaros made a plan to bring hundreds of kilos of cocaine into the country by sea, from Saint Kitts to Newfoundland.

Kollaros knew of a man who purportedly owned a sailboat brokerage and ran a side hustle bringing cocaine from the Caribbean to Atlantic Canada. His name was Joe, and he was exceptionally well connected. Over the previous year, he'd peddled his shipping services to drug smugglers across the country. With an Ottawa restaurateur, Joe had hatched a plan to bring in 3,000 kilograms of cocaine from a pickup point off the coast of Antigua. With a 60-year-old career criminal from Montreal, he'd plotted to move 500 kilos of coke along the same route. And with a pair of Nova Scotia brothers connected to the coast guard, he'd created a lookout system to ensure that his boats could evade law enforcement.

Kollaros was in contact with Joe about the possible Saint Kitts shipment, and he introduced Joe to "the man in charge": Wedding, who lived a short walk from Kollaros's Montreal apartment. When Joe met Wedding, he knew immediately that he was dealing with a sophisticated criminal. Wedding asked Joe detailed questions about the storage capacity of his boats and helped him design a plan to transfer the contraband from a large research vessel, which would pick up the drugs in Saint Kitts, to a fleet of smaller fishing trawlers, which would bring the haul to shore, inconspicuously, in Newfoundland.

The only hitch in the plan: Joe was really an RCMP operative, referred to in court documents as "Undercover Officer Joe," who'd infiltrated Canada's extensive underground drug-trading networks as part of an initiative called Operation Harrington. The sting was designed to target the Mexico-to-Canada cocaine trade, a route that had ballooned in size and become so lucrative that it could be run, on the Latin American side, by only one person: Joaquín "El Chapo" Guzmán, the most powerful drug lord in the world. The semi-literate child of a farming family in the Mexican state of Sinaloa, El Chapo had become a billionaire by building up the regional Sinaloa Cartel into the biggest drug-smuggling enterprise in history.

At the time of the Harrington sting, the Sinaloa Cartel was doing business in 50 countries, and it was responsible for the majority of the narcotics that moved across the US-Mexico border. In Sinaloa, the cartel basically ran a parallel state. It owned hundreds of businesses, from water parks to daycares; it financed roads and schools; and it bought off the very officials who were supposed to bring it to justice. The cartel was also legendary for its acts of brutality—kidnappings, public decapitations, shootouts at funerals in which entire families were slaughtered. As head of the cartel, El Chapo had presided over 34,000 murders, built a secret network of subterranean railroads at the US-Mexico border and been arrested several times, only to break free by, for instance, hiding in a prison laundry basket or directing associates on the outside to tunnel him out of his cell.

In the early 2010s, El Chapo was specifically targeting Canada for his exports. The domestic price of cocaine was high, and because Canada wasn't then a focal point of US drug-trafficking investigations, he considered the country a safe place for his subordinates to meet with international smugglers or with suppliers of drug precursors. To that end, he'd made inroads with Canadian contacts, people with extensive knowledge and power in the local drug trade. When El Chapo had sent high-ranking deputies to Montreal, they'd met with Kollaros—and probably also with Wedding.

But, on April 20, 2015, before any cocaine could actually enter the country aboard Joe's ships, the RCMP pounced, issuing 15 arrest warrants, including ones for Wedding and Kollaros. They were both charged with conspiracy to import and traffic cocaine, and Wedding got an additional charge for trafficking. The size of the combined conspiracies was staggering. People living in at least seven Caribbean and Latin American nations were implicated in the Harrington sting, which involved an estimated 15 tons of cocaine, worth at least $750 million.

The Harrington defendants suffered a range of fates. Some pleaded guilty and got lesser sentences; others went to trial and wound up serving hard time. It's unclear whether Kollaros cut a plea deal with the Crown, but he ended up serving a mere day in prison after getting credit for time in remand. That's not to say he got off lightly. On the evening of November 7, 2018, Kollaros was hanging out at Café Cubano, an old-school coffee shop in Montreal's Little Italy, when a man strode in and shot him. Kollaros died in hospital later that night.

The murder has not been solved, although one person—Wedding—had obvious reasons to want Kollaros dead. Kollaros knew all the details of the Saint Kitts plot and could testify against Wedding at a later date. Plus, it was Kollaros who had foolishly brought Joe, the undercover operative, into the Saint Kitts operation in the first place. If Wedding plotted the murder, though, he surely did so from afar. In April of 2015, when the RCMP showed up at his Montreal condo to arrest him, he had already left the country.

POLICE BELIEVE THAT Wedding fled Canada directly into the arms of the Sinaloa Cartel and went into hiding, probably in Mexico, under their protection. In exile, he was bolder than ever. According to the US Department of Justice, he built his drug smuggling enterprise into a billion-dollar organization, which now moves 60 tons of cocaine per year—worth nearly half a billion dollars—most of it through the United States and into Canada. He has collected an impressive list of aliases: RW, James Conrad King, Buddy, Giant, Public Enemy, El Toro ("The Bull") and El Jefe ("The Boss"). And he's become the kind of person who kills, sometimes carelessly, without compunction.

Jaspreet Kaur Sidhu, a 28-year-old Caledon woman, became one of his many victims. One night in November of 2023, she was getting ready for bed when she saw a masked man in her hallway. She had a full house: her father, Jagtar, and mother, Harbhajan, were visiting from India and staying in the rental home she shared with her brother, Gurdit, who happened to be out that evening.

Jaspreet recalls the events of that night only in fragments. She remembers hearing her mother scream. She remembers the sound of shots being fired, followed by a horrifying silence. She remembers attempting to stand up, keeling over as a bullet pierced her leg and then crawling, bloodied and semiimmobilized, across her bedroom floor to pick up the phone, prop herself up on a dresser and dial 911. A friend who lived downstairs came outside when he heard the shots and saw a gunman escape into a pickup truck. The vehicle was later found, abandoned and in flames, on a rural stretch of road 20 minutes away.

Jagtar died before the paramedics arrived at the home. Harbhajan, who'd been hit with 22 bullets, died in hospital 13 days after the attack. And Jaspreet, who was hit 13 times, remained paralyzed and unconscious for a month before awakening and slowly regaining her mobility. She and Gurdit were devastated by the attack. Who on earth would want to kill them and their kindly parents?

It wasn't until almost a year later that the FBI and the Ontario Provincial Police would offer them an answer: they believed the killings had been ordered by Wedding. Their home was owned by a company that has been linked to illegal trucking activities. Wedding may have been trying to retaliate against the previous residents or the owners for a stolen drug shipment. The Sidhu family were the victims of mistaken identity.

In order to run his lethal operation, Wedding had amassed a vast and complex web of subordinates and collaborators. One such mid-level operator was Jonathan Acebedo-Garcia, a Colombian Canadian who grew up in Montreal, where he worked for his family's cleaning company. In 2009, US agents searched Acebedo-Garcia's car at the New York–Ontario border and found 23,000 hits of ecstasy laced with meth. Acebedo-Garcia pleaded guilty to conspiracy to traffic drugs and got a four-year sentence, which he partially served at Reeves County, in Texas. That's probably where he met Wedding, who was serving time there for the San Diego operation. By 2024, according to police, Acebedo-Garcia was working directly with Wedding's second in command, Andrew Clark, a 30-something elevator mechanic from Toronto who'd left Canada for Mexico in 2022. Acebedo-Garcia communicated with Clark over Threema, an encrypted messaging app, to help arrange Wedding's drug-trafficking operations from afar.

On February 20, 2024, at Wedding's and Clark's direction, Acebedo-Garcia visited an auto body shop in the GTA, where police say he met with Hardeep Ratte, the Brampton-based owner of a long-haul trucking company, and Ratte's nephew, Gurpreet Singh. At the meeting, court documents allege, Ratte and Singh agreed to truck shipments of cocaine from southern California into Canada for a flat rate of $220,000 per load. Representatives from Ratte's trucking business would drive down to LA to meet with guys from the Wedding enterprise. Acebedo-Garcia would provide Wedding's men with a dollar-bill serial number; the guys from the trucking company would use that number to identify themselves. Wedding's associates would then hand over a shipment of cocaine—up to 350 kilos per run—which had been stashed in safe houses around LA. Ratte's guys allegedly planned to smuggle the contraband into Canada via secret compartments in their trucks.

While these shipments were being arranged, Wedding and Clark were busy eliminating their enemies. Clark had been grooming a young, boyishly handsome man named Malik Cunningham to work as an assassin. He had even flown Cunningham, who'd recently been released from the Toronto South Detention Centre, to Mexico for military-style training in small arms, long guns and target shooting. Then he sent Cunningham back to Canada with a lengthy hit list.

Cunningham's first assignment from Clark, for which he was paid $100,000, was to drive to the Niagara home of Randy Fader, a 29-year-old American and Canadian citizen, and, as Clark put it in his instructions, "blow this guy's top off." On April 1 of last year, he did just that, shooting Fader execution-style in his driveway before fleeing the scene. Exactly what Fader had done is unknown, but clearly he'd made an enemy of the Wedding enterprise. That job now complete, Clark, communicating over Threema under the pseudonym Mero Wero, started preparing Cunningham for more lucrative hits: $200,000 to murder "a realtor in Van," more than twice that amount for "some Arabs" in Toronto and $1 million for a person in Dubai—all of them had antagonized El Jefe in some way.

On April 14, 2024, Cunningham slipped up. He drove the same car he'd used as his getaway for the Fader murder to a GTA funeral parlour where attendees were mourning the victim of a recent homicide. York Regional Police say they spotted the fraudulent plates and, believing the car to be stolen, pulled Cunningham over and arrested him. When they searched it, they found four cellphones, multiple rounds of ammunition and $100,000 in cash. On Cunningham's phone, they found the Threema messages between him and Clark.

Police had a second lucky break in the Wedding case. In early 2024, they convinced Acebedo-Garcia to flip. He was the ideal informant—trusted, well connected and enmeshed in the organization. At last, they had a way in. Drawing on information from Acebedo-Garcia, the authorities commenced Operation Giant Slalom, a cross-border investigation into the Wedding criminal enterprise. Last summer, they raided LA safe houses, stopped truck drivers at the US-Canada border, and picked up Ratte and Singh—the guys from the Brampton trucking company—at their Ontario homes. Law enforcement confiscated nearly two tons of cocaine, worth more than $30 million. And on October 8, the Mexican navy descended on a restaurant in Guadalajara and captured Clark, who was later extradited to the United States. All told, 14 men, eight of them Canadian, were arrested. Cunningham has been charged with murder. Ratte and Singh are charged with conspiracy to export, possess and distribute controlled substances and continuing a criminal enterprise. All three are in custody but have not yet entered pleas. Clark is facing nine charges, including murder and attempted murder. He has pleaded not guilty to all counts.

The State of California scheduled a trial for May of this year, with Acebedo-Garcia as the star witness. But, on January 31, Acebedo-Garcia was having lunch at El Indio, a shopping mall in Medellín, Colombia, when a man carrying a handgun with a silencer walked up and shot him dead. Acebedo-Garcia's murder threw the case against Wedding's associates into disarray. His testimony would have been the centrepiece of the trial, the thread that sewed the various scraps of evidence into a coherent narrative. Without him, the state has to find a new strategy—or a new star witness. The trial has been postponed until February of 2026.

THE FBI HAS successfully infiltrated Wedding's networks, rounded up some of his closest collaborators and coordinated a manhunt across multiple countries, but Wedding himself still eludes them. They believe he's somewhere in Latin America, and they've added his name to their roster of 10 Most Wanted Fugitives, a list that once included Osama bin Laden and the legendary Boston crime boss James "Whitey" Bulger. The US State Department is now offering $10 million—the same amount it offered for El Chapo's sons—to anybody who provides information that leads to Wedding's arrest.

Still at large and still at work, Wedding is like a malevolent ghost: in Canada, he's absent in the flesh, but his presence is felt. His name came up again in June, in connection with Operation Pelican, a series of coordinated Peel police raids on trucks stationed in the GTA or attempting to cross the Canada-US border. The busts led to nine arrests and the seizure of 479 kilograms of cocaine.

The FBI has released two recent photographs of Wedding. The contrast between these images and the Olympic press shots from 23 years ago is jarring. Gone is the bright-eyed, baby-faced dreamer; in his place is a scowling, bulky, mustachioed man. In one shot, he's wearing a $1,000 Louis Vuitton T-shirt and what appears to be an LA Dodgers cap—a reference, perhaps, to the city where he made his debut as an international drug smuggler and where he still runs a network of stash houses. Kalina, the man who arrested Wedding in San Diego, believes that the former Olympian is living his best life—ensconced in a mansion, wealthy beyond his wildest dreams.

But, as Wedding has become more dangerous, he's also become more endangered. Facing tariff threats from the Trump administration, Mexico has ramped up efforts to capture cartel leaders, using special forces and the navy to avoid relying on corrupt local officials. The addition of Wedding's name to the FBI's Most Wanted list means that the US government will spend essentially whatever it takes to hunt him down. When the world's richest country decides it wants somebody that much, it usually gets them.

Wedding can't even rely on his allies to protect him. El Chapo was captured and extradited to the US in 2017. He's locked up in a maximum-security facility in Colorado. On July 25, 2024, Ismael Zambada, a top lieutenant in the Sinaloa Cartel, was reportedly kidnapped by men working for El Chapo's son, Joaquín Guzmán López, and both have since been arrested. The rupture threw the cartel into civil war, leading to highway blockades, shoot-outs and aerial bombings. In one macabre spectacle, members of one Sinaloa faction sent a cooler decorated with wrapping paper and bows to a rival faction. In it was a severed human head. Since the infighting began, cartel leaders who once walked around openly in Sinaloa have gone into hiding or fled to other Latin American countries.

Wedding's story is surely nearing its denouement. Perhaps he'll be captured by special forces and brought to LA to stand trial, at which point his parents and sisters—who live normal lives as engineering consultants and gerontologists and health care administrators—may get to see him, likely for the first time in over a decade. At a minimum, he'll face life in prison. Or maybe he'll be murdered by rivals before law enforcement can get to him. The last act of his story will likely be sensational. Perversely, Wedding will have achieved his dream: he will have solidified his place as Canada's most famous snowboarder.

On January 26, 2026, the FBI announced that Ryan Wedding had been arrested in Mexico City. He is currently in the United States, awaiting trial. Prior to Wedding's arrest, Mexican authorities raided various properties belonging to Wedding and seized millions of dollars worth of luxury goods, including 62 motorcycles and two Olympic gold medals. It's unclear who the medals originally belonged to.

SIMON LEWSEN is a magazine writer from Canada and an assistant professor at the University of Toronto. This year, he won a National Magazine Award for Best Profile.

Cal Raleigh Is Carrying the Mariners with Glute Force

STEPHANIE APSTEIN

FROM *Sports Illustrated* • SEPTEMBER 2025

After every Mariners win, the 26 victors gather for a brief ceremony. Baseball is a team sport, but everyone involved understands that on any given night, one person was probably more valuable than everyone else, and only one person can receive the footlong pair of gilded testicles, hanging from a chain, emblazoned with a trident, that accompany the poetic title Nuts of the Game.

This season, the most valuable player has usually been catcher Cal Raleigh, who entered the stretch run with the major league lead in dingers in the scorebooks, the Home Run Derby trophy on his mantle and history in sight: With his 42nd long ball, he surpassed Todd Hundley of the 1996 Mets for the single-season record by a switch-hitting catcher. Up next was the Royals' Salvador Pérez's 2021 mark of 48 by a catcher, which he eclipsed on Aug. 24. With six weeks remaining, Raleigh still held an outside chance at the American League single-season home run record, which the Yankees' Aaron Judge established at 62 three years ago. Raleigh sat a tenth of a point ahead of Judge for the AL lead in win probability added, a measure of how clutch he's been. [Editor's note: Judge has since overtaken Raleigh in WPA.] Raleigh is a perfect fit for *Sports Illustrated*'s Power List issue. And he did it all while shepherding a pitching staff beset by injuries to a 3.95 ERA, seventh in the AL. Seemingly every night he does something that makes his teammates gape—something Nuts-worthy.

"We should call it the Cal Award, probably," says righty Logan Evans.

But unfortunately it's Raleigh, 28, who gives out the Nuts, which means he's almost never the one receiving them. If he hits a game-winning home run, he honors the reliever who kept it close.

Doesn't it seem kind of ludicrous to create a player of the game award and all but exclude the guy who's usually the player of the game? "It's not about that," Raleigh says. "It's more about bringing everybody together at the end of the day and trying to enjoy a win for a few minutes, because it's so hard in the big leagues to win. You gotta be able to enjoy it. And there's always people that contribute, whether it's one pitch or one swing. Maybe it was doing something little that goes unrecognized. So for me it's not always about rewarding the guy who hits a home run or two home runs—it's more about rewarding a guy who does their job well."

Raleigh has been doing his job well since 2022, the year he hit a towering walk-off shot to put an explosive end to what was then the longest playoff drought in North American sports. He's been famous since July, when he became the toast of All-Star week, with his prodigious power and remarkable rear end, which led to the best nickname in baseball: the Big Dumper. Raleigh spent his whole life preparing to be good at baseball without giving much thought to what might accompany that success. In a lot of ways, his reality changed nearly overnight. But his attitude has not.

Says president of baseball operations Jerry Dipoto, "I've never worried less about someone being able to handle it."

RALEIGH HATES THE premise of this story. First, he disputes the idea that he's famous. "I wouldn't say that," he scoffs. So he became the first catcher to win the Home Run Derby, with his dad, Todd, pitching to him and his 15-year-old brother, Todd Jr., catching, while nearly six million people watched from home. So he's been in a T-Mobile commercial, signed endorsement deals with Nintendo, a local hospital chain and—best of all—a portable toilet brand, Honey Bucket. Todd Sr. and Cal's mom, Stephanie, lined up for a bus during All-Star week only to realize that it was wrapped in their son's face.

"I'm just a pretty average guy," Cal insists.

But what's worse is that people keep trying to tell him he's not. Longtime friend Bret Baldwin, who grew up with him in Cullowhee, N.C., and is now an engineer nearby, tries to imagine how the interview went. "'Please don't ask me another question about why I'm so good,'" he guesses correctly. Make no mistake, Raleigh is polite for the entire 12 minutes, plus another five a couple of days later, but he visibly winces at the attention. "Nice to see you again," he lies, before appearing to weigh the merits of turning and walking away.

Naturally, his teammates find this behavior hilarious. Every day or two, righthander Logan Gilbert shakes his head at his friend. "Fame," he pronounces gravely, "has changed you." (He is not the only one who has assigned himself the task of keeping Raleigh in check: "Everybody's been cheering for him a bunch recently, so I've been trying to boo him a little bit to keep him down," says righty Bryce Miller.)

"It's funny, because he's the last guy to actually change," says Gilbert with a laugh. "He really does handle it very well—but I'm trying to convince him otherwise."

The people close to Raleigh often find themselves in the unusual position of having to remind him that he's a superstar. "He's the prince of Cullowhee," says Baldwin. The neighboring town of Sylva, home of Smoky Mountain High, which Raleigh attended, recently declared July 14, 2025, to be Cal Raleigh Day. Raleigh is such a major celebrity there that he's made Baldwin a minor celebrity; people regularly recognize him and ask for details on Cal's life.

Meanwhile, Raleigh says it has never occurred to him to use his name to get a coveted dinner reservation. (He's cautious even when he eats at fast-casual restaurants that charge extra for various toppings. "Sometimes if I want guac, I'll get it," allows Raleigh.) Earlier this year, when he and three teammates were headed to dinner, he ordered them an UberX, the company's cheapest option. Raleigh signed a six-year, $105 million extension before the season, backup catcher Mitch Garver points out. "Order an Uber Black," he says. Raleigh only recently upgraded from the Toyota 4Runner he bought used to a new Toyota Tacoma.

"I've always been more of a cheap guy," he acknowledges. "I like coupons."

Dipoto suspects that it's this attitude—plus a few dozen clutch home runs—that has so endeared him to Seattle. Raleigh looks and acts more like the clubhouse attendant putting baseballs in buckets than the slugger putting baseballs in the stands.

His dad says, "Twelve months ago, on this calendar day—he's the same guy." He's not quite the same player, though.

HE COULD ALWAYS catch. The son of a baseball coach who spent eight years at Western Carolina and then four at Tennessee, young Cal grew up studying the game. "I love the nuances," he says. By middle school, he was calling his own games. "You didn't shake," recalls Baldwin.

Cal was the captain of every team he ever played on. He was a Division I–caliber basketball player, his father recalls, but he drove his coaches crazy by passing up clean shots. "He'd go rebound it and kick it back out and want his buddy to experience some of that," Todd recalls.

Cal came by that naturally. When Todd coached his son in travel ball, he always sat him for the first game of a tournament. "I just never wanted that to be a thing," Todd says. "He probably had less at-bats than anybody else on that team. We'd get in deeper into the tournament and I remember parents finally complaining, 'Hey, you've got to play him. This is ridiculous.' But I think he always liked it, too. He didn't want it to be, like, *Oh, I'm getting more at-bats because of who my dad is.*"

On the drive back from games, they rarely discussed strikeouts and home runs. All Todd wanted to talk about—and eventually, all Cal wanted to talk about—was whether the team had won. "In high school, if he didn't have a great game and they won, he was fine," Todd says. "He'd be the first guy jumping up and down happy. So it's not an act."

Dipoto got his first glimpse of that attitude in 2019, when he visited the High A Modesto Nuts on a day Gilbert was pitching and Raleigh was off. The GM noticed the catcher of the future crouched on an overturned bucket of baseballs, taking notes on Gilbert's outing the way other pitchers are often assigned to do.

After the game Dipoto brought it up with the coaching staff. "Why do you have Cal charting?" he asked.

The pitching coach laughed. "We don't have him doing that," he said.

When Dipoto asked Raleigh about it, the catcher explained he was just trying to learn more about how the pitcher saw himself so that he could refine his game-calling. By the next year, the Mariners were assigning all their young catchers to chart their young pitchers.

Those relationships pay off every day. Since the start of 2018, the year Raleigh was drafted out of Florida State, Dipoto has made 121 trades, according to a tracker maintained by Yahoo Sports' Jordan Shusterman, but of Seattle's top six starters, five were drafted and developed by the team. They are Raleigh's best friends; several of them have been his roommates.

"He doesn't let them make excuses," says Mariners pitching coach Pete Woodworth. "He doesn't let them stray. He keeps them accountable. As soon as they start veering off track, he slaps them in the face and gets them back." Many pitchers, he adds, "want to make it more complicated than it is. [Cal says], 'This is who you are. This is what you're good at. Let's just do that better.'"

That strategy fires his pitchers up. He does not play the cat-and-mouse game, always trying to fool the hitter. He calls for the pitcher's strength, again and again. "If something's working, he's not going to go away from it until they prove they can hit it," says Miller.

And Raleigh extends that same level of focus to every pitcher, "even the ones who only throw one inning," says Woodworth. "He sits down with them and lets them air out the s--- that goes on inside their crazy little brains, and then gets them back to what's simple and what's successful."

It has not always been so easy for him to do the same at the plate. He struggled early, facing a different sort of power issue: He managed just a .532 OPS in 47 games in 2021 (after slugging .608 in Triple A). He looked even worse to start '22. When the team sent him back down, his career batting average was .166 and his slugging percentage was .294. Cal had been cut from teams as a child, and his father always brushed off his complaints: "Just get better." He delivered the same message now. Around the same time, Mariners catcher Tom Murphy dislocated his left shoulder, forcing the team to call Raleigh back up, ready or not.

In his sixth game back, he socked a go-ahead home run. "I think it really gave him confidence to just say, you know, 'I gotta go,'" says Dipoto. "'I'm not worried about what anybody else is thinking.'" Raleigh had an .807 OPS the rest of the way and delivered that cathartic, playoff-ushering bomb against the Athletics, the 26th of 27 he'd hit on the season.

But nothing foretold this year. It took an assist from the greatest Mariners hitter ever to unlock this one. When Raleigh struggles at the plate, he tends to get too far forward. Instead of waiting for the ball, he lunges at it. He's late on fastballs and early on off-speed pitches. As this season began, Seattle director of hitting strategy—and Hall of Fame DH—Edgar Martínez set Raleigh up with a chest-high tee that he placed near the catcher's front foot along with a short bat. The idea was to force him to stay upright. "What it did was amazing," says hitting coach Kevin Seitzer. "Oh my gosh."

What it did was create one of the most lethal hitters in the sport. Left-handed and right-handed, Raleigh stays back in the box and crowds the plate. He pulls the ball in the air nearly 40% of the time, more than any other hitter, and he barrels up some 20% of the balls he hits, which ranks in MLB's top 10. He will probably never compete for the batting title; nearly every swing is engineered to produce a dinger. And a lot of them do.

But when Raleigh and his father discussed his goals for the season, they didn't spend much time on home runs hit or even on shutouts caught. Cal decided he wanted to take on more of a leadership role.

A few days before he signed his extension, Raleigh stopped by Dipoto's office at the Peoria, Ariz., facility, dressed in full uniform, and took a seat. For two and a half hours, he ran through an exhaustive audit of the organization. This was the player who spent the moments after the Mariners were eliminated from playoff contention on the final day of the 2023 season criticizing the team's lack of spending. "Sometimes, you have to go out and you have to buy," he said then.

He'd already become someone Dipoto checked with before he acquired a player, because Raleigh keeps detailed reports on most everyone in the league. So it was no surprise that he knew all the prospects' names and the status of all his teammates' contracts. He wanted to know whether the team he was committing to was committed to winning. Dipoto explained that Seattle had never been much of a destination for free agents but that he intended to keep improving the big-league roster via trades.

Four months later, when Dipoto sent two pitching prospects to the Diamondbacks for first baseman Josh Naylor, he got a text from Raleigh: "A++."

As much as Raleigh prefers to lead by example, he's starting to understand the power of his voice. "He doesn't talk much, but when he talks, it's an impact," says Seitzer. "He breathes life into people with just his presence." So Raleigh has started speaking up more in hitters' meetings and in the dugout during games, even if it's just to offer enthusiasm. And he encourages his teammates to celebrate the victories with the postgame ceremony he dreamed up.

The city, meanwhile, has fallen in love with him and with his club. The Mariners staged a campaign to get Raleigh to the All-Star Game, donning BE A PEACH, VOTE CAL shirts—complete with emoji—and using a butt-themed walk-up song playlist. Raleigh finished with the second most votes in the league after Judge and became Seattle's first elected starter since designated hitter Nelson Cruz in 2015. Local restaurants have debuted meals named after him. Fans regularly tell Raleigh they've named their children after him. Sometimes it all feels like a lot. But he understands what fans understand: He is leading a team that could make Seattle go nuts.

STEPHANIE APSTEIN spent 15 years covering baseball and Olympic sports at *Sports Illustrated*, where she wrote seven cover stories. She has twice won top honors from the Associated Press Sports Editors. She graduated from Trinity College with a bachelor's in French and Italian, and has a master's in journalism from Columbia University. She lives in New York City with her husband, the writer Andy McCullough, and their son, Robbie.

Bola Cheia

CHRIS FELICIANO ARNOLD

FROM *The Believer* • DECEMBER 18, 2025

Opened in 2020, the COPA Soccer Training Center in Walnut Creek, California, is a 117,000-square-foot, three-story-high labyrinth of sensorenabled practice spaces where boys and girls ages one through nineteen can refine the individual skills necessary to attract scouts from major European clubs.

Perched above the glass entryway, a gargantuan soccer ball spins slowly like a planet. Seven days a week, morning, noon, and night, families from around the Bay Area orbit the drop-off/pickup circle. Young athletes in yellow-and-black COPA jerseys scan their membership badges at the front desk before reporting to the areas designated for their age group and skill level.

Athletes ages six to nineteen are organized into training groups by age and ability, following tailored routines designed to push their physical comfort zones and leverage the neuroplasticity of their developing brains. COPA stands for Comprehensive Objective Performance Assessment, and true to its name, there are few spaces in this building where an athlete's performance is not being comprehensively assessed. On the thirty-yard synthetic SpeedTrack, a barrage of lasers analyzes their speed and gait. In the COPA skills.lab—the only one of its kind in North America—athletes step into a 360-degree array of screens, ball launchers, and motion sensors that can replicate almost any in-game scenario. In the COPA Cube, players enter a turf box surrounded by a grid of targets that light up at random so athletes can hone their passing skills with video game–like intensity.

Data from each station is fed into proprietary technologies that calculate an athlete's COPA Score, an objective summation of skills and potential—balance, ball control, decision-making, and more—augmented by kinesiologic measurements like maximum oxygen consumption and bone density. Teams from the Bundesliga, Major League Soccer, and NCAA Division I schools are keen to access these scores and evaluate players at seasonal scouting events. Even having a COPA Score to begin with signals to clubs that a player—or at least their parents—are dead serious about soccer. A good COPA Score can land somebody a tryout, a scholarship, or a contract, making all the pickups and drop-offs worthwhile.

When I enrolled my son William, he was almost four—still six years away from having his data fed into the machine. I tell myself that I will unenroll him from COPA long before then. For one thing, I cannot afford this place much longer. Also: I brought him here for all the wrong reasons.

LET ME EXPLAIN. I was born in Brazil, and then I was adopted and moved to the United States in 1981, at the twilight of the military dictatorship. When I was six or seven, my parents gave me a soccer ball, but, growing up on a farm in Oregon, I had few kids to play with, and the ball lay deflated in our gravel driveway. So despite my pedigree, I am a bola murcha (a flat ball)—I have no game. I don't want that to be true for my kids, who are Brazilian Mexican. Soccer—futebol, o jogo bonito—was my birthright. It was taken from me. I want to give it back to my kids.

The best I can do is make sure they touch a soccer ball at an early age. I want them to be able to send the ball anywhere, to make it do magic—a magic I have never felt. I want them to feel at home in their minds, in their bodies, in their blood. I don't know how to do that other than by making them feel at home on a soccer field.

Twice a week since early spring, William and I have walked past the weight room and the SpeedTrack and the skills.lab and the COPA Cube to Jungle Turf 1, where the one-to-three-year-old athletes gather to learn the fundamentals of the beautiful game. Jungle Turf 1 is a turf field surrounded by jungle wallpaper featuring a gorilla, a snake, a sloth, and other animal friends. On top of the supply closet, which is painted like a village hut, a monkey watches the action, tail arched like an S. The objectives for the Jungle Turf 1 athletes are very simple: Dribble the ball to the monkey. Water break. Dribble the ball to the parrot. Water break. Dribble to the sloth. Water break.

The kids here do not have a COPA Score. They play for fun. They play for stickers. If they listen to Coach Amanda, at the end of practice they get a sticker to add to their badge. Most of the children in this age group are still learning not to pick up the ball with their hands. "No hands," says Coach Amanda. "No hands," say the parents lined up at the perimeter of the field.

The parents at COPA are a mural of Bay Area immigrant ambition. People bring their kids to COPA to connect them with home while also exposing them to a sort of Silicon Valley engineering marvel that can happen only here. At the end of each session, Coach Amanda—over-patient and underpaid—drags out a mini net and pretends to be an alien while a swarm of three-year-olds peppers her with errant shots. We parents applaud each goal that gets through, a radiant love emanating from the sidelines. Planet Soccer is a good planet, despite war and famine beyond the Jungle Turf. A fair, well-lit planet where everyone gets a sticker. A planet with no real grass.

COPA IS THE most American way possible to train your kid to play soccer. As in most other domains, the United States is trying to engineer its way to soccer relevance through data-driven, objective, skills-based education, money, and immigrant talent. COPA is a space where, like in so much of America, play and joy and the natural world—swimming in a lake or kicking a ball across actual grass—have been replaced by automation, surveillance, status, and award seeking. I should get a sticker for bringing him here.

When William earns five stickers, he moves up to Level 2, and I take him to Dairy Queen for a hot fudge sundae. At that point, he is still learning how to balance his toe on a stationary ball without falling over. When he earns ten stickers, he moves up to Level 3, and I take him to Dairy Queen for a hot fudge sundae. At that point, he is learning to dribble from animal to animal and back, pause, and put his toe on the ball. Next, he learns how to dribble fast or dribble slow from the parrot to the net—and shoot to score. When he earns twenty stickers, he moves up to Level 4, and I take him to Dairy Queen for a hot fudge sundae. By then he is four years old, full of hot fudge, and we move him to the four-to-five-year age group, over there on Jungle Turf 2, where another Brazilian kid, age four and a half, looks prepared for the World Cup. For the sake of privacy, I'll call this kid Max. Max does not wear a COPA jersey. He wears a canary yellow Brazilian national jersey with bright blue shorts. He is light on his toes, already developing his own style and flair, punting the ball into the net from anywhere in the room while his mom works on her laptop.

During sideline chit-chat, I ask Max's mom how he got so good. She says he's here five days a week, and when he's not here, he's on YouTube, watching soccer, copying what he sees. Indeed, he looks like a soccer prodigy in a YouTube clip. When Max is finally connected to the COPA Score machines, he is going to melt the sensors. Someday an army of German coaches will fight over him.

It makes me feel good to see Max here, because it means that, even though I've taken this American route to the jogo bonito, it's good enough for real Brazilians if I sprinkle in a little YouTube.

In Brazil, at least the part of Brazil where I would've grown up, the best players are forged in the streets, on uneven terrain, on cramped five-by-five futsal courts, where they learn to improvise. They develop the kind of muscle memory that you can learn only by playing with bare feet. They learn the kind of creativity that you can learn only in mixed-age-group pickup games with no adult supervision. You don't earn stickers; you earn respect. You earn a nickname. If you cry, it's your teammates, not your dad, who comfort you. Who knows who your dad is, anyway? Those players are forged the way I would've been forged if I had never left Brazil.

TWENTY YEARS AGO, the first time I returned to Belo Horizonte, the city of my birth, I picked up a blue soccer jersey—Cruzeiro—at the bus station. The next day, I met my birth mother for the first time, and her son, and her other son, and her daughter, my younger half brothers and half sister. After we'd gotten through the initial tsunami of emotions, my half brother Ramon, two years younger than me, rushed us back to the bus station to pick out an Atlético Mineiro jersey. The Felicianos were not Cruzeirenses. The Felicianos were puro gallo. The working-class team in BH.

When my brother found a jersey that fit me, he put on his Atlético jersey, and we took a picture together, and our mother beamed. On another planet, our mother would've watched us play futebol together in the alleyway with the creek running past. On another planet, we would've watched championship matches together. But on this planet, she saw me once as a baby, and then again, twenty-five years later, as a grown man who could barely speak his mother tongue. While my brothers played barefoot soccer in the alleyway, I was knocking baseballs around a sheep pasture.

And this is the awful metaphysics of our dilemma. We never would've been together in Brazil. If I had stayed in Brazil, if my father had not abandoned my mother, Ramon and Renato and Rosana would not have been born. If I had stayed in Brazil, my son William would not have been born. In some way, I never would have been born, or at least I would have another name, another life, my original life, for worse or for better, who's to say, but one thing you can say is that if I had been born and kept, instead of born and given up, then I would not be me, or at least not the me I know now, and that many people I love—including my own children—would not have been born. And there is nothing I can say or do, or would want to do, to undo all that, but maybe there is something I can do to bring us all full circle so we are on the same planet—Planet Soccer.

That's a lot of pressure to put on myself, and it's a lot of pressure to put on little William, who still needs his mother to go to sleep, and I tell myself that it's OK if I am here for all the wrong reasons, as long as he is here for the right reasons: hot fudge sundaes. But after a really good practice, I can tell he wants more. COPA is doing the job of filling him with something that I cannot. Confidence with the ball. Moves. I want him to own the ball. I want him to own Brazilian and Mexican and the space in between. I want him to own William.

I do not want soccer to own William. So far he wants to come to COPA. He wakes up some days and asks, "Is this a COPA day?" The older kids, the ones with COPA Scores, do not look like they are happy to be on Planet Soccer. I do not hear the sound of much laughter here. Their parents, if they are here at all, are on their smartphones. All the playfulness has been sucked out of the turf. This is a place for skills training, not play. This is a place to be improved, rated, sold off to the highest bidder.

By June, when Coach Amanda kicks the ball his direction, William can stop it with his foot and balance like a statue. Look up. Take action. When he tries to score a goal on Coach Amanda, he knows, somehow, how to juke her. He moves across the turf with the ball on a string. During some practices, he is tired, sleepy, rolling on the ground. During other practices he is focused, a look of determination and joy on his face like I've never seen. He is playing with a full ball—a bola cheia—and he knows it.

One night after dinner, William tells me he wants to go out to the backyard to play soccer.

"I'm great at soccer," he tells me.

"You are," I say. "You've been practicing."

And no matter what happens with soccer, I can already tell he is going to be great at being William. He doesn't even know the difference between Jungle Turf 1 and Estádio Maracanã. He doesn't know the difference between California and Oregon, between the United States and Brazil, between Coach Amanda and some future coach that might yell at him. But already he knows that a goal is something special, that not every ball flies true. A goal is a magical concoction of aim and force and luck. Like a life. If you score a goal, you should celebrate. I don't know how he knows that, but he knows. It's not something that comes from his papa, who has never scored a goal. It comes from a place inside him that has no name, no shame, no home or away. And as long as I can steer him clear of the lasers and the sensors, from being assigned a score, then I can keep his soccer Brazilian soccer—creative, joyful, poetry—and then maybe he'll stick with it. In a few years, he is going to feel it in his bones, in a place before memory, in his bare feet, and he is going to step onto a field with confidence, with flair, splitting defenders, elastico, vai vai vai vai vai, William, and he will cry when he loses, and he will cry when he wins, and he will nutmeg some kid named Chad from Walnut Creek, gol de placa, and he is going to dance, and his heart will be full, and our hearts will be full, finally, bola cheia, bola cheia.

But that's just my imagination. You could fill an ocean with my dreams for him. That he does not know those dreams is a grace. Another grandma, whom he has never met, another language that he has never spoken, a whole universe of ice cream treats he has never tasted, a whole new city with streets like veins. Someday we will visit, and I will roll out the ball, and he will play with his cousins in Bairro Santa Teresa, and if he plays long enough, an afternoon, a weekend, a summer, he will earn his nickname.

CHRIS FELICIANO ARNOLD is the author of *The Third Bank of the River: Power and Survival in the Twenty-First-Century Amazon*. He directs the MFA in Creative Writing program at Saint Mary's College of California.

The Dark Side of Sports Betting and Its Impact on NBA Players: Death Threats, Racism and Venmo Requests

JAMES L. EDWARDS III

FROM *The Athletic* • FEBRUARY 12, 2025

After every game, when the duties of that night are complete and Jalen Brunson has a chance to unwind, he opens his phone to dozens and dozens of messages on social media.

It doesn't matter if he scores 40 points or 20 points. It doesn't matter if the New York Knicks win by 30 points, two points or lose. The bulk of the messages tend to be the same: They threaten him and his family, including his months-old daughter. They call him racial slurs. They demand money.

Brunson could do what he's paid to do: play well and win basketball games. And yet, the star guard has spent many postgame nights sifting through harsh messages from people who wager money—sometimes large sums—on things they can't control.

"Genuinely threatened?" Brunson asked himself, pondering for a moment, after the question was posed by The Athletic. "I've never felt genuinely threatened, but there has been some really disrespectful s— said. It's a lot of people who don't have profile pictures. There is part of me that has thought about airing them out, but s— always comes back around."

Now that sports gambling is legal in many states and widespread, this kind of abuse has become increasingly common and unavoidable part of players' lives. It's an unintended consequence of opening up this revenue floodgate.

In 2018, the U.S. Supreme Court overturned a federal ban on sports betting at the state level, clearing the way for several states to legalize it. That made it so accessible that people can wager larger sums of money from their phones while sitting within the comfortable confines of their home, a bar or even an arena as they're inside watching the game in front of them. Per The American Gaming Association, the industry made $10.92 billion in revenue in 2023, and states collected almost $2 billion from tax revenue.

The NBA announced last year that it would allow fans watching games on its streaming app to track betting odds and click through to make bets with the league's betting partners, FanDuel and DraftKings. (The Athletic has a partnership with BetMGM.)

Under the NBA's collective bargaining agreement, players can invest in sports betting and fantasy sports companies, but their ownership stake must be less than one percent in any company that takes NBA bets. Players, however, cannot gamble on games in their league.

Last year, Toronto Raptors forward Jontay Porter was banned from the NBA for what Adam Silver termed "a cardinal sin" of betting on the league's games. Miami Heat guard Terry Rozier is under federal investigation for possibly manipulating his performance in a 2023 game as part of illegal sports gambling scheme. The league was alerted to suspicious betting surrounding Rozier but "did not find a violation of NBA rules," a league spokesperson said.

When legal sports betting really started to take off, and was new to almost everyone—including the players—Brunson got concerned about the messages he was receiving. Couple the eagerness of fans who could freely wager from home with the direct access to athletes through social media, and Brunson admittedly struggled to comprehend what was going on.

The league has processes in place that allow players to report incidents to their teams and/or the league office, an NBA spokesperson told The Athletic. NBA security also monitors social media for threatening messaging and works with teams to identify persons responsible and, if necessary, involve law enforcement. Multiple players who have talked to The Athletic have said they weren't aware of the protocols in place.

Even then, there isn't anything that can stop players from receiving these messages directly to their phones, not without making their accounts private or not having social media all together.

"It's gotten to the point where it's somewhat comical to me now, but, at first, I was like...What the f—?" Brunson said.

Detroit Pistons center Isaiah Stewart began his NBA career around the same time online sports betting launched in Michigan. At this time, during the COVID-19 pandemic, spectators weren't allowed in arenas. So, a lot of Stewart's early interactions with fans came via social media, where people were upset about something he did or didn't do on the court that lost them a bet.

"No, not at all. That's their decision," Stewart said by telephone when asked if there is ever any guilt when someone tells them they lost a bet. "They chose to put money and bet on our games. You find it funny, until there's a line that they cross when it's not funny.

"They've said a lot of crazy things like from bringing up family, to commenting on my wife, my son."

When in college at Marquette, Knicks rookie Tyler Kolek said he would receive hateful messages after every game.

"I've been told, 'Go kill yourself,'" Kolek said. "I've gotten worse than that, but that's a common one."

Washington Wizards guard Corey Kispert—who came into the NBA in 2021—said he and his teammates receive messages almost nightly, usually after losses. The Wizards have yet to have a winning record since Kispert entered the league.

Kispert said it's often the same people, all of whom have no profile pictures and no username that suggest who they truly are. Death threats are common.

"No, normally I don't [report death threats]," Kispert said. "I mean, these people are pretty much anonymous on social media. We just kind of feel like we can let it go. It's the dark side of it all."

Milwaukee Bucks forward Kyle Kuzma finds the interactions he receives on social media humorous.

"I don't really read the messages," Kuzma said. "It might be on Twitter. I think it's really funny, honestly, because, yeah, you can win money, but you're also wasting money, too, at the same time. It's funny because I said something the other day, and it's like we get threats and we get called names, and people never think about like maybe they're bad at picking the parlays?"

For Knicks guard Josh Hart, there rarely is a difference between him getting 10 rebounds in a game or nine. In the majority of instances, one rebound won't determine if Hart did his job successfully; his job being to help the Knicks win basketball games. However, for @sportsbettor12345 or John Doe in Long Island, Hart only having nine rebounds instead of 10 can potentially be the difference between that person being able to pay their mortgage that month, or even worse.

"I get everything," Hart said. "People say, 'I hope you die.' They wish injury. Racial stuff."

Hart and his teammates never let someone's betting anger or need dictate how they perform. Yet, it's nearly impossible for these 20-somethings who are online to not be impacted one way or another.

Hart, admittedly, has played into someone's anger before, prior to sportsbooks being open across the country. It was back in college, and while he doesn't remember the bet that someone lost due to his performance, he recalls the person sending a message with their Venmo attached so that they could get repaid for their financial loss.

It backfired.

"It was in Providence, and someone told me I messed [some bet up], so I sent them $1 on Venmo," Hart said. "Then I started getting a bunch of Venmo requests, and I was like, 'All right.'"

The Golden State Warriors' Trayce Jackson-Davis gets people demanding money regularly.

"'What's your Venmo, bro? You sold my parlay,'" he said of the messages he gets. "'You could have grabbed one more rebound or you could have had one more layup.' That happens all the time. Or people behind the bench will be like 'Trayce, I need 10 boards from you tonight!'"

New York guard Miles McBride tries his best to ignore any gambling-related messages that he gets. However, McBride added that most of his gambling interactions with fans come during the offseason, when he's trying to blend in as a normal civilian. People will come up to him and say, "You won me a lot of money!" or "You sold me one time." And, no matter which side of the track a fan is on, McBride attempts to not feed into it.

"I think the first-bucket bet might be the one I notice all the time," McBride said. "I see guys high-fiving in the stands and it's just a regular layup. I think it's funny."

Last month, with the final seconds winding down on the Orlando Magic beating the Knicks inside Madison Square Garden, New York guard Cam Payne hoisted a 3 that turned what would have been a 103–91 Orlando victory into a 103–94 Magic win. The shot gave Payne eight points on the night.

In the grand scheme of things, Payne taking and making that final 3 had no impact on the game. Yet, for one reason or another, whether it was the point differential, Payne's point total or the total points scored in the game, the shot came with repercussions from betting fans.

"Everyone is mad at your boy if he doesn't play well or doesn't make shots," Payne said. "They be on me about their little parlays.

"It's funny that people are out there looking for that instead of just watching the game. It's just funny to me. We don't ask you to bet your money."

The NBA's—and other sports leagues'—big-picture approach to lean into the legalization of sports betting has helped create these possibilities. It's also impacted in-arena experiences with fans screaming at players and coaches based solely on whether they lost or won a wager. Team security does not confront abusive fans. That responsibility rests on arena security. Fans are often given verbal warnings when first breaking the NBA's Fan Code of Conduct, which the league promotes at every game. A second and third incident by a spectator could lead to them being kicked out of the arena.

Ultimately, there is only so much the league can do to limit interactions or abuse related to betting. The league can't police a player's social media account. And asking players not to check their accounts is unrealistic in the modern world.

Gambling is now part of the fabric of collegiate and professional sports, and there is likely no turning back. After all, the love of money is the root of all evil, and there's a lot of money in sports gambling.

"That's what I get upset about," Knicks guard Mikal Bridges said. "When I lose someone a bet, [I get hate messages]. I don't get anything when I win them a bet.

"Where's my money at?"

JAMES L. EDWARDS III is a staff writer for The Athletic covering the New York Knicks. Previously, he covered the Detroit Pistons at The Athletic for seven seasons and, before that, was a reporter for the *Lansing State Journal*, where he covered his alma mater, Michigan State, and high school sports. He hails from Flint, Michigan.

The Longest Journey

CASSIDY RANDALL

FROM *The Atavist* • JUNE 2025

"It is important to affirm, and prove, that we go to the mountains to live and not to die, that we are not fanatics but firm believers, and that the few accidents which occur are hard but not useless lessons."

—Italian alpinist Guido Rey

ONE

The tent quaked in the howling wind. The storm had raged for three days, trapping Lena and Ruby Rowat at a narrow notch in the mountain ridge. By now the ceaseless sound of flapping nylon had become maddening. When the storm was unleashed on March 25, 2001, the sisters had only just skied to this pass, called Manatee Col. They hastily assembled a tent; there'd been no time to build up enough snow to create a windblock. Snow now piled against the shelter's walls, threatening to collapse and bury them. When the women went outside to shovel it away, they threw themselves through the door to keep their sleeping bags from being covered in snow, which could soak the down that kept their bodies warm. They couldn't afford to be careless. The nearest town—the British Columbia ski mecca of Whistler—was at least a four-day journey south on skis, up snow-draped peaks and down unpopulated valleys.

Lena, 28, and Ruby, 30, lit a stove inside the tent to cook food and dry their gear—a calculated risk, given that the tent wasn't flame-retardant. But the heat from the stove and their bodies melted the snow beneath the floor, and it began to dip like the hull of a canoe, pooling water and pitching the sisters toward each other as they slept. Above the rampaging wind, they could hear the muffled roar of avalanches around them.

Such dangers might explain why no one had done what Lena and Ruby were attempting on this expedition: traverse North America's Coast Range, a giant's backbone of mountains stretching nearly 1,000 miles from near their home in Vancouver all the way to Alaska and the Yukon. Some veteran mountaineers and skiers thought that it was impossible to ski it in one go. The Coast Range was remote and glaciated, shot through with raging rivers, almost laughably difficult to access, and notorious for unholy elevation gain, from sea level to peaks as high as 13,000 feet.

Then there was the wild scale of it all: Many considered it the longest nonpolar ski journey ever attempted. Some called it the longest technical ski traverse in the world. It demanded months of arduous travel and route finding. Anyone who tried it would have to navigate crevasses, avalanches, and the storms that broke across the mountains like waves. Traveling the entire length was the equivalent of climbing and descending more than eighteen Mount Everests over a distance equivalent to nearly fifty marathons.

Yet Lena Rowat thought it could be done. Outwardly, Lena lived a life of epic adventure: skiing, mountaineering, through-hiking, cycling across the continent. She was known in Whistler's ski community as a six-foot-tall powerhouse with insane endurance, game to try almost any mountain objective. She wore thrift-store clothes, preferring bright tights and flowery dresses over brand-name gear, and sometimes shed clothing altogether to ski naked. She dyed her short hair—once bright blue, now bleached white—and danced on tables at parties, without any need for alcohol or drugs to let loose.

But underneath the hard-charging, fun-loving exterior, she mostly felt lost and depressed. She had no structure in her life, no steady job, and was often overwhelmed by a bottomless feeling of isolation. The mountains were the only place where her brain calmed. Which was one reason she was excited to tackle the Coast Range traverse: It had the tantalizing potential to fill her inner emptiness.

She just needed her sister, equally capable in the mountains, to join as her partner. The two had had matching facial features, but Ruby was much shorter, with a gymnast's compact body, and hair dyed a deep magenta. Lena liked the idea of achieving this first together. Other than their mother, she knew of very few women in the world of mountain sports, and sometimes struggled to find adventure partners—simply, she assumed, because she was female. Lena liked that she and Ruby could model the kinds of possibilities for women and girls that the two of them didn't have growing up.

Except it seemed that it would be men who completed the Coast Range route first. Somehow, after so many years when a full traverse was thought impossible, a young Canadian alpinist had dreamed the same dream at the same time. His team of four men left four weeks ahead of the Rowat sisters.

The women had raced to begin their own journey, and three weeks later they were pinned down by the storm. Now, in the besieged interior of their meager shelter, Lena's stomach began to roll with nausea. In the hours that followed, it worsened. She had to exit the tent repeatedly to relieve herself. The storm showed no signs of abating as Lena's illness intensified. In that moment, dejected mentally and cut down physically, she considered abandoning the attempt altogether.

But she couldn't go back now. Not after all the work that had gone into planning the expedition. Not when all that waited back home was crippling loneliness and the lurking sense that she'd failed.

Lena wasn't the only one in adventure sports who'd battled demons. Such endeavors often draw the misfits, the slightly crazed, the traumatized. Acute levels of risk, like those found in mountaineering, ski touring, whitewater kayaking, and climbing, can offer a tantalizing opportunity to mask a void—or, for people like Lena, fill it. Walking the thin line between life and death demands the kind of focus that can cause the demons to fall away entirely, and help athletes feel part of something bigger than what plagues them. But many never take the next step and figure out what's behind an interior wound, or do the deep work to heal it.

Lena would do both—but only after her Coast Range journey brought her face-to-face with death.

LENA WAS BORN in the aftermath of a snowstorm. In 1972, Nona and Peter Rowat spent Christmas and New Year's in a rustic cabin at the base of the Whistler ski resort, north of Vancouver. Nona was nine months pregnant with Lena, and had sworn to press pause on skiing; she was due any day. As a family doctor and a pioneer of preventive medicine who'd publicly supported midwifery decades before it was recognized as a medical profession, she knew how to take care of herself and her unborn baby. But a New Year's Eve storm delivered so much fresh powder that Nona couldn't resist. At the end of a day on the slopes, she went into labor. Lena was born just after midnight on January 2, 1973.

It was a fitting entry into a family that prioritized outdoor adventure. Ruby and Lena learned to ski by the time they were school-age. Soon they were carrying their own backpacks on multiday trips on Vancouver Island's rugged West Coast Trail, through rain and mud and mosquitos. With such activities came risk. When Lena and Ruby were in middle school, Peter took the girls on a winter backcountry trip. He taught them to dig a snow cave and melt water with a stove, which Ruby said released so much carbon monoxide they nearly suffocated. A few years later, as the family returned with friends from a wilderness hut in the Tantalus Range, a torrential storm brought flooding that caused Lena and another girl to be swept off their feet as they crossed a swollen creek. Lena still has a clear memory of being submerged in the water, desperately clinging to a branch at the creek's edge, her feet hooking her friend to keep her from being carried away.

As Lena and Ruby grew older, they appreciated that their parents instilled in them the passion and the skill set—not to mention the capacity to handle themselves when things went sideways—that were key ingredients for staying safe outdoors. But it also seemed to them that their parents too often prioritized their own desires over the needs of their children. (Nona and Peter once left two-year-old Ruby tied to a tree, watched over by a friend's dog, while they executed a nearby multi-pitch climb.) Lena often felt like she only deserved love when she was getting after it in the mountains. At the same time, she felt unprepared for regular life, with its responsibilities and rules. Worse, she lacked the ability to relate to others. Lena struggled to connect with people beyond her family. She had few friends growing up.

Things briefly improved during college. She made friends and experienced her first romantic relationships, which were with other women. One lasted a year and a half. When it ended, Lena blamed herself. She noticed her baseline mood lowering, her emotions sinking beneath the surface.

After graduating, Lena moved back to Vancouver, into the house where she grew up. Her parents had moved to San Diego when Peter, a neuroscientist, took a job at the University of California campus there. They leased most of the house to tenants, and Lena paid a nominal rent to live in the basement. With her family gone—Ruby, a talented gymnast, was traveling the world as a trapeze artist—Lena had next to no social contact. She lacked a steady job too, following a short stint planting trees and a brief try at medical school. She felt useless, without purpose.

She wished there was even one person who wanted to spend time with her or cared about what was going on in her life.

The only thing that gave Lena relief was skiing. She volunteered on the ski patrol at Whistler, biking or hitchhiking nearly 75 miles each way from Vancouver. She soon bored of the resort runs and began skiing outside the ropes. Avalanche education was new and hard to obtain, and Lena's parents paid for her to take the only course she could find. She slept in her car in the parking lot during the weeklong instruction, taking naturally to the dirtbag lifestyle pioneered by climbers and ski bums.

In the winter of 1998, Lena and one of her only friends, Merrie-Beth Board, ski-toured in the backcountry outside Whistler as often as they could. After she'd descended several big lines, people said that Lena was good enough to go pro in the burgeoning sport of big-mountain skiing. But being in the backcountry gave her an elusive joy she was reluctant to saddle with obligation. Plus, she could hardly handle everyday tasks let alone chase sponsorships.

And God, she was still so lonely. On top of Lena's stunted ability to connect with people, the seasonal nature of mountain towns made social attachments ephemeral for everyone, contributing to a feeling of isolation in a place with few mental health services to turn to. Not that mountain culture in that era was ready to prioritize mental health. The mostly male community overwhelmingly prized strength, speed, stoicism, and infallible expertise. A willingness to show vulnerability was—and too often still is—sacrificed as the cost of belonging.

And so Lena sacrificed. By the late 1990s, her depression was so deep that she found herself sometimes thinking about suicide.

Then, in the summer of 1999, Peter took his daughters to climb Mount Waddington, the highest peak in the Coast Range Mountains at 13,000 feet. One day on that expedition, Lena gazed at the glaciers spilling out in every direction. She thought how easy it was to travel on them through the mountains. She pulled out a map of the range. The glaciers seemed to stretch from her home in Vancouver all the way to Alaska, into the Saint Elias Mountains, up and over Mount Logan (Canada's highest peak), and down to the Gulf of Alaska. You could strap on a pair of skis and just keep going.

From that moment on, Lena's plan was to connect the entire stretch over several years, in two-month segments. That's how Peter tackled long traverses too, traveling in March and April when conditions were optimal. Here, she thought, was a project that would take three or four spring seasons to complete. A sense of direction that would span years.

TWO

Lena didn't leave on the expedition immediately. Ruby needed to block out enough time away from performing to join her sister. In the meantime, Lena floated through jobs and undertook a last-minute cycling trip on a rickety second-hand bike, riding 2,500 miles from Florida to her parents' San Diego home. Then, around Christmas in 2000, she heard that another local skier was planning a Coast Range traverse—and aiming to do it all in one go.

His name was Guy Edwards. He was the ex of a woman Lena had hiked nearly a thousand miles of the southern Pacific Crest Trail with in the summer of 1997. He was known as Fast Eddie, renowned in both the American and Canadian mountain communities for his climbing feats on ice, snow, rock walls, and boulders. He had an almost hyperactive energy and an effervescent personality. Like Lena, Guy preferred fluorescent secondhand clothing to technical apparel. He painted his toenails. He had a monkish dedication to traveling light and held several climbing speed records. But he wasn't chasing fame with his records and first ascents. Like many in the B.C. coast's outdoor community, he believed that a person's accomplishments should fly under the radar.

When Lena heard what Guy was planning, she called his house and left a message on the answering machine: She wanted in on the trip, and maybe Ruby could come, too. Guy returned Lena's call in early January. His team was aiming to reach Skagway in Alaska, he said, a 1,200-mile journey over seven months. It was short of Lena's vision of going all the way to Mount Logan—an additional 420 miles—but she was still interested. He said he'd have to speak to his other teammates first.

Guy had been planning the traverse for months and had already assembled an all-star team of alpinists: Vance Culbert, John Millar, and Dan Clark. Guy and Vance connected years earlier through the Varsity Outdoor Club (VOC), a cadre of climbers and mountaineers at the University of British Columbia. He and Guy had done expeditions together, including climbing Waddington without any maps, testing their route-finding skills up the complicated mountain. Guy and Vance left from their back doors in Vancouver; kayaked nearly 50 miles up Bute Inlet; skied 55 miles to the peak through trail-less rainforest; and after climbing to within 65 feet of the summit, bushwhacked to a logging road, where they hitched a ride home. The trip exemplified the human-powered ethos that prevailed among the coast's adventure community at the time; fueled by environmentalism, they eschewed helicopters, ski lifts, even their own vehicles when on expeditions.

Dan Clark grew up in Calgary and had learned to climb in the Rocky Mountains. He'd skied other long expeditions, including a first-ever traverse in the Columbia Mountains west of Banff. When he heard that a few guys were planning an epic journey across the Coast Range, he drove out to persuade Guy to let him join the team.

The VOC also placed John Millar in Guy's orbit. Only 22, John emanated a quiet maturity. He was the middle child of a largely absent father, both physically and emotionally; John's mother, Eileen, had raised him. He was a sensitive kid who grew into a big youth, ultimately reaching six-foot-five, with explosive emotions. At the University of British Columbia, he discovered an outlet for his unwieldy inner life: Climbing, skiing, and mountaineering provided a focus for his energy and immense strength. He learned quickly and became just as strong an alpinist as Guy, although he broadcasted his accomplishments even less.

Lena endured another restless week before Guy called her back a second time. He apologized, but his team was only a month out from departure and already too far along in their planning—which included 24 food caches, nine of which would be dropped by helicopter or ski plane—to add additional members. He kept her number just in case.

In tears, Lena called Ruby in Montreal. Could they at least do the first of their spring traverses—more than 400 miles from Vancouver to Bella Coola—this year? It seemed improbable. The men had spent nearly a year planning; Lena and Ruby would have just weeks. And Lena's capacity for the complicated logistics of a three-month expedition was close to nil. Had Ruby said no, the idea might have imploded right there.

But Ruby said yes. She spent hours each day on the phone counseling Lena through her depression and anxiety as Lena organized nearly two dozen buckets of food into daily rations and grouped them by traverse section. They also had to pinpoint locations for food drops and find pilots to handle them. Perhaps most important, Ruby needed to obtain a pair of telemark skis, made for touring. Though she had some experience in the backcountry, she had never tele-skied before. Yet she didn't think twice about undertaking a massive expedition on unfamiliar equipment, in perilous terrain, with limited options for getting back to civilization if something went wrong. Neither did it seem to bother her that she'd just broken a rib performing. After all, this was a Rowat-family adventure.

On March 2, four weeks after the men left, Lena and Ruby stepped into their skis and began skinning—skiing uphill using long strips of synthetic material stuck to the bottom of their skis for traction. They were undaunted by the enormity of the journey before them. Lena's brain didn't roil. She didn't sense the ever present welling of tears. Heading up into the heights with her sister, she was singing at the top of her lungs.

THREE

Three weeks later, inside the storm-racked tent on Manatee Col, the Rowat sisters dug out their satellite phone and desperately dialed their father, hoping for moral support, advice, and a weather forecast. Lena's stomach had settled some, but the fact that they were trapped by the storm for days had deflated her confidence.

Through a crackling connection, Peter Rowat told his daughters that the storm wouldn't clear for a while. But, he reminded them, conditions were often calmer below the ridgeline. And one more thing, he said. Guy Edwards had called the Rowats' house from his own satellite phone.

The men's expedition had hit a snag, too; they'd run into a storm of their own a couple of weeks prior. It pinned them down for a few days as their food supply dwindled. Once the weather calmed, they raced to a logging camp for one of their food caches. Desperately low on provisions, the group were traveling in the dark when Dan skied off the lip of a drainage ditch and slammed hard into the ground below. He came up bleeding and unable to shoulder his pack, let alone ski. They arranged a float plane for him to see a doctor, hoping he'd soon rejoin the team. But Dan had fractured two cervical vertebrae in his neck. He was lucky he wasn't paralyzed. His Coast Range traverse was over.

The men replaced Dan with a skier named Kari Medig, but he was only available for a portion of the trip, and the team needed a fourth to climb technical sections in pairs. Guy had called to ask if Lena wanted to join for the northern stretch. The invitation sparked her spirits. She asked her father to tell Guy that she would be there as soon as she could. She only needed to reach Bella Coola with Ruby—after three weeks, they were just shy of halfway there—then she could join for the 620-mile leg to Skagway. The sisters quickly took their father's advice to abandon the ridge, packing up their snow-drenched gear in the gale. Five hundred feet below camp, the wind disappeared. The snow let up as they descended farther.

Days stretched into weeks. More unstable weather forced more idle time in the tent. In the rainforested valleys, they slogged through the thick, slushy snow skiers refer to as elephant snot and bushwhacked the sharp spears of a plant called devil's club, with spines that can pierce skin even through sturdy clothing. Higher up, they contended with avalanche danger and crevasses. Ruby once stepped through snow into the empty air of a thinly covered chasm, her heart nearly stopping before she stepped carefully backward onto solid ground.

It wasn't all misery, though. Under the spring sun, the sisters traveled topless and skinny-dipped in glacial pools. Lena occasionally skied in a bright print frock she called her party dress. Several inches taller than her sister, she moved with the long strides of a giraffe. Ruby was an accomplished athlete herself, yet she often found herself lagging behind. When Ruby led, doing the hard work of breaking trail through the snow, the women found that their pace matched if Lena took on just a few pounds from Ruby's pack. Despite substantial experience in the mountains, Lena's self-doubt had kept her from seeing just how capable she was. "I think she realized, for the first time, that she was stronger than her older sister," Ruby told me. "That trip helped launch her confidence in some respects, that she had that competence out there."

Yet both felt their relationship fraying. Lena wasn't just moving faster because her legs were longer. She wanted to join Guy's team, and could seem impatient to do so. For Ruby, the 400-mile journey from Vancouver to Bella Coola—an enormous feat in itself—was the goal. As was spending time with her sister. After the call to their father, Ruby sensed the dynamic with her sister shift. "This was something we said we'd do together," she said, "and then suddenly Lena was just keen to get on with these other people."

By the time they reached the tiny settlement of Bella Coola, the Rowats had covered more than 400 miles in 54 days—a day faster than the men. Ruby gave Lena her skis, since Lena had damaged her own. The sisters hugged goodbye on the side of the highway. Then Ruby caught a ride south with family friends to return to the life she'd built. Alone on the road, Lena stuck out her thumb to hitchhike north, toward a life she still needed to create.

Lena met the team in Terrace, British Columbia, where Guy, Vance, and John were staying to regroup and make repairs. Lena and John knelt on the floor of a house to examine a pair of busted skis. Lena had met him before, back in January; though he'd turned down her request to join the expedition, Guy invited her to come look at maps with his team. But in Lena's anxious and depressed state, she retained none of her first impressions. She'd been apprehensive walking into the Terrace house as a new team member; she didn't know the others well and had no idea if they'd get along. Now John turned to her, his chin wispy with the thin beard of an adolescent. "Let's see if we can find a Leatherperson," he said.

Lena stared up at him as he lifted his full height off the floor. The name of the tool he'd referred to, a sort of Swiss Army knife on steroids, was Leatherman. Who was this guy who'd thought to say Leather*person* instead? She could tell it wasn't to impress her. It just seemed to be the way his brain worked.

With the mountains as his guide, John had grown from a troubled youth into a good and jovial man. At potlucks, he was always first to do the dishes—then mischievously hide them in obscure spots in the kitchen. In Yosemite during one climbing trip, he stepped in when a group of policemen roughed up a drunk climber on crutches. John asked them to stand down; they threw him in jail for the night. Vance called him a warrior monk. Guy called him a superhero with morals.

Despite feeling welcomed by John, worries about the expedition gnawed at Lena during those few days in Terrace. Would she be able to keep up? Ski well enough? Be a capable team member? What would they think of her if she couldn't?

Finally, the team of four headed into the mountains. They hadn't gone far when Lena skied over a dip in the slope, bumped into Vance's back, and fell backward in her heavy pack. She looked like a stranded turtle. Everyone, including Lena herself, burst into laughter. She felt the tension ease, like a pressure valve releasing.

The feeling wouldn't last. A few days later, the men pulled out collapsible sleds—helpful for moving gear over flat terrain. Lena and Ruby had brought one, too, but opted not to use it. Now it took Lena a long time to assemble hers as the men skied off. Once underway, she had to stop repeatedly to adjust it. As she fell farther behind, anxiety rose in a sour tide.

"It was an abandonment trigger for me," Lena recalled. "A lot of my childhood was, 'You better keep up or else.'" When she was older, she noticed that being able to go far, fast, won her positive feedback. But if her teammates paid any mind to the trouble she had with her sled, no one said anything about it.

Over the next few weeks, Lena began to feel more comfortable. She skied in her party dress. She skinny-dipped in glacial ponds. Evenings, she sat with the others watching the sun set over the spires and ramparts of mountains few people had laid eyes on. And she proved herself a valuable member of the team. Once, while navigating a complex icefall—a steep section of jumbled ice—Guy was in the lead, tied onto a rope with Lena. He stepped onto a pile of snowy ice to jump across a narrow crevasse. When it collapsed, he disappeared into the void. Lena sat down immediately to use her body as an anchor until Guy could pull himself out.

Lena also experimented with ways to navigate the Coast Range's numerous rivers, whose banks were choked with tangled alder and thickets of devil's club. After bushwhacking a difficult stretch, she inflated her sleeping pad and placed her pack and climbing gear on top—including her sharp crampons and ice axe. Then she waded into the river to swim while pushing the makeshift raft ahead of her. The men had begged her not to do it; it would be catastrophic to lose everything in the river or be swept away herself. Lena was undeterred, and paddled past the men as they struggled onshore. "She did things her way," Vance said. "Which often turned out for the better, even though there was a high degree of risk involved."

On June 1, about a month after she'd joined the men in Terrace, Lena and John were walking together when he turned to Lena, pulled her in, and kissed her.

Lena felt a jolt of thrill—and surprise. Not because previously she'd been with women; if she was honest, she'd fallen in love with all three men on the expedition. She'd thought she and Guy might end up together—John was several years younger, and Vance was already in a relationship. But Lena had come to know John as a strong, quiet goofball. He was caring and selfless; without fail, he was the first to wake up on frigid mornings to make something hot for the rest of them. He was completely himself, and he made Lena feel appreciated for who she was. So when John kissed her, she relaxed into the moment.

It had been a bold move on John's part. He was painfully shy around women. By the time he was 22, he hadn't even kissed a girl. Inexperienced though he was, John was mature enough to want to avoid upending team dynamics with what could turn into a budding romance. He suggested they keep their mutual attraction secret, confined to nights when they were paired up in the tent rotation or during rare moments alone. Lena went along with it. Guy and Vance remained cheerfully oblivious. And though Lena and John's relationship didn't really exist outside of intermittent nights spent pressed against each other in the scant privacy afforded by nylon walls, the loneliness that had strangled Lena for years began to loosen its grip. Soon, John became the love of Lena's young life.

Weeks later, in the long midsummer light of southeast Alaska, the small party of skiers blazed like beacons of color against the glistening pale of the Stikine Icecap. Their figures were dwarfed by its expanse and the stark silhouette of the great spire they skied toward. Like an ancient stone monolith, the Devils Thumb rises more than 9,000 feet from a glacial basin dubbed the Witches Cauldron. Its sawtoothed massif—a forbidding wall of rock and ice—had called to alpinists for decades and was one of the most challenging climbs on the continent. To this day, fewer than fifty people have made it to the summit.

The team had no intention of merely passing by the Devils Thumb; to climb it, even by an established route, was still a great prize in alpinism. The men had arranged for a food cache and some climbing gear to be dropped there, just enough for two climbers at a time to make the attempt. Vance went first with his girlfriend, Cecelia Mortenson. A competent mountaineer who'd just returned from a solo traverse in the Himalayas, Cecelia had met up with the team at a fishing lodge on the Stikine River. The pair were turned around before the summit ridge by an impassable pinnacle of rock. Next went Guy and John, the group's strongest climbers, choosing a different route straight up the face; they, too, were stymied.

That left Lena. She wanted to climb with John, but he was exhausted from his attempt. Vance offered to go back up with her. It was only after they'd ascended the first steep snowfield that Vance realized Lena had never climbed a technical alpine peak before. "She was so confident in herself, she just believed she could do anything," Vance said. Still, to realize that he was on the Devils Thumb with an inexperienced partner, far from any help should something go wrong, was unsettling.

They spent a long afternoon and night—a dusky twilight so far north—ascending, including a pitch of aid climbing, which Lena had never done before. Under Vance's direction, Lena learned to step up and pull on pieces of a webbing ladder and loops that Vance fixed in the rock and ice. They crested the knife-edge summit ridge, empty air dropping away for thousands of feet on either side, as the sun lit the basin.

But just before the summit, they were stopped by a pillar of smooth rock. The only way around it was to traverse the wildly steep, snow-covered north face, and the day was too warm for the snow to support their weight. They were forced to turn around. Vance built a snow anchor for them to rappel off a steep pitch. He explained that if the snow anchor appeared to hold his weight, she should pull out the backup anchor, called a picket, so as not to leave any gear on the mountain. As he rappelled down the pitch, Lena saw the snow anchor give only the slightest bit. She pulled the picket, tied onto the rope, and leaned her whole body back into space.

The snow anchor failed immediately. Vance watched, horrified, as Lena sailed over his head, somersaulting down the nearly vertical rock of the south face. The rope screamed through his hands, the friction burning his gloves as he grasped at it desperately. As Lena catapulted downward, her life didn't flash before her eyes. Instead, a mantra played in her head: Try to stop, try to find handholds, don't give up.

Miraculously, the rope tied itself into a knot and arrested her fall after more than 100 feet. Lena came to rest on an angled snow patch. She sat up in the sudden stillness, shocked to be alive and amazed that Vance still had one end of the rope. She climbed back up to him as he belayed her. When she reached him, he was in tears. "I was a total wreck," Vance said. "I almost killed Lena." She appeared to him as calm as a windless day. (The feeling of free-falling would haunt her in flashbacks, every time she rappelled, well into the future.)

When the pair made it back to camp, they passed along the climbing gear to Guy and John, who were eager for a second attempt, without disclosing Lena's near-death experience. They only told the others what had happened when the men returned the following morning after another unsuccessful try. For Guy and John, the failure to summit the Devils Thumb was the only disappointment of the entire journey. As they skied away, the image of that tower of ice and stone stamped itself on their brains.

On July 16, the Coast Range team stepped into the Alaskan mining town of Skagway. The streets bustled with cruise-ship tourists, so the team couldn't have stood out more: They were dirty and disheveled, with skis strapped to their backs in the middle of summer. In the preceding five and a half months, they'd traveled more than 1,200 miles. They navigated avalanching slopes, icefalls, crevasses, and storms, using paper maps, compasses, and the still-developing technology of GPS. They climbed 14 major peaks, including two first ascents. And they completed what many consider the longest technical ski traverse in the world.

But when they got to Skagway, there were no reporters, no welcoming party. Fanfare would have been anathema to them anyway. None of them were after glory. This wasn't the culmination of some competition. It was a love affair, an homage from a few bold skiers to the mountains they considered home. Later, when word got out that the Coast Range had been traversed, the same people who'd said it was impossible "bowed their heads, calling it the greatest ski ever completed, anywhere," wrote Geoff Powter, then editor of the *Canadian Alpine Journal*. "They said these young skiers were the next great generation, that they'd set the stage for a whole new era of exploration."

Now that it was over, most of them were keen to move on. Guy and John were ready to get back to rock climbing. Vance was headed to graduate school. But Lena felt that the expedition had given her direction, taught her to function through the chaos in her brain. She'd connected with people meaningfully for the first time in her life. And it had delivered John. Lena didn't want it to end. She could have kept going forever.

FOUR

After Skagway, Lena had a new objective: completing the pieces of the traverse she'd missed. But without companions for the endeavor, she felt herself begin to drift again. John tossed her a lifeline. He invited her to come to Vancouver and learn to rock-climb with him and Guy. The three of them lived in a rental house dubbed the Mansion, which overflowed with a rotating cast of climbers connected to the VOC. Only four names were on the lease, yet at one point 17 people got their mail there. John had once claimed the kitchen closet as his room.

The bustling house meant that Lena and John were rarely alone. Even when they climbed together, it was often with Guy or other housemates. In the few months they cohabitated there, she and John made only one trip that was just the two of them. It was to Mount Sedgwick, a hard-to-access peak in the Squamish wilderness that generally called for what one local mountaineer had called "two days of extreme-level sufferfest" to summit. When they'd reached the peak, Lena sat in John's lap, the whole of the B.C. coast laid out below them, and they enjoyed a quiet moment together. Despite having spent little time alone together, John was certain enough of his relationship with Lena to introduce her to his mother, Eileen, at her house on Quadra Island, north of Vancouver. In Eileen's kitchen, Lena and John danced to the ukulele notes of his favorite song, "Somewhere Over the Rainbow."

By the fall of 2001, Lena was restless and making plans to undertake what she considered the complete Coast Range traverse: from Haines, Alaska, to Mount Logan, the roof of Canada at 19,551 feet, and back down to the Gulf of Alaska. She asked John to join her, but he was more interested in climbing than skiing, and about to join an expedition dubbed the Endless Summer—a group of climbers sailing all over the world and summiting peaks from Alaska to Antarctica. He left for New Zealand in mid-September. The decision and the distance would have ended many relationships, and Lena still battled her belief that people didn't really love her if they didn't want to go on adventures with her. As she mulled over their relationship, Lena decided to join the expedition, too, in late January. But by then John was getting ready to leave it—which left her to suspect that he didn't want her there.

The pair overlapped for just two nights in Ushuaia, Argentina, where John proudly gifted Lena a sweater he'd knit. Lena loved it—both the sweater and the gesture, which helped ease her angst about their prospects as a couple. On their first night together again, they slept on a mattress in a storage locker by the dock; the second they spent in a high valley, holding the tent down against a fierce wind.

Lena returned to Canada in March and left for her Logan traverse in late April 2002. The logistics of this expedition were easier. The long stints of glacier travel were more straightforward, and there were teammates to help. She'd enlisted Kari Medig, who'd skied a portion of the Coast Range traverse before Lena; Merrie-Beth Board, with whom Lena explored the Whistler backcountry; and Jacqui Hudson, a VOC member who was dating Guy. Also, her brain felt calmer. She'd begun to develop a community around her. And she still had John. Although he wouldn't be joining, he drove Lena and the others down to Bellingham to catch the ferry to Alaska.

Most people who climb Mount Logan set up a base camp on its flank and ascend via the King's Trench, considered the easiest route up the mountain. But Lena's team planned to ski nearly 280 miles from sea level in Haines and ascend the more difficult East Ridge. Once underway, the Logan traverse was not nearly as exciting to Lena as the others had been, although the team did nearly run out of food at one point, and Jacqui fell 25 feet into a crevasse while dragging a sled. There was little of the sense of newness around every bend that the southern part of the range had held; instead, it was a slog across the mind-boggling enormity of flat glaciers. And where Lena had enjoyed a dreamy group dynamic with the Coast Range team, this quartet—all strong personalities—rubbed each other raw at times. Merrie-Beth was training to be a ski guide and tended toward group decision-making, Jacqui said, "Whereas Lena will just ask for what she wants or tell you what she's going to do. So she and Merrie-Beth butted heads a lot."

Still, the team completed the Logan traverse in 55 days and 420 miles. There was only one piece of unfinished business on the Coast Range.

In April 2003, Lena, John, and Guy returned to the only peak they'd failed to summit during their traverse: the Devils Thumb in Alaska. They wanted to complete the Northwest Face, a massive 6,500-foot, nearly vertical wall that avalanched ice and snow. The climbing community considered it both the last great unachieved challenge on the continent, and, in the words of local Petersburg climber Dieter Klose, "a perfect place to commit suicide."

Lena, still more of a skier than an alpinist, had no plans to try the Northwest Face. Instead, she enlisted her father for an attempt on an established route up the south face, while Guy, John, and a climber named Kai Hirvonen tackled the more perilous route. Once the expedition was over, Guy planned to head to Nepal. In John's journals, he wondered whether he should be done pushing dangerous limits in the mountains. He'd been thinking about medical school.

After a few days of boating and skiing to the mountain, the group spent one more night together in its shadow. Lena pulled out her harmonica and played John's favorite song, "Somewhere Over the Rainbow," as they all sat in the long light of a northern sunset. They skied out the following morning under gleaming skies. After John, Guy, and Kai broke off on their own, Lena tied a surprise goodie bag to a rock for the men to find on their way back. She didn't worry much as they skied away. That was one of the things her parents had ingrained in her—the Rowats were experts at underplaying physical risk.

Six days later, as she slept after the climb with her father, the whine of a chainsaw invaded Lena's dream. When she woke, she realized that the sound was a helicopter landing so close that it blasted the tent walls with snow. Her heart sank with a sick certainty. Kai emerged from the helicopter with search and rescue personnel and said, "We're looking for John and Guy."

Thank God, she thought. They're not dead yet, then.

After peeling off from Lena and Peter, Guy, John, and Kai had set up base camp at the foot of their route and spent three days assessing conditions on the Northwest Face. On the evening of the third day—climbing at night was safest, because warm snow and ice can be unstable—they approached the wall under clear skies, carrying several days' worth of food and fuel. At the base of the wall lay an enormous pile of avalanche debris. It made Kai so uneasy that he decided to turn around. "There was something in my body screaming at me not to go," he said. "I'd never sensed that in my entire life." He was embarrassed and ashamed to let John and Guy down. They'd spent so much time saving for the trip, planning it, and getting to the remote location. "We took planes, we took boats, we skied," he said. But he felt that it was too dangerous.

John urged him to reconsider. "It's not that bad," he said. "You should come."

But Guy said gently, "I get it. No worries."

Kai skied back to base camp, where he watched the tiny lights of John's and Guy's headlamps ascend the rampart into the night. He stayed up for an hour, following their progress, before he turned in. As the days passed, he kept a close eye on the mountain but couldn't make out any figures or headlamps. Finally, after three days, he skied out alone—covering in a hurried 12 hours what had taken three days on the way in—and summoned a rescue. Then he came to find Lena.

The helicopter airlifted Lena and Peter out to Petersburg, where Lena began making calls. People flew up and gathered in the small town: both of John's parents; John's sister, Jerusha; his brother, Hamish, who'd been on a ski trip in southern Argentina when he'd gotten word that John was missing; and Jacqui, even though she and Guy had broken up by then. The group took turns looking for the climbers from the helicopter.

When Jacqui first glimpsed the Northwest Face's restless ice and hanging glaciers, she thought only one thing: They're dead. There was no way anyone could survive such a pitiless place. The scale of it played tricks on Eileen. Flying over the peak, she told the pilot she would just step out of the helicopter onto the snow and ice to look for John herself; the pilot told her they were 100 feet in the air. Jerusha watched her father get out of the helicopter to scream at the mountain, and at John for losing himself to it.

After two days with no sign of John or Guy, the local search operation ceased its efforts. Eileen used her own money, borrowed from John's grandparents, to hire a helicopter and keep looking. After another five days, that search was called off, too. It was presumed that John and Guy had been swept away by an avalanche and buried at the base of the massive wall.

Still, some in the climbing community secretly hoped that they'd show up on some logging road trying to hitch a ride home after summiting the unclimbable face, having given everyone the slip. For years afterward, the sound of helicopters in the mountains dropped Lena into the hope that it was John and Guy, alive, coming to reunite with her.

FIVE

On a late September day in 2024, more than two decades after that expedition to the Devils Thumb, I joined Lena to hike an unforgivingly steep route to an alpine lake above her home in Squamish, north of Vancouver. She was 51 and still possessed much of the youthful drive that had propelled her across the impossible spine of North America. Her long legs ate up the slope effortlessly. As she led me upward, she told me stories about her past.

After John and Guy died, Eileen's house on Quadra Island became Lena's haven. She spent weeks there, the two of them grieving alongside each other. For a long time, Lena would awake with the sudden memory that John and Guy were gone. It was like a punch to the heart. It took all day for Lena to finally, somehow, feel OK. But as she went to sleep she'd collapse into grief again, then repeat the whole process the next morning.

When she wasn't on Quadra, Lena was at the Mansion. If the climbing house had once been full, now it burst at the seams with people coming together to remember John and Guy over potlucks and at parties, sitting on the floor and painting each other's toenails in homage to their lost comrades. This was a community acquainted with loss; John had seven or eight friends die in the mountains by the time he went to the Devils Thumb for the last time. But this one seemed to hit especially hard.

As Lena suffered her way through grief, the outdoor community's support buoyed her. As it tightened around her, she felt part of it in a way she never had before. The loss also brought her closer to Hamish and Jerusha, whom she'd barely met before those horrific days in Alaska. John's siblings and his mother became her adoptive family; Eileen told me that she lost a son but gained a daughter.

Finally, here was the thing that Lena had been missing for so much of her life: deep connections. From beyond the grave, John and Guy had given her this. "Having that community helped calm my mind," she told me, "and allowed me to then home in on midwifery"—the vocation her mother had championed. "I remember thinking when they died that it was so good I had something I could work toward." For the first time in her life, Lena had purpose outside the mountains.

Not that she pulled back entirely from outdoor adventure after John and Guy died. Between 2006 and 2009, Lena assembled two expeditions to finish the sections of the Coast Range traverse she'd skipped when she hitchhiked from Bella Coola to Terrace, which included the most technical stretch of the route. When those sections were complete, Lena Rowat had gone farther in those mountains than anyone else.

In 2014, eleven years after John's death, Lena married a man with a matching appetite for adventure and a calm temperament that provided balance for hers. They now have a nine-year-old adopted son. She's worked as a midwife since 2008.

Would that all things in life were tied up in such neat bows. When John and Guy died, Lena shut out her parents and Ruby, a move that devastated her sister—Lena's closest companion during her youth and her teammate on the leg of the Coast Range traverse that had launched the best years of her young adulthood.

Nor did Lena's demons fade away easily. She suffered with them for years, until at the age of 50, she committed herself to therapy to confront her tangled attention span and the depression that plagued her after John died. She's honest about losing her train of thought when responding to a question. She still has a hard time completing chores and what she calls "administrative tasks" at home, and spends time outside before she has to pick her son up at school. She talks a lot about internal family systems, about what makes for a healthy one. She knows that she hurt Ruby, but also that she needed other people at the point in her life. They're both trying to heal their relationship.

As we topped out at a lake gleaming like a jewel, surrounded by the stark beauty of the south end of the Coast Range, Lena told me that she no longer felt she had to prove her lovability through her prowess at extreme adventures. She goes into the mountains now to connect with herself, with her husband and son, and with her friends. She sometimes feels that John and Guy are with her. She still has the sweater John knit for her; she wears it around the house when she wants to be cozy. She keeps a photo collage of both of them on the wall in the living room. She says there was once a part of her that wished she'd been the one who died doing something she loved, with someone she loved—so she wouldn't have to go through the travails of the rest of life. But she doesn't feel that way anymore.

Lena knows that it's a long path she's on, exploring these internal reaches. In some ways, it's a path that began all those years ago when she stepped into her skis to walk the whole of these mountains; it took that long to get where she is now. But pilgrimages rarely end with a single moment of transcendence.

More often, transformation comes when the journey leads back home, to the minutiae of everyday life.

That fall afternoon, Lena shucked off her flowery skirt, edged out onto a hanging flake of rock, and jumped naked into the green water thirty feet below. When she emerged, she was laughing, the glorious sound of it rolling to the sky.

CASSIDY RANDALL writes on adventure, environment, and the West. Her latest book, the survival epic *Thirty Below*, won the Banff Mountain Grand Prize and the Banff Award in Mountain Literature; and her last book, *The Hard Parts*, with Paralympian Oksana Masters, won the National Library Association Award and was named one of the best sports books of the year by *The Times*. Her journalism has appeared in *Vanity Fair*, *Rolling Stone*, *National Geographic*, *The New York Times*, *Men's Journal*, *TIME*, *Men's Health*, *Esquire*, and *Outside*, among others.

How Legendary Historian Robert Caro Is Fueling OKC's Title Run

BAXTER HOLMES

FROM ESPN • NOVEMBER 26, 2025

Five days before the Oklahoma City Thunder opened training camp following the franchise's first-ever NBA title, Sam Presti sat down at a table inside the team's practice facility about 10 miles north of the team's downtown arena.

"Morning everybody," the Thunder's general manager said at 10 a.m. local time as the assembled media settled in on Sept. 25.

Wearing a black button-up shirt, Presti cleared his throat and reached for several sheets of paper in front of him, squaring them up.

Presti read for the next 12 minutes, talking about the growth of the NBA and the challenges ahead for the Thunder's forthcoming season, which he referred to as Chapter 18, a nod to the team's 18th season in Oklahoma. The occasion marked Presti's annual preseason news conference, one of the rare instances in which he publicly addresses the media.

Though he is perhaps the most highly regarded executive in the league, Presti is just as known for his discomfort in the spotlight. He prefers to remain hidden in the background. But he makes these news conferences count, and they often last for two hours.

"As has been the case since the first time I sat in front of the media in Oklahoma City in 2008, I'll sit here until the last question is asked, until you guys start asking me questions like, 'What books are you reading?' and things like that, that's when I'm probably going to call it," he said in 2022.

And, despite his protestations, that led to an annual tradition.

It unfolds like this: At the end of the news conference, someone will ask Presti what he has read over the previous several months, and the GM will oblige.

This season, as the news conference reached nearly two hours, that tradition began anew.

Presti sat back and began to catalog. He "dabbled" in a few things, he said, including work from Joan Didion and a 1923 collection of essays by the French architect Le Corbusier called *Toward an Architecture*. He said he'd read *The Science of Hitting* by Boston Red Sox legend Ted Williams and the author John Underwood.

The diversity of subjects was typical. In past sessions, he has talked about jazz drummer Art Blakey, Antarctic explorer Ernest Shackleton and Max Perkins, the editor for Ernest Hemingway, F. Scott Fitzgerald and Thomas Wolfe.

But there's one author whose work Presti has repeatedly cited: a legendary historian who has won two Pulitzer Prizes, and who since 1974 has been working on an acclaimed, multivolume biography about the life, legacy and impact of former President Lyndon Johnson.

That author is Robert Caro, and Presti has not only referred to his books as inspiration, he has also frequently cited Caro's iconic philosophy and process as a guiding light for how he has built the Oklahoma City Thunder into a potential dynasty the franchise and its fans hope will also span multiple volumes.

As for his NBA admirer, Caro said he's honored.

"I am truly touched," he told ESPN, "if you want to know the truth."

The public admiration began in 2020.

On a Zoom call in his hotel room on the Walt Disney World campus inside the NBA's bubble, Presti said he was beginning his days by working out and then "trying to make a dent into that Robert Caro book," which at that time was *Master of the Senate*, Caro's third in his series about Johnson.

"It's one of those books where my wrist gets tired before my eyes," Presti said of the 1,167-page tome that focuses on Johnson's tenure in the U.S. Senate from 1949 to 1960, including his efforts to pass the landmark Civil Rights Act of 1957.

Four years later, in his opening statement on Sept. 24, 2024, as the Thunder were about to embark upon their inaugural NBA championship season, Presti cited Caro's mantra.

"One of my favorite authors, Robert Caro, has a great saying about research, where he says, 'You have to turn every single page,' and I really like that relative to what it is that we have to do in order to discover the team," Presti said.

"We have to really understand and go through every iteration to ensure that we're not shutting off potential pathways that could really help us or get us to another level, whether it's now or in the future.... I think by turning every page, you give yourself every opportunity."

Later, in the same opening statement, as he talked about the admirable depth on the Thunder roster and how he thought the team could leverage it for a long run, Presti repeated Caro's mantra.

"If we're turning every page, as we talked about, we'll find some things out of that, as well, if we stay curious about it."

Minutes later, he repeated it again. "We recognize that in order to be exceptional, in order to be that team, you have to be willing to be an exception, and for us that means staying curious, staying open, knowing you can't find it if you're not looking and turning every page."

He wasn't finished.

Later, when asked about midseason additions via trade, Presti stated: "I think we need to turn every page, to use Caro again. We have to see. In order to see that, it'll take time. I don't know if we'll have the ability to do that. But we have to, as I said before, be curious about that."

Call it executive-speak, call it unnecessary repetition, call it the biggest of clichés, but Presti and the Thunder believe in it—and it informs everything they do.

From there, the mentions have continued, including on June 30, just eight days after the Thunder defeated the Pacers in Game 7 of the NBA Finals, when he described how proud he was of what the team had accomplished, and how everyone was consumed with the pursuit of progress, rather than outcomes or adulation.

"I think that is a credit to their maturity and a credit to the leadership that [Thunder coach Mark Daigneault] and his coaching staff demonstrated, not just this year but over the course of time," Presti said.

"Very much pace-setting and not clock-watching, not looking at timelines or external expectations, really just turning every page."

PRESTI IS FAR from alone in his admiration for Caro.

Caro's four-volume series on Johnson has sold more than 1 million copies, and there are museum exhibits devoted to the writer and his work.

All six of his books have been featured on the cover of *The New York Times Book Review*, and the last one, released in 2012, was reviewed in *The Times* by former President Bill Clinton. None has gone out of print; last year, *The Power Broker*, which turned 50, sold more than 40,000 copies in its 74th printing.

Late night talk-show host Conan O'Brien, one of Caro's biggest fans, told *The Times* of Caro's work, "The Lyndon Johnson books by Caro, it's our Harry Potter."

But it is Presti's repeated vocal appreciation of Caro's exhaustive approach that is notable.

Over his 60-year reporting career, Caro has interviewed thousands of people and turned over hundreds of thousands of pages.

Consider his first book, *The Power Broker*, a biography of Robert Moses, an urban planner who wielded extraordinary power over New York City and within the state. Over a seven-year period, Caro conducted 522 interviews and wrote more than 1 million words. He also went broke, and his wife, Ina, was forced to sell their home.

But the 1,296-page tome was groundbreaking. It won a Pulitzer Prize, among numerous other awards, and is considered one of the greatest biographies in history.

The book changed Caro's life.

Presti isn't the only Caro fan in the NBA, either; his former boss in San Antonio, Gregg Popovich, is also an admirer.

In the Venn diagram of the NBA and Caro aficionados, you'd be hard-pressed to find a more ardent admirer than Sam Hinkie, the former president and general manager of "The Process" Philadelphia 76ers from 2013 to 2016.

"Robert Caro," Hinkie told ESPN in 2015, "is my favorite author."

Such a fan of Caro is Hinkie that, in 2020, Hinkie named the Menlo Park, California-based investment firm he founded 87 Capital, a reference to Caro's second book on Johnson, *Means of Ascent*.

In Silicon Valley, if someone starts reading Caro's work, odds are that they'll be connected to Hinkie. Last year, Hinkie ran a book club where members read 100 pages of *The Power Broker* each month, then gathered to talk about it.

Hinkie first encountered Caro's books in his late 20s. He devoured them quickly.

"I'm drawn to the doggedness and the duration of what he did," Hinkie said.

To Hinkie, Caro is singular—a "one-in-a-million writer, and a one-in-a-billion researcher—in the same person," Hinkie said. "Then you get this nonfiction that reads like literature, which he purposely trained himself to do, which makes it more interesting and more memorable and makes the 1,200-page book not as daunting as it otherwise might be."

As it relates to the NBA, team-building and the role of a general manager, Hinkie said Caro's "turn every page" mantra—the one of which Presti is so fond—could be translated to simply staying open-minded to what can be learned.

Or, as Presti often says, to remaining curious.

But just as Presti holds Caro in high regard, Caro feels the same about basketball.

The game, he says, has long served as an undercurrent to his life and his work.

IT'S EARLY ON May 24, and the night before, Caro's beloved New York Knicks had lost another close Eastern Conference finals game at home against the Indiana Pacers. He'd watched at home as the Pacers won 114–109, taking a 2–0 lead in the best-of-seven series.

"That was a bad night," the then-89-year-old told ESPN. "It's really worse than the first game, because you felt they're just faster than us, younger than us."

These days, stories about Caro focus on his efforts to finish the fifth and final volume of his series about Johnson. Today, Caro says he's on page 982.

"I'm not nearly done yet," he adds. "It's going to be another very long book. Part of the reason is when I did the research, I tried to turn every page."

He is taking a rare break, though, to discuss a passion outside his decades-long examination of power.

"I love basketball," Caro says. "I'm not very good at it, but I love it."

During his teenage years at the Horace Mann School in New York, Caro also loved football, but he says he wasn't very good at that either, so he became a sportswriter.

He maintained that tradition at Princeton, where he filed an 800-word sports column titled "Ivy Inklings" three times a week for *The Daily Princetonian* newspaper. ("It was always running too long," he says of his column.)

In the mid-1960s, Caro began a Nieman Fellowship at Harvard University, where he kept a small office on campus while playing on a local basketball team.

"I have a tip for your readers: At the age of 30, don't play basketball," Caro said. "I hurt my back [and] my Nieman year was brought to an end. Friends of mine had to bring me home lying in the back of a car. That was sort of the end. I do want to say, though, that I had a terrific jump shot. I'm not sure everybody appreciated it, but I did, anyway."

Caro's love of the game continued in New York in the early 1970s when he attended games during the Knicks' championship seasons in 1970 and 1973.

"Walt Frazier, to me, was something so special," Caro said before digging into the particulars of Game 7 of the 1970 NBA Finals, when the Knicks beat the Lakers to win their first NBA title.

"You know, in that game the numbers that came out—I'll never forget—are 36 and 19. Walt Frazier scored 36 points and had 19 assists. I can remember to this day. Between the 36 points of his own and the 38 points that he got for other guys, that's 74 points! And he would come down the court and almost deliberately go along the baseline and, very slowly, as if he had a whole half court laid out in front of him, he would make the pass or score.

"It's one of the memorable nights of my life."

Caro's philosophy, he said, began in 1959, when he worked as a young reporter at *Newsday* on Long Island.

"One weekend, because everyone else was on vacation, I got to do an investigative story," he said.

The paper's managing editor was a veteran journalist from Chicago named Alan Hathaway. Caro told him he didn't know anything about investigative reporting.

"And he looked up at me [and said], 'Just remember one thing—turn every page, never assume anything, turn every goddamn page,'" Caro said.

That principle would shape Caro's approach and his career.

"And there are times in my life when I hear his voice saying that, like when you're down at the Lyndon Johnson Library [in Austin, Texas], and you call for the files on something and they bring you out 8 million pieces of paper that you're going to go through," Caro said. "And you say, 'Oh, I'm going to skip this box.' And then you suddenly hear Alan's voice—'Turn every page, do everything.' And I can't tell you how many times by doing that I found stuff that helped my work, helped me understand Lyndon Johnson."

Over the years, Caro has repeatedly heard from people in all walks of life who have conveyed how much his research process has meant to them.

"I have to tell you, without exaggerating, I get a lot of letters from people saying they've adopted that as their motto or they understand what it meant. So to have [Presti], who is a great basketball executive, say that, I'm very touched by it."

And regarding his mantra's place in the Thunder's 2025 championship?

"It's flattering to think my motto played a role," Caro said, "but it's players and coaches that win championships—not authors."

AS THE THUNDER were in the midst of their postseason run to a championship, a man named Steven Taylor enjoyed breakfast at a diner in downtown Oklahoma City.

Taylor, a former Chief Justice of the Oklahoma Supreme Court, is the father of Wilson Taylor, the Thunder's director of logistics.

He's also close friends with Presti and loves Presti's hours-long news conferences. A couple of years ago, Taylor told him someone ought to have the transcripts printed and bound into a book of their own, perhaps one that could help teach management or leadership.

In September, as Presti sat before the media, his opening statement referenced a specific theme—that the team's success from the previous season wouldn't carry over.

Here, he used a play on the Caro philosophy.

The Thunder, Presti said, needed this time to turn the page.

"Effectively turning the page allows us the necessary renewal to treat this coming season with the respect it deserves. To maximize this coming season, we have to voluntarily divorce ourselves from the success of last season or it will hold us back."

As he finished his opening salvo, after finding the miniscule space between turning every page and turning the page, and repeating it again and again, he outlined his expectations for the coming season and the Caro-inspired process he believed the Thunder would need to undertake to meet them.

"If we want to pursue excellence, we have to let go of last year and start again, turning every page, stacking every day with no guarantees, and of course, no silver platters," he said, adding, "Chapter 18 is yet to be written. Last season we talked about nothing being expected but anything being possible, and that's how we feel again this year."

Then he thanked everyone and opened it up to questions, saying he'd stay there as long as they wanted.

BAXTER HOLMES is an ESPN senior writer who focuses on the NBA. He has covered the Los Angeles Lakers, the Boston Celtics, and previously worked for the *Boston Globe* and *The Los Angeles Times*.

High School Football Teams in Los Angeles Affected by ICE Raids: 'Everybody's on Edge'

ERIC SONDHEIMER

FROM *The Los Angeles Times* • JULY 22, 2025

On the day immigration agents swooped through MacArthur Park in armored vehicles, wearing tactical gear and riding on horseback, Contreras Learning Center football coach Manuel Guevara said more than 20 of his players skipped summer practice.

"Kids were messaging me their parents don't want them to leave their house," Guevara said.

The fear among families with students attending three downtown Los Angeles high schools minutes apart—Contreras, Roybal and Belmont—is real.

"Everybody's on edge," Guevara said.

Players don't know if their parents will feel safe enough to watch games from the school bleachers this fall.

As official football practice begins on Monday, three downtown Los Angeles head coaches—Guevara, Roybal's Michael Galvan and Belmont's Kenneth Daniels—have been in constant communication and united to help their players and parents deal with ICE raids. No one knows when the raids might subside or how the ongoing anxiety might affect teams this fall.

One of the first raids happened outside an elementary school across the street from Contreras. A 17-year-old Contreras cross-country and track athlete, Nory Santoy Ramos, was detained and later deported to Guatemala with her mother after showing up for an immigration appointment. Families in the area rely on afterschool programs that are facing budget cuts. Students continue to deal with issues involving homelessness, gangs and drug use at nearby MacArthur Park.

Even though all three coaches said players feel safe on campus, with Los Angeles Unified School District Supt. Alberto Carvalho vowing to make schools "safe havens," coaches are most concerned about students' commutes to and from school.

"A piece of me worries about them getting home safe," Roybal's Galvan said.

Guevara said one Contreras player told him he's 80% certain his mother is going to leave and take him with her because of ICE fears. He's had kids message him this summer that they couldn't come to practices because their parents feared for their safety.

The *Times* has confirmed U.S. citizens are among those who have been detained during immigration raids in Southern California that have continued for more than six weeks. More than 2,700 people have been arrested during the raids and more than two-thirds of those detained had never previously been convicted of a crime.

"I understand their plight," Guevara said. "I was brought here when I was 1. I became a citizen when I was 17. It's not like you can tell anyone in this situation, 'Suck it up.' It's a completely different animal. Our area is targeted."

Belmont is struggling to field a football team this fall. School enrollment is down to less than 700 after once being a school of more than 6,000—the largest in the county—until Contreras and Roybal were built. Athletic director Carlos Calderon said four sports that have been practicing on the Belmont campus this summer—cheer, girls volleyball, cross-country and football—have been affected by parental safety concerns.

"We've seen a deduction in kids coming to practices and increase communication with parents and having them call us [to say,] 'We don't feel comfortable in kids coming to practice,'" he said.

Calderon, who helps coach cross-country, has had athletes train on the school track instead of running the hills at Elysian Park to assuage parental fears.

Daniels said after one summer practice, when he learned an ICE raid was unfolding nearby, he instructed players to leave school from the back entrance instead of the front entrance.

"It's really affecting us," he said. "We're not getting the numbers we need to get the workouts in."

Belmont has 20 football players signed up, but only about half have been showing up for workouts. The team usually adds players once classes begin Aug. 14. Daniels, a walk-on coach, is already consumed by the challenge of building a new house in Altadena after his burned down during the Eaton fire.

"Nothing has been easy in 2025," he said.

Galvan said he's had players miss practices to go shopping for family members who feel they have to stay home. Others had medical appointments delayed because parents didn't want to leave their homes.

"In all of my 25 years of teaching in the area, I've never experienced anything like this," he said. "You just don't know. It's hard to explain. How do we get through one day?...We're taking it day by day."

The Garfield-Roosevelt game, known as the East L.A. Classic, draws the largest L.A. high school football attendance each year. It's scheduled for Oct. 24 at a site to be determined and officials want to make sure fans attending feel safe, so a decision on the site and security arrangements in light of continuing ICE raids are being taken into consideration along with budget.

"We will continue to follow district guidelines to ensure the well-being of our entire school community," Garfield athletic director Lorenzo Hernandez said in a text message. "Our priority is—and will always be—to keep students and families safe, informed and supported."

Said Galvan: "We definitely have to approach this season differently and see who we can accommodate and support the kids and balance understanding the situation and keeping them safe. It's going to be on a weekly basis how we approach each game."

Skipping summer practices won't prevent a team from going forward. But if players start missing practices this fall, that will cause problems, because practices are needed to help prevent injuries and get athletes into the proper physical condition to participate.

Guevara still remembers July 7, the day of the MacArthur Park show of force. He addressed players who showed up to practice and were going home.

"Be vigilant, be careful," he told them.

It's a message likely to be repeated again and again this fall.

ERIC SONDHEIMER enters his 50th year covering high school sports in Southern California in the fall of 2026. He joined *The Los Angeles Times* in 1997 as prep columnist after first working as a stringer for the *Los Angeles Daily News* starting in 1976, then full time in 1980. He also was with *The National* for 18 months as a West Coast correspondent, the nation's first daily sports newspaper. He's a member of the Los Angeles City Section Hall of Fame and Southern California Jewish Sports Hall of Fame and has been honored seven times by the California Prep Sportswriters Association for best prep sports column. He's the co-author of the book *College Football's Most Memorable Games* and is finishing up a memoir about the highs and lows of being a horse racing owner.

Chasing Ghosts with Dale Earnhardt Jr.

KENT BABB

FROM *The Washington Post* • MAY 22, 2025

MOORESVILLE, N.C.—For as long as he can remember, Dale Earnhardt Jr. has had a recurring dream. He's at some racetrack, in a garage or the pits, and there's his daddy talking to some guys.

Dale Sr. is in flannel and jeans, like he just came off the farm. He looks the same as the day he died: eyes still narrow, hair just as dark, creases rippling off his mustache like rings in a pond. Junior wants to walk toward him, maybe ask a question that's been percolating for years.

But he can't move.

"I want to go, 'Hey!' But that's not working," he says. "I'm as close as I can get."

Ancient civilizations believed dreams were spiritual rendezvous points where the dead could check in on the living. Until recently, Junior says, he could count on one of these visits about once a year. And since he's not allowed at his dad's actual grave, he always tries to avoid waking up.

He just stands there, watching and listening, for as long as he can.

BEFORE JUNIOR'S BIRTHDAY one year, he glanced in a mirror. The face staring back was old. Sun spots, gray hairs, lines around his lips and eyes. NASCAR's cocky boy wonder, with his cap perpetually backward and his tips forever frosted, was long gone.

"I don't *feel* this old," he told me last fall. "I kind of got to this point in my life before I expected to."

Middle age is sneaky like that, and though Junior is still lively and trim, he's just another husband and father whose glory years are gone. A big night used to be mainlining Bud Heavy until sunlight slipped between the pines outside his secret drinking hole. Now it's a koozie hiding a nonalcoholic brew.

In October 2023, Junior turned 49. That's the same age his dad was in 2001, when, before the last turn on the last lap of the Daytona 500, Dale Earnhardt Sr.'s car bumped into Sterling Marlin's, sending the iconic No. 3 careening into the wall at 160 mph.

"We've lost Dale Earnhardt," NASCAR President Mike Helton said when he announced, two hours after the crash, that Dale Sr. was dead.

Seventeen million people had watched it live, a seemingly minor collision that turned haunting the moment driver Kenny Schrader looked through Earnhardt's window and frantically waved for emergency personnel. In the quarter-century since, Schrader has never spoken about what he saw.

Until then, crashes were as intertwined with the sport as cigarettes and beer. (Its top two levels: the Winston Cup and Busch series.) Wrecks at racetracks claimed the lives of eight drivers in the 1980s and '90s, and initiating contact and walking away from crashes was why Dale Sr., nicknamed "The Intimidator," was so popular.

Now, after a wreck he couldn't walk away from, NASCAR had no choice but to confront and overhaul its outdated safety mechanisms. No driver has died since.

"A horrible thing," Junior said on his podcast, *The Dale Jr. Download*, in 2023. "The whole sport had to go through it."

Beneath something so unprecedented was a most relatable thing: a shell-shocked young man who had lost his dad. Gone in that same instant were the answers to a million questions, lessons to be learned, the hope of some beer-fueled conversation that would smooth out wrinkles of the past.

"They were just developing this relationship," says Kelley Earnhardt Miller, Junior's older sister. "To have that pulled out from under him, to have it taken away, was a second tragedy."

It's a lonely feeling, and one I happened to know. Fourteen months after Junior's dad died, so did mine.

Michael Babb wasn't famous, but as a bass guitarist for a 1970s Southern rock band, he had come close. After High Cotton broke up, my father came home, bringing addictions to drugs and alcohol with him.

I was 15 when, for the first time, I confronted him about his drinking, and we got into a fistfight. I never listened to High Cotton's record, deciding it couldn't possibly be good. He loved NASCAR, which meant I hated it. I was into *real* sports, and when I shared my dream of a career writing about baseball or football, he didn't understand.

I was studying journalism in college in 2002 when my grandmother called. "They think he's gone," she said. His heart had become enlarged, and while he was painting a house one day, it just stopped.

He was 51. That's all I know, and because a pipeline of information got shut off, that's most of what I ever will.

I'm 43 now, and since the day my dad died, there has been something unsettling about the idea of turning 51. I've learned this is common among people who've lost a parent young, or what is called an "off-time" death. Psychologists suggest these feelings of anxiety and fear, alongside a gradually intensifying urge to learn about your bloodline, are like a final stage of grief. And it's one that most people, and in particular men, rarely talk about or explore.

I did want to talk about it, preferably with someone who understood. And though I never took to NASCAR, I knew Junior and I belonged to the same unfortunate club. I wondered if he thought about it, if he dreaded turning 49, how he was coping as he approached the age his daddy was.

So, before his birthday in 2023, I asked if he'd be open to talking. He said yes.

Of the dozen stops on North Carolina's "Dale Trail," none is more important and solemn than a quiet grove in downtown Kannapolis. Dale Earnhardt Sr. grew up here and put the town on the map, and following his death, it became the epicenter of despair.

Now, past cypress shrubs, are seven stairs that represent the number of Dale Sr.'s Cup championships. Benches are grouped in sets of three, a nod to his car number. At the center is a nine-foot bronze statue.

"OUR FRIEND AND CHAMPION," reads one of the plaques.

In places like this, the homegrown star belongs to everyone. Especially when, like Kannapolis, the place is one of a thousand Southern mill villages that sprouted a century ago, spun cotton into yarn and then, when the textile industry cratered, plunged into decay.

Dale Sr., a high school dropout, actually worked those looms. He married young and had his first son, Kerry, at 18. But he didn't know how to be a husband or a father, so he abandoned both and took off for some dirt track to chase his dream.

Earnhardt fans love all that, because their fantasy was his life. He achieved wealth and superstardom in America's most blue-collar sport, doing so with a defiance and fury that made you either love or hate him.

By the time Kelley and Junior were born, both to Dale Sr.'s second wife, Brenda, the local legend had gone regional. He skipped out of town to enter races outside Charlotte or Atlanta, paying entry fees instead of his bills, and the last car that drivers wanted to see in their mirror in those years was the damn No. 3, because that meant they were about to get passed or knocked out of the way.

Dale Sr. didn't see racing as dangerous. That was a myth, he once declared, propagated by "Yankees." When NASCAR started requiring drivers to wear a five-point harness in 1976, the response to nearly a dozen deaths over the previous decade-plus, Dale Sr. said the added safety measures made the sport *more* hazardous.

"The only reason I broke my collarbones was because I had my safety straps on," he told a reporter in 1980, the year he won five races and his first Cup championship.

The folks back home loved that, and soon the whole sports world was taking notice. By the end of the 1980s, a million people a year were attending NASCAR races, more tuned in for live broadcasts and Fortune 500 companies were angling to sponsor top drivers.

Dale Sr. went back to Kannapolis when he could, but never for long. He skipped his kids' bedtime, soccer games and high school graduations. When Dad was around, Junior made sure Dale Sr. saw him playing with toy cars and turning cardboard into a miniature speedway.

"Always wanting that attention," Kelley says now. "Wanting to be noticed."

Dale Sr. had become a hero to millions of kids, including his own. Kelley stopped fighting for her dad's affection, but Junior never did. After races, he could often be seen elbowing through the crowd to be photographed next to his dad.

When that didn't work, a teenage Junior found new ways to get Dale Sr.'s attention. He smoked cigarettes and played video games with friends from nearby Mooresville, which they called the "Dirty Mo." Dale Sr. liked Hank Williams Jr. and Alannah Myles; Junior preferred the Stone Temple Pilots and Rob Base. He slept past noon, let the dishwasher and trash overflow, assembled an impressive collection of soiled dishes under his bed.

For better or worse, it all led to the heavy sound of Daddy stomping toward his room.

When Junior was 6, Dale Sr. had started his own racing team, Dale Earnhardt Inc., and bought hundreds of acres near Kannapolis. NASCAR was becoming a national curiosity, with Dale Sr. as its pitchman, carrying the brand in commercials for McDonald's and Coca-Cola. In time, every speedway in America overflowed with shirts and flags and decals with the slanted "3," and kids built models of Earnhardt's menacing GM Goodwrench car.

Junior, meanwhile, got himself sent to military school. That didn't take, so Dale Sr. got his son a job changing oil at Dale Earnhardt Chevrolet, but he quickly got fired. When Dad tried connecting with Junior by bringing him to the track or letting him get behind the wheel of one of Dale Sr.'s cars, Junior showed only a talent for wrecking them.

In the 1990s, Dale Sr. was trying to break Richard Petty's record of seven Cup championships. His son was living in a double-wide, smoking and drinking with his buddies, on his daddy's land. One day Dale Sr. stormed in and scolded Junior for wasting his life, and the two went at it.

Junior erupted, accusing his father of caring more about strangers than his own family. His son? The kid saddled with the same name? He couldn't even get the attention, Junior told him, of a "pimple on your ass."

HIDDEN ON JUNIOR'S property, along the banks of a narrow creek, is a vast graveyard. There are at least 80 bodies out there, scattered across an unmarked wooded area accessible only by ATV.

Here, in rural North Carolina, lie the charred remains of the car Juan Pablo Montoya crashed into a track dryer during the 2012 Daytona 500, the tub of an IndyCar that Will Power once wrecked and quasi-recognizable cars once driven by Tony Stewart, Jeff Gordon and Mark Martin.

"I've never paid a dime for any of them," Junior says. "They're just trash."

So why collect them? What's the point in dispatching Sonny Lunsford, an old buddy with a flatbed, to haul away somebody else's junk?

In 1998, Junior got serious enough about racing that his dad gave him a shot to drive one of his cars full time in the Busch Series, essentially NASCAR's top minor league. Considering Junior's clearest talent was destroying these hyper-engineered machines, he had no idea why.

The only advice Dale Sr. gave him? "Don't lift," he told Junior, because success requires fearlessness. Cars are often separated by inches, even as they try to avoid (or initiate) contact while approaching 200 mph on turns with gravity-defying inclines. No matter the consequences, good drivers never lift their foot off the accelerator.

Yes, sir. Junior won seven races in 1998, when he was just 23, and six more the next year, claiming consecutive Busch Series championships. He showed a familiarly aggressive style and a rare gift for feeling the air open up around his car, flying past competitors and, in 2000, into the big leagues. Damned if he didn't win two Cup races, same as his daddy.

Still, it took getting to Victory Lane for his dad to tell him he was proud. If Junior didn't win, Dale Sr. didn't show up.

Junior was 26 when the 2001 season began. That year's Daytona 500, the most important event on the NASCAR calendar, featured Junior and Senior sitting sixth and seventh, right next to each other, as they started their engines. Both were among the favorites to win, with Dale Sr. trying to win Daytona for the second time in four years.

On the last lap, Junior's teammate Michael Waltrip was leading, and Junior was in second. That's when he saw his dad's car in his rearview. But he wasn't trying to pass or wreck him. In third place, Dale Sr. was blocking Sterling Marlin from a late surge, protecting a win for the team he owned.

Junior doesn't remember much about what came next. After he and Waltrip crossed the finish line, someone said something about a crash. A golf cart took Junior and Danny Earnhardt, Junior's uncle and a member of Dale Sr.'s pit crew, to a van. Then a crowded hospital lobby, where he saw anguished faces and a curtain. He looked behind it and saw his dad, who had been pronounced dead.

Junior doesn't remember the trip back to Kannapolis, either, or convening with extended family at his grandmother's house. Instead of processing what happened, he distracted himself by trying to be everyone's rock. No one saw him cry. A week after Daytona, he was at the track in Rockingham, North Carolina, acting as if nothing happened.

Thousands of fans waved flags with Dale Sr.'s No. 3 on them, and 23 seconds after the race started, Junior crashed into the wall. It isn't grief he recalls feeling. It's numbness.

"I didn't care if I died," he says. "I didn't *want* it to happen, but I was miserable in general all the time. I didn't give a f---."

Two months later, during a practice in Fontana, California, he crashed again. He says it took that wreck to "get my s--- together" and focus on not dying. But there were other stresses back home.

Dale Sr.'s last will and testament hadn't been updated since 1992, when Kelley and Junior were 20 and 18. It transferred the entirety of his estate—the race team, the property, nearly two dozen trademarks—to Dale Sr.'s third wife, Teresa, whom he had married after divorcing Junior's and Kelley's mother. Junior's car and his No. 8 now belonged to his stepmother.

Kelley says she and Junior were never invited to look through sentimental possessions, childhood items or family photos. Teresa rejected their input, she says, when planning Dale Sr.'s funeral and choosing a grave site.

His final resting place is less than a mile off Highway 3, behind a tall screened fence, down a dirt road, protected by cameras and more fencing. Not far from a pond is a walkway that leads to a mausoleum with EARNHARDT stamped in gold. Kelley says Teresa invited her and Junior to see it after their dad's interment.

Kelley hasn't been back. She says it's understood that she and her brother are unwelcome. "She's so extreme," she says of Teresa, "that we might get arrested."

I tried to reach Teresa Earnhardt directly but couldn't. Her lawyers declined my interview requests and did not respond to a question about whether Kelley and Junior actually are prohibited from visiting their dad's grave.

Junior, for his part, says he "might have" gone back by himself once. Fueled by some combination of liquid courage and that Earnhardt defiance, he admits, he invited himself to "sit and think."

That was at least 20 years ago, he says, around the same time NASCAR was issuing sweeping changes in the wake of Dale Sr.'s death. Drivers complained about having to wear head and neck restraints, and cars had to be outfitted with stronger roll bars and carbon fiber seats. Speedway walls were updated with upgraded barriers that dissipated energy during a crash.

Cars were expensive enough before the changes, but by 2002, teams were cutting full shells off car bodies to replace them with the newly mandated materials. Junior hated the idea of sending those shells to the scrapyard, so whenever he wrecked, he asked Sonny to tow the car home and dump it in the yard. Other teams offered their cars, too, and a collection grew: Darrell Waltrip's No. 11, covered in leaves and twigs; Mike Wallace's No. 52, sitting among the skinny trees; Kevin Harvick's No. 29, resting in peace behind Montoya's.

There is, noticeably, nothing ever driven or owned by Dale Sr. Teresa controls those things, too, and Kelley suspects that's the real reason her brother did this.

"There's just this longing," Kelley says, "to put pieces together."

Junior shrugs at that theory, but it's hard to deny what the assemblage amounts to: a graveyard he doesn't have to sneak into. Each car body is a rusting monument, just five miles from his dad's more traditional memorial, to stories and recollections and moments in time. He built a place he can visit whenever he wants, for as long as he'd like, thinking about things such as the oddities of grief and how it leads a son to gather up twisted metal because it's one of the only ways to feel close to his dad.

JUNIOR DREADED TURNING 40, in part because that's when he thought people naturally slow down. Some drivers go so far as suggesting that having kids makes you two-tenths of a second slower, but considering there's no evidence for this, it's just a convenient excuse for these Peter Pans to put off responsibilities while they chase each other for a living.

When he was in his 20s and early 30s, nobody staved off adulthood quite like Junior. Before the graveyard, he had Sonny build a 1,000-square-foot tree house on his land, which he calls Dirty Mo Acres. He added a paintball course and a small herd of bison. A bit farther down the hill, he started dreaming up plans for the town of Whisky River.

"We needed a place to party," Sonny says of Junior's bachelor paradise. Specifically one that, unlike the local bars, had no last call.

At Junior's direction, Sonny brought in three 18-wheelers' worth of reclaimed Kannapolis timber and spent nine months constructing an Old West main drag: barbershop, mercantile, post office. The hub was a saloon, naturally, across the street from a church and the jail. "We didn't even *start* until 10, 11 o'clock at night," Sonny says.

While Sonny built, Junior kept the pedal down. Five months after his dad's fatal crash at Daytona, Junior dominated the same track to win the Pepsi 400. Then the Daytona 500 itself three years later. This cemented him as NASCAR's most beloved figure, named the sport's most popular driver for the first time in 2003. Nobody else won the award for 15 years. Budweiser was paying $1 million per race to sponsor Junior's red No. 8 Chevy, which, like his dad's black Goodwrench car, was becoming inextricably sewn into the fabric of Americana.

It was Junior, after all, who had won in Dover, Delaware, 12 days after the terrorist attacks of 9/11—and then circled the mile-long oval with an American flag dancing outside his window.

He was, like his dad, a perfectly imperfect brand ambassador—relatable, sure, as the guy who fired up his car at Pocono Raceway with a gash on his head after a drunken swan dive into the shallow end of a pool. He occasionally started his own engine with a breakfast Bud and a lung dart and once scoured his house for anything carbonated because he demanded the hot tub have more bubbles.

At his 30th birthday party, in 2004, Junior's buddies rented out an Irish pub in Mooresville. They closed it down, a Marilyn Monroe look-alike sang "Happy Birthday," and somehow a few of them wound up in a boxing ring, where a professional bull rider gave Junior a black eye.

As he refused to grow up, 30 wound up being the age he stopped winning.

Junior blew off postrace analysis meetings to play *Madden* in his bus and had so much beer delivered to him that the distributor accused him of reselling it. His fans ignored the fact that, over a 108-race stretch, he won just three times. He withdrew, sparred with reporters, told girlfriends that he was never settling down.

Yet people were buying so much merchandise and companies were so keen on sponsoring him that Junior averaged about $20 million in yearly earnings. He made a cameo in Will Ferrell's *Talladega Nights*, flew to Monaco for dinner with Jay-Z and Beyoncé before appearing in a music video and traveled to nearby Concord, North Carolina, in his private helicopter to race NBA legend Shaquille O'Neal in a made-for-TV spectacle.

On the flight back to Mooresville, he looked through the window at a field below.

"There's Daddy," he told Mike Davis, his longtime road manager and branding specialist.

In 2007, Kelley and Junior got tired of working for a company their father started but was now controlled by their stepmom. They announced they were starting their own racing team, JR Motorsports, and leaving behind Junior's famed No. 8 Bud car. When Junior won in Brooklyn, Michigan, in 2008, his first victory in two years, it was in a No. 88 owned by Rick Hendrick and sponsored by Amp, an energy drink.

He wouldn't win again for four more years. In 2012, he crashed during a tire test at Kansas Speedway, leaving him with the first of several of concussions that would force him to miss starts for the first time. His reaction time and peripheral vision weren't sharp, and he was experiencing balance problems that, because Junior is *Junior*, he measured in beer.

"Small headache," he wrote in his phone's Notes app, which became the basis of *Racing to the Finish*, his 2018 memoir. "Drunk, one beer feeling."

"I got out of the car and felt 1 or 2 beers drunk," he wrote another time.

"Felt lazy and 1 beer drunk rest of the day."

He occasionally appeared on what was ostensibly his own podcast, except Davis and another guy hosted it. The guy it was named for wanted almost nothing to do with it.

"Kind of got ugly," Junior said after finishing 30th at Watkins Glen.

"Tough luck," he said after placing 35th at Chicago.

"Frustrating," he said after not finishing at all in Charlotte.

Before the 2014 season, Steve Letarte had become as much life coach as crew chief. Because it wasn't age that was slowing Junior down. It was immaturity, brain injuries and increasing self-doubt. That year at Talladega Superspeedway, where Dale Sr. won 10 times, Junior went into the pits before stomping the accelerator in an attempt to make up time.

Then, up ahead, he saw a massive crash unfolding. He did the one thing Daddy told him he couldn't: Junior lifted. And the worst part? There was no crash. He had avoided a collision that existed only in his imagination.

"My team was like, 'What was that?'" Junior says now. "I really couldn't hide what I'd done. They knew. They watched it. That's when I was like, 'Hmm, I wonder if I'm going to do this much longer.'"

With Letarte in his ear, Junior, 39, won four races in 2014. That October, Kelley and Junior's girlfriend, Amy Reimann, threw him a blowout party for his 40th. The band 21 Pilots played, Kid Rock mingled, and the night came alive out in Junior's woods.

Everybody congregated in the saloon at Whisky River, drinking and singing and pounding the keys of an old red piano. At some point long before sunrise, the guests noticed the birthday boy was gone, having slipped into the darkness after walking past a painting of an aging cowboy.

My dad, like Junior's, is a frequent subject of my dreams. He is as I remember: beaten-down and resentful, frizzy gray hair, knuckles swollen with rheumatoid arthritis and flecked with paint.

He's frozen in time, even as my 20s and 30s have come and gone. Eight years ago, I became a father myself. I want to know more about the old band and why it broke up, to tell my two daughters about him, to answer questions about him and therefore myself.

The dreams often end with me feeling guilty. He's at home, surrounded by guitars he rarely plays. But not wanting to bother him, I just haven't called.

I explain this to Junior.

"Teresa said something really interesting one day very recently after he passed away," he says. "She said that missing someone you love is selfish, because you want them there for *you*. I always kind of kept that in the back of my mind. It made me try not to be selfish.

"But I *do* miss him. God, I wish he was here for me. I want him. I want to hug him. I want to talk to him, and I need him."

Once he accepted this, he realized that there's nothing selfish about grief. So he stopped caring about what anybody else thought and tried to think of new ways to connect.

These days, people close to Junior joke that, if you're up late trying to score some obscure piece of Dale Sr. memorabilia on eBay and keep getting outbid, it's probably Junior who's outbidding you. Indeed, the last username you want to see in an auction history is DMA7488, who has bought and sold more than a thousand items since 2013 and, with an estimated net worth of $300 million, isn't about losing.

Vintage racing hats, early Dale Sr. shirts, scale models of cars his daddy once drove. Most sellers have no idea it's Junior, but one figured it out. Junior bought so many of the seller's die-cast cars that the two started emailing, and they recently spent an hour on the phone discussing the details of a custom 1976 No. 8 Chevy, the first car Dale Sr. raced at Daytona.

His phone is a portal, taking him to racing fan sites to look for photographs Junior has never seen. Pictures of the icon or the ghost? That's not the objective. It's the man. Junior says he has a dozen photo streams, organized by "chapters" of his dad's life. There, in "Dad 70s Sportsman," is a bushy-haired kid whose car is sponsored by a construction company. Here, in "1980–81," is a young man toasting victory with a Coke cup.

"What hotel did they stay in?" Junior wrote on social media, alongside a black-and-white picture of the actual Chevy Nova his dad drove. "Did they eat at any local restaurants? Who all went down there with him? Was he nervous? I want to time travel."

These folders are precious, to be sure. But there's one he rarely shows anyone. "Just Dad" contains photos of Dale Sr. lounging at home or tinkering in his shop. Junior shows me a picture of his daddy at sunset, that familiar profile backlit as a fishing line drops into Lake Norman.

Junior is smiling.

"Just being a person," he says.

In 2015, the portal took him to 18th-century Bavaria, where Johannes Ehrenhardt Sr. and his son boarded a passenger ship bound for Philadelphia. Two decades later, Johannes Jr. would be granted a tract of farmland in the British colony of Carolina. There, he would turn over the same dirt where, much later, his descendants would plant seeds and play games and, starting with Junior's grandfather, lay rubber.

Junior was so moved that, standing next to Amy in the ancient chapel where the Ehrenhardts once worshiped, he dropped to a knee and proposed marriage.

He was 40 and engaged, two things he once believed would slow him down. But he won three times in 2015, after reaching victory lane just eight times in his 30s. The next season, he finished second in three of his first eight races.

Then his concussion symptoms returned. There were no horrific crashes. Just dozens of minor ones, each jostling his neck and head. He struggled to tie shoelaces and buckle a belt, and his reaction time and vision had dulled.

"Angry for no reason," he wrote in his Notes app. He told no one, not even Amy.

"Close to puking," he wrote later.

"Seems to be getting worse."

He pledged to donate his brain and was ruled out for the final 18 races of 2016. During his time off, he took interest in a new project: actually hosting his own podcast. His plan was to interview racing buddies and the sport's pioneers, and soon "Dirty Mo Acres" was adding a dedicated studio. As time passed, Junior noticed that his questions and guests seemed to follow a trend.

"We're at that part of our lives," he says, "where we're reconciling with our past."

After my dad died, I felt an urgency to accomplish every goal and live as much as possible before age 51. I needed to be established in my career, to have started a family, to see the world in what felt like a truncated time. Even as I notched those things, I wondered what my dad would've thought.

You never stop wanting to impress your parents, even after they're gone. There's a longing to speak as equals.

"I would love to say, 'Hey, when I pissed you off that day,'" Junior says, "'you were right. What an a--hole I was. I was not using my head.'"

But when all you have are memories, yours and those held by others, you protect them. Concussions were now threatening Junior's long-term brain circuitry, and after the 2017 season, he retired. When he spun out at Daytona, after the front of Kyle Busch's car sent Junior's careening into a wall, that was it.

However much time he had left, he didn't want to spend it in pursuit of more wins. He wanted closure. Junior had traditionally avoided conversations about his dad's death, partly because he didn't remember much about that day. Now armed with a microphone, he interviewed guests about the things they remembered, trying to bring a blurry picture into focus.

Mike Helton, the NASCAR president in 2001, described the moments before his announcement that Earnhardt was gone. "We just lost the greatest driver we've ever had. What am I supposed to say?" Helton said.

Then came Kenny Schrader, who, after peeking into Earnhardt's car window after the wreck, frantically waved for emergency personnel. Schrader had never revealed what he had seen, and Junior didn't want him to do so on the podcast. Instead, he wanted to read Schrader something.

"You're one of the few to see the darkest moment for my dad," he said, reading from a laptop. "You have intimate knowledge of those moments; you are a keeper of that delicate information.

"I feel pain for you to have to carry that memory. But you carry it for me. You carry it for Kelley.... I know you might sometimes wish that you weren't the one, but I'm glad it was you."

And Sterling Marlin, whose collision with Earnhardt had preceded the crash and, in the weeks afterward, spurred death threats.

"I hope that you've carried no sliver of guilt," Junior told him.

Junior turned 46, an age his grandfather Ralph had died before reaching, and kept asking questions.

"What were some of the not-so-great things about him?" Junior says. "We've been talking about how insane amazing he was all these years, and sometimes it's fun to talk about how real he was."

So Junior and Kelley asked their mother, Brenda, why she and Dale Sr. had divorced. He was addicted to racing, yes. But there was also a clear avoidance of responsibility. His own father's fatal heart attack had shaken him, kicking off a few years of emotional instability and financial distress. Rather than confront his own grief, he distracted himself—driving, tinkering or disappearing into the woods.

Hank Parker Sr., a pro fisherman and one of Dale Sr.'s closest friends, came on to tell Junior about one of their hunting trips. As they were waiting for a deer, Parker's son called, and Parker told his boy he loved him. Dale Sr. looked jealous.

"I don't know how to love my kid like you love your kid," Parker said his friend told him.

"He was never able to express to you how much he loved you," Parker went on. "Never was able. You always felt like he loved you when you won and he didn't when you didn't win."

Junior just let him talk.

"I've always wanted, somehow," Parker continued, "to get you and grab hold of your shoulders and tell you how hurt he was that he didn't know how to express his love for you.... It also showed me a side of him that was sad."

Last year, Junior's longtime crew chief, Tony Eury Sr., was his guest. It was the same day JR Motorsports announced that, after Teresa Earnhardt let the trademark expire on the old No. 8 Bud car, Kelley and Junior had bought it back. He and Eury were talking about Dale Sr.'s fateful decision so many years ago to put Junior, after all those wrecks and so many arguments, into one of his cars.

"You knew he wasn't happy. He let you know," Eury said. Dale Sr. wasn't sure Junior even wanted to race. "I said: 'Dale, they're kids. Put him in it. Spend your money on him, and we'll go see.

"'We'll know in a year if he's got it or not.'"

It's September 2024, the end of summer, sunset on a humid Friday. Junior is 49. Since retiring from full-time racing, he does one or two tracks a year. This time it's Bristol Motor Speedway, where, in 1979, Dale Sr. got his first win.

Junior won't say it, but everyone knows this is his last NASCAR race. There's something poetic about a circle closing here, at the precise moment a new rotation begins. Junior and Amy's two young daughters, 6-year-old Isla and 3-year-old Nicole, are here on pit road, smelling the singed rubber and hearing the air guns, as Daddy stands next to his car.

He picks up Nicole and points toward the speedway lights, then his blue No. 88 car.

"I'm trying to see if it might register with my girls that I did that. That I *do* this," Junior says. "This is what our family does."

Junior kisses Amy and high-fives Isla. Then he climbs in and buckles his head and neck restraint. Junior knows it won't be long before his girls start asking about the man they see in so many pictures, eyes hidden by sunglasses, usually looking fearsome. That'll be a good day, he says, to ride over to Kannapolis and, because they can't visit the grave, show them the statue.

It belongs to everybody, he'll explain, because "The Intimidator" was everybody's. But Papa Dale? The man Junior has spent the past decade getting to know? He's theirs, and the two little girls with strawberry hair don't have to share him.

"He was this guy. He did this thing. Then he died," he'll say.

"I hope that one day, they go: 'Hey Dad, tell me about Daytona. Tell me about winning the Daytona 500 in 2004. Tell me about going to Victory Lane when you were a kid. What was like that?'

"I want them to get to a point to where they're asking me about that part in my life. It may take some time. There's a lot to talk about."

As I wrote this story, I reached out to my dad's old bandmates, to ask about the man I never got to meet.

Before he was my dad, they said, Michael was a prankster who'd do anything for a laugh. The band toured the East Coast, opening for the Doobie Brothers and the Allman Brothers, and a disagreement with Ted Nugent's road crew nearly led to an onstage brawl, lead singer Jeff Logan told me. Logan and Phillip "Flip" Myers, the band's drummer, disagree on why things eventually fell apart. Too little money, Jeff says. Creative differences with legendary producer Allen Toussaint, Flip says. They recorded a second album that was never released.

"We were damn close to breaking through," says Flip, who's 76. "I think about it every day."

Not long after we spoke, a package from Jeff arrived: an 8-track of High Cotton's first record, a remastered CD, a half-dozen pictures of a man in his early 20s, lively and grooving. I handed the packet to Lilah and Lucy, my daughters. The guy with the dark hair flowing from beneath a cowboy hat? That's Grandpa Michael.

That day in Bristol, Junior finishes seventh and climbs out of his car. Someone hands him a water on pit road, and he drains it and asks for a beer. Fans line a walkway, yelling for an Earnhardt one more time, and drivers walk over for high-fives and hugs. Junior empties the one can, so somebody brings out a cooler. He reaches in and slips another Bud (Select) into a koozie.

This was a race, sure. It was also a goodbye, the kind drivers used to not get. Junior changes out of his fire suit and into a T-shirt and jeans, opening a third beer as he walks over to mingle with fans. A staffer hands Junior his glasses, and lines ripple across his cheeks as he smiles for selfies.

It's nearly midnight when Amy and several friends join, another party just getting started. I ask Junior about the podcast guest he wants most, the one he can never have. But if he could, what would be his first question? What is it he wants to ask his father?

He pauses, thinking about it, and smiles.

"How'd I do?" he says.

LAST OCTOBER, JUST three weeks after Bristol, Junior woke into what felt like a dream. His dad wasn't in this one; in fact, the visits stopped around the time Junior turned 49. Instead, he was in a beach house in the Lowcountry, a wife and two daughters next to him in bed.

It was his 50th birthday.

He made it, reaching an age his daddy never did, the last person to ever pass the great Dale Earnhardt. The family spent a lazy day on the coast.

"Just Amy and my girls," he says.

They went to a local joint with a balcony, and Kelley Venmoed Amy to buy her little brother a drink. The four of them sat there for hours, all Junior wanted, just feeling the breeze and listening to his girls for as long as he could.

KENT BABB is a sports features writer for ESPN, where he explores the intersection of sports with cultural and social issues. He has written two critically acclaimed books: *Not a Game*, the definitive biography of Allen Iverson, and *Across the River*, a narrative examination of poverty, violence, and high school football in post-Katrina New Orleans. He lives in Northern Virginia with his wife and two daughters.

How the StudBudz Are Revolutionizing the WNBA

KATIE BARNES

FROM ESPN • SEPTEMBER 23, 2025

"I went over there to de-escalate the situation," Natisha Hiedeman says.

With her pink hair poking out of her blue hood, she's explaining her role in an incident at the end of a Minnesota Lynx–Seattle Storm game. The details don't matter much. But here goes: Hiedeman's Lynx teammate Kayla McBride fouled Erica Wheeler on a drive to the basket. McBride scooped up the ball and tossed it in frustration toward Wheeler. Seattle's Skylar Diggins rushed toward McBride. Hiedeman stepped in and had a few words for Diggins.

"I was like, 'You know what? That whole little crush that I thought I had…it's out the window. It's gone.'"

Courtney Williams, sporting sunglasses and matching pink hair, busts out laughing in her perch next to Hiedeman. She grabs her teammate's chair, shakes it and stomps her feet on the floor.

"You know what she told me?" Hiedeman continues. "'Shut up. I know you still like me.'"

Williams. Just. Can't. She gets up and staggers out of the frame as Hiedeman cackles at the camera that's livestreaming the conversation.

This is StudBudz. They're open. They're honest. They're Black. They're gay. They're masculine. They're beloved. And they're always recording.

At the start of the season, Williams and Hiedeman unleashed StudBudz accounts on Instagram and TikTok. From there they took their banter to Twitch. They streamed 72 straight hours during WNBA All-Star Weekend, which catapulted them into the mainstream and spawned merch like "Everyone watches StudBudz" T-shirts. Napheesa Collier even flaunted a giant StudBudz chain on the bench during Minnesota's Aug. 21 game in Atlanta.

In a season deprived of a full suite of Caitlin Clark magic, in a season that saw the rise of the Lynx, in a league that has only recently embraced the variety of its players' identities, the StudBudz have become the biggest thing in the WNBA.

THE PINK HAIR is everywhere.

At Barclays Center in Brooklyn, Renee Agosto and her 13-year-old daughter, Bailey, wear pink wigs and Liberty T-shirts at the New York-Minnesota game. "They're authentically themselves," Agosto says. "I think that's such an amazing thing for young girls to look up to. And their laughs are contagious."

At Mohegan Sun Arena in Connecticut, Darlene Cummings wears a StudBudz shirt and pink wig to a Lynx game. "I fell in love with the StudBudz," Cummings says. "I just love how open they are."

At the Minnesota State Fair, Andrew Heller rocks a Williams jersey as he walks around the grounds. There are still a few games to go in the regular season, but he already is making plans. "I'm going to have to get some washout pink hair dye for the playoffs," Heller says.

The Lynx gave out pink wigs for Minnesota's final regular-season home game. The Target Center stands looked like strawberry icing had been shot from dozens of T-shirt cannons.

Collier and McBride added pink highlights to their own hair.

Hiedeman's mom, Ann Gevaert, has even been swept up by StudBudz fervor. "People want to take pictures with me," Gevaert says. "They're like, 'That's Tee's mom!'" She has been gifted T-shirts with her daughter's face on them and a "Stud Bud Mom" bracelet. She wears the bracelet to every game. "It's just so fun," Gevaert says.

"THAT DAY WAS just not the day for me," Hiedeman says.

It's late May, early in the season, and practice was rough. Williams and Hiedeman struggled. Turnovers on offense and porous on defense. Coach Cheryl Reeve let them have it, Williams says.

"It was one of them days, man," Williams says. "It's just like 'Damn, Twin, do I suck at basketball?' That's what it be feelin' like. 'Damn, did I f--- this up?'"

They both teared up during and after practice.

Wanting to rid herself of what she considers to be bad energy, Hiedeman calls Williams on FaceTime and runs the clippers through her blonde curls. First, she dyes her hair a light purple. Then she goes pink. Williams cheers her on.

Williams and Hiedeman trace their friendship to Connecticut, to 2019. Williams arrived in 2016, after she was drafted eighth by the Mercury and traded to the Sun later that season. Three seasons later, she welcomed Hiedeman, drafted 18th by the Lynx in 2019 and traded to the Sun on draft night. Williams invited the rookie out to celebrate her 25th birthday that May. They had a lot in common: Neither came to the WNBA from major college programs—Williams played at USF and Hiedeman played at Marquette. Neither grew up in basketball hotbeds—Williams is from Folkston, Georgia, population less than 5,000. Hiedeman's hometown is Green Bay, Wisconsin. Both call themselves studs, a term used to describe Black, masculine and queer women.

"Man, she my baby, Bro," Williams says. "She came in as a rookie just tryin' to find her way. And we just immediately gravitated to each other."

They reunited for a season in Connecticut in 2022, but their friendship popped the past two seasons in Minnesota because, well, they have time to hang out.

"We're both single," Williams says. "People laugh every time I say that, but the reality is being single is the major part of why we're able to get so close. 'Cause reality is, we know gay relationships. When you're in a gay relationship, you're with 'em every day. You in each other's skin every day."

If Williams was in a relationship, she wouldn't get out of bed to go out with Hiedeman at 11:30 at night. They wouldn't talk as much (they've been known to text and chat all day). "I'm on the phone with Tee more than anybody," Williams says.

They figured they couldn't be the only people who would be entertained by their banter. So, they turned a camera on themselves.

Before launching their livestream, Williams and Hiedeman told their teammates their plans. To show their support, many Lynx players paraded through their hotel room and hopped on the first stream. There was a (bad?) freestyle to introduce McBride, and a dissection of whether Alanna Smith's outfit sent gay or straight signals ("It's giving stem," Williams said, a mashup of stud and femme). There was lively discussion about who on the team Collier would hypothetically let her daughter date. ("Not these two," Collier joked, motioning to Williams and Hiedeman before specifically explaining her stance to Williams. "You'd send her back to the '50s. She'd have to cook and clean and take your dogs out.")

So, after that rough practice and after Hiedeman dyes her hair, Williams tells viewers on the stream that she will dye her hair to match if they get to 1,000 subscribers. The StudBudz are on the road in Seattle when the subscriber count crosses the threshold. They have hair dye sent to their room and dye Williams' hair on stream.

"I wanted to be a woman of my word," Williams says. "So, we had to order the stuff to the hotel room and dye my hair, just me and Tee."

"WE FINE AS S---," Williams tells me one day in August. "We put it on. We got that vibe about us. We ain't never hurtin' for no women."

It's not just the pink hair. Or the sunglasses. Or the baseball hats. Or the hoodies. Or the chains. It's aura.

Williams and Hiedeman routinely talk about "baddies" on the stream. They talk about what they look for in women. (Spoiler: Also, baddies.) They streamed a double date. For now, they remain single, much to the dismay of some fans.

At Barclays Center, Charlotte McKinley clutched her homemade sign, waiting to get a glimpse of pink hair from her seat near the player tunnel. "Here 4 the Studbudz," her sign read in black marker on one side of the poster board. She flipped it over to the declaration on the other side. "Down bad 4 Natisha Hiedeman."

McKinley, 28, is a professional dancer in New York. She said she started getting into the WNBA about six months ago but got serious about it within the past three months, in part, because of the StudBudz.

When Hiedeman started walking toward the tunnel and McKinley's seat, McKinley waved her sign and shouted to Hiedeman. "I have a gift for you," she said when Hiedeman got close enough.

McKinley reached into the deep V of her denim vest and pulled a folded piece of paper from her bra. Written inside was her phone number.

Hiedeman put the piece of paper in her pocket, took a selfie with McKinley, and ran up the tunnel toward the locker room. When she saw Collier, Hiedeman handed her the paper and said someone wanted Hiedeman to give it to her.

Collier opened it up and laughed. "No, they didn't," she said.

Back in Minnesota a few days later, Hiedeman tells me she hasn't texted McKinley. "I'm just in my single era right now," she says.

She smirks. "It's not the first time."

The first Pride initiative in the WNBA didn't happen until 2014. The first of its kind in American professional sports, the initiative highlighted the pressing need to serve LGBTQIA+ fans. The relationship between the WNBA and queerness among its fan base and players had been historically fraught. Early marketing campaigns highlighted femininity, whether it was authentic or not for the players being showcased, something that Sue Bird and Diana Taurasi have spoken about in recent years. In 2002, Lesbians for Liberty staged a kiss-in at a New York Liberty game to protest what they saw as lesbian erasure.

There were Pride nights before 2014 and there were openly gay players before then too, the first of whom was Sue Wicks in 2002. Three-time MVP Sheryl Swoopes shared she was in a relationship with a woman in 2005 (though she has since identified differently), Seimone Augustus came out in 2012, Brittney Griner was openly gay even before she was picked No. 1 in the 2013 draft. But in the past 10 years superstars like Bird, Taurasi, Elena Delle Donne, Candace Parker, Chelsea Gray and many others have turned a spotlight on queer players in the league.

Still, the WNBA fanbase has mostly been served conventionally feminine players, even among those who are part of the LGBTQIA+ community. Another word for marketability is desirability. The StudBudz's queer ethos flips assumptions about attractiveness to fans and sponsors alike. Masculine women, they say, are sexy, too.

Williams has pointed out the missed opportunities before. When five WNBA players were highlighted in the *Sports Illustrated* Swimsuit Issue for the first time in 2022, the presentation of those five players was markedly feminine. "I love *Sports Illustrated*'s attempt to be more inclusive and amplify women in the W," Williams wrote on X. "At the same time though it would of been raw to see a sleek lil sports bra & some shorts swaggin'. There's more than one way to look sexy, and I hope in the future we can tap into that."

It's a sentiment echoed by coaches and other players, too.

"When I was first in [the WNBA], there was so much attention on the league being successful," Reeve says. "That translated to societally pretty players doing things that society at large viewed as marketable. So, you look at the queer players at that time having to be something they weren't because they were told, 'Well if you don't, then this all may go away.' To see that we've evolved into a space where you can show up to work, be who you are and be celebrated for it, I think it's a special time."

Liberty guard Natasha Cloud cosigns.

When asked about the appeal of masculine women, she smirks and flexes her arms. "My s--- gonna sell too," she says.

"There's just as many women screaming about us. The investment should be there. I just feel like the W is dumb for not doin' it, 'cause why don't you want to be paid?"

The StudBudz have attracted some brands on their own. They recently dyed their hair "period red," for a partnership with Kotex and managed to have fun with a topic that has traditionally been taboo. At one point, Williams is dead over Hiedeman's cramp-combatting technique: Laying down in the shower. "Who does that? I ain't never heard of that," she says. (Don't worry. The red was, shall we say, cyclical. They're back to pink now.)

Williams sees their content as filling a need for some, and she understands that StudBudz, despite the claim on their T-shirts, might not be for everyone.

"I think everybody get to kinda see how we vibe, how we talk to women. Because, one, where you ever really see that? You see all these datin' *Love Island* and all these different things. But it's like you rarely see, like you said, gay interactions. Maybe that might not be what you want to see, and that's cool. You don't gotta watch that stream. Watch another one."

"You guys are amazing," WNBA commissioner Cathy Engelbert says to Williams and Hiedeman during WNBA All-Star Weekend in July. The StudBudz stream the entire weekend. Literally. And it's impossible to look away.

There's a moment between Diggins and Hiedeman when Diggins comes over to say hi on the orange carpet. "What's a Stud Bud?" she jokes as she approaches them. Diggins and Hiedeman hug, while Williams gives a knowing side-eye because of, well, the crush heard round the internet.

The StudBudz dance with Reeve, draping their arms over their coach's shoulders, bopping along with her to the music. Reeve throws her head back and laughs. Coach and players, from different generations, and all three members of the LGBTQIA+ community.

They hang out with Clark.

"Oh, we're live!" Clark yells as she daps up Williams on the stream.

"We've got Caitlin Clark in the building!" Williams yells at the camera. Clark tells Williams and Hiedeman that she has been watching the stream at home.

The moment starts a meme for the StudBudz who begin to joke that they will "call Caitlin Clark" whenever they need help with anything, like getting into an Indy club.

Williams dances with Angel Reese, and I mean dances.

And with "Knuck If You Buck" thumping in the background, the StudBudz dance with the WNBA commissioner.

"They pulled the curtain back and showed that we're all friends off the court," Collier says. "We're competitors on the court, so that's why it feels so feisty. But off the court, we're all cool."

All-Star Weekend launches the StudBudz into a different stratosphere. According to Google Trends, "StudBudz WNBA" search interest in the U.S. increased over 5,000% in July compared to June. During All-Star week, the query "StudBudz merch" increased over 5,000% in U.S. search interest compared to the previous week.

None of it would have happened without basketball success as the foundation.

"We want to bring this organization back to where it's always been," Williams says.

The Minnesota Lynx are among the most successful franchises in WNBA history. They won four championships in seven years: 2011, 2013, 2015 and 2017. Those teams were anchored by a core of Hall of Famers: Lindsay Whalen (2022), Seimone Augustus (2024), Maya Moore (2025) and Sylvia Fowles (2025). Whalen and Rebekkah Brunson, who was also a member of those championship teams, are both on the Lynx staff this season.

The Lynx made it back to the WNBA Finals last year for the first time since winning the 2017 title, but they fell in five games to the New York Liberty.

Williams is the starting point guard for the top-seeded Lynx, who are up 1-0 in their semifinal series against the Phoenix Mercury. Hiedeman is her backup, but they often share the court. Game 2 is Tuesday in Minneapolis.

For the StudBudz, the Lynx's championship heritage is important, and adding to it is their primary focus.

Since the calendar flipped to September, Hiedeman is averaging 14.8 points per game, including 18 in the Lynx's Game 1 win over Golden State in the first round. Primarily known for knocking down 3-point shots early in her career, Heideman is shooting 57.7% from inside the arc this season.

"Cheryl and them, they created that culture and carried that through years," Hiedeman says. "She obviously wants the best players to play for her. But she's also looking for the best people. When you do that, the culture is obviously going to be amazing."

Williams averages 6.2 assists, second most in the league. Many consider her "middy" to be the best in the game, but this season she's shooting 38.9% from beyond the arc at a career-high volume. She had 23 points, 8 rebounds, 7 assists and 5 steals in Minnesota's 82–69 Game 1 win over the Mercury.

"I think you see in my game now, how I just elevated my game since last year," Williams says. "Even havin' Whalen come in, and havin' that mixture of her and Cheryl be in my ear, it's just done elevated my game so much for sure."

They're both quick, pesky defenders and average a combined two steals per game.

"On-court success is what we're all here for," Reeve says.

"Courtney has established herself as one of the best point guards in this league. Without that, our franchise isn't where we are. We lost a key bench player from last year's team, and Tee's evolution has helped fill that void. The confidence and the things that she's giving us have been really vital to our success."

That's not to say that the StudBudz haven't presented some challenges for Reeve.

"I feel like my boundaries have been stretched," Reeve says. "Sometimes it goes well and sometimes it doesn't. I know I've been difficult for them at times, really trying to challenge them to come to my side a little bit. There's a little bit of give and take in there because I think there's certain things it takes to win a championship. Learning how to coach those two and them teaching me a little along the way has been fun."

Their commitment to Minnesota's championship chase has never been in doubt.

"It's not something we've had to talk about or worry about," Collier says. "When we're on the court together, we're focused on winning. We're not focused on anything else."

This season, the Lynx had the best record in the league, won the most games in franchise history and secured home-court advantage through the playoffs. They swept the Valkyries in the first round.

If Minnesota wins the WNBA championship, prepare for a StudBudz party.

The camera will be on.

KATIE BARNES is a senior writer at ESPN and author of *Fair Play: Trans Athletes and the Fight for Fairness.* An award-winning journalist, Katie writes at the intersection of sports and gender, focusing on in-depth storytelling. They are a graduate of St. Olaf College and reside in Connecticut with their wife, daughter, and cat.

Two Nights Playing with Fire at Patrick Mahomes and Travis Kelce's Steakhouse

LIZ COOK

FROM *Defector* • DECEMBER 16, 2025

KANSAS CITY, Mo.—As celebrity restaurant mascots, athletes offer a tidy sense of vertical integration: Why not supply the very calories they need to expend on the field? I'm surprised there are so few successful models. We have all mostly forgotten (or agreed not to talk about) George Brett's restaurant in Kansas City, Brett Favre's Wisconsin steakhouse, or those 31 Papa John's franchises Peyton Manning coincidentally shed two days before the NFL dropped the pizza chain as a sponsor.

Still, tables have been reliably booked at 1587 Prime—a mashup of Patrick Mahomes's and Travis Kelce's jersey numbers, along with a word that vaguely connotes "beef"—since it opened in Kansas City in August. I left an eight-year gig as a KC restaurant critic in 2023, but the mania surrounding the opening was enough to summon me out of retirement. Like a washed-up former detective, I couldn't resist stumbling half-drunk into my old precinct for one last job.

In some respects, a flashy celebrity steakhouse means the same thing everywhere. But it means something else in Kansas City, a cowtown whose economic engine was its stockyards, once the second-largest in the country, and which has struggled for years to cultivate a high-end dining scene. We have some great restaurants, but fundamentally, we're a city that loathes to dress for dinner. (I felt a swell of civic pride when I learned Travis proposed to Taylor Swift in shorts.) I wondered how Noble 33—the Miami-based fine-dining restaurant group tasked with executing 15 and 87's vision—would fare here.

In a pure business sense, they seem to be faring just fine. On a recent visit, a server told me that a group of Taylor Swift fans had waited six hours for bar seats, hoping they might catch a glimpse of the singer housing a truffle grilled cheese. Taylor didn't show. I wish the restaurant had something else to offer them.

If nothing else, 1587 Prime looks nice. The 238-seat, two-story restaurant inside the Loews Kansas City Hotel is riddled with luxury tropes. Everything is bathed in a charmed, golden light. The stairs are marble, the tables are marble, and the servers all wear smart white coats and black ties. The leather-backed menus are enormous—perilous. Manipulating them at a small table covered with expensive glassware made me feel like a horse on roller skates.

Music is ostensibly a theme. Every night, local musicians perform short sets of Motown, jazz, and soul hits, and the performers are universally talented. They're also chastely miked. The live backing band is never loud enough to compete with diners' conversation, and while the singers roam around the dining room, they seem trained in the art of extremely brief eye contact that asks nothing of you in return.

The same can't be said of the patrons. Every time I looked around the room, diners looked back with the defiant stares of people who are used to being watched. The restaurant seems to be drawing in its target clients: people who fly private. On my first visit, our server—a very friendly woman named Debbie—told us she had two tables that had flown in just for dinner.

"There's this thing I learned about," she said. "Did you know they have an Uber Jet?"

I did not. I sensed that Debbie and I had both learned this against our will.

To be fair, one of the reasons I kept looking around the room was that everyone's drinks were on fire. This was, I learned, The Alchemy ($22), a cocktail the restaurant created for Taylor Swift, a woman who has never had to use Uber Jet.

I ordered one, too, and a dedicated server brought out a martini glass with some steel wool tangled around the stem. (Something else to know about 1587 Prime: there are at least two employees whose main job appears to be setting things on fire.)

"How many tables order this every night?" I asked.

"Almost all of them," she said, with just a hint of resignation.

She lit the drink. The steel wool pulsed with a warm, luxurious shimmer before almost immediately fizzling into a cold pile (yes, this is a metaphor). "The stem might be a little hot," she warned, pawing the nest away from the glass. The drink tasted like a Cosmo someone had strained through a French Vanilla Yankee Candle.

The Alchemy is in a section of cocktails titled "The Players," named for the steakhouse's famous guests. For Mahomes fans, there's the "Showtime" ($19), a rum and coconut cocktail made with a "Coors Light syrup" that I tragically could not taste. I preferred Kelce's "Big Yeti" ($24), a nocino-enhanced old fashioned with bitter chocolate notes.

There is a fourth cocktail in the section, named after Brittany Mahomes. I will not be tricked into commenting on it.

The drinks were designed by beverage director Juan Carlos Santana, who's led menu design at other Noble 33 haunts. This is the only way I can explain why a steakhouse cocktail menu features a "Noble Margarita" ($18), or why the house martini ($23) is laced with fino sherry and fennel-infused Italicus (a sweet, sunny bergamot liqueur). It's a lovely, nuanced cocktail, and it seems to have been designed in a lab to piss off martini drinkers.

If you're after a more traditional martini—say, gin and vermouth—you can order the martini "your way" for an extra $10.

"Isn't this a service most bars offer for free?" my husband asked.

Sure. But most bars don't come with a "Martini Cart Experience." The first part of the Experience is using a checklist and a golf pencil to select your ideal spirits, vermouths, and enhancements, whether that's truffle brine (an additional $5), caviar-stuffed olives (an extra $12) or an accompanying "caviar bump" ($21).

The second part of the Experience is waiting for the cart. The restaurant only has space for one cart per floor, which can create backlogs when multiple tables order martinis. On my first visit, my table waited a modest 12 minutes before the cart became available.

The Experience concluded with a bartender scanning my checklist, building the martini, shaking it (you read that correctly), and straining it into a glass that had been chilled by a light-up contraption resembling a Simon. With the upcharge for the truffle brine, the martini was $38.

Much of the menu at 1587 Prime reads like magnetic poetry for people with expense accounts. If you'd like, you can order a black truffle grilled cheese ($27), truffle fettuccine ($39), tuna tartare with a truffle ponzu ($29), fried chicken with truffle honey ($25). You could not bring a truffle pig within a mile of this place; it would die instantly from a seizure.

Wagyu? You got it. There's wagyu pastrami ($42), a wagyu cheesesteak ($65), a bowl of wagyu meatballs and spaghetti for two ($68). There's a wagyu carpaccio ($33) that *also* has black truffle sliced thickly over the top, like very expensive bagel chips.

Even dishes without any obvious high-end flourishes are given a luxury veneer. I liked the homey roast chicken ($37), which had crisp skin and a simple, savory pan sauce. For some reason, the restaurant calls it "marble chicken."

"You've heard of 'chicken under a brick,'" my server said. "Well, this is chicken cooked under a marble slab."

"Is the chicken actually cooked under a marble slab?" I asked.

"No."

Wealth has always been about signifiers, but no one said they had to be this lazy. That ethos might even extend to the hiring of executive chef Ryan Arnold, who Noble 33 appears to have found by googling "country clubs near me." Arnold's previous gig was at the St. Joseph Country Club, a country club in the satellite town of Country Club, Missouri. (Hey, it's good SEO.)

Arnold seems like a talented chef, and to his credit, some of the more gimmicky-sounding dishes actually work. The wagyu meatballs ($28, available not just in the spaghetti entree but as a standalone app) were the best thing I ordered at 1587 Prime. They were indecorously soft, with an almost 'nduja-like texture; the bracing heat from the accompanying arrabbiata sauce sliced cleanly through the richness of the beef and the melty snow cap of mozzarella and Parm.

Even the "A5 wagyu katsu sando" ($68), a dish my server tried to dissuade me from ordering, was well-composed. The "sando" is in fact four stamp-sized bites arranged on the plate like modernist finger sandwiches—Girl Dinner, but for Marie Antoinette. Each bite of wagyu was buttery and plump, with a super thin crust to give the beef a hint of structure. A swoop of Osetra caviar on top added brininess to the richness. A sleaze of gold leaf added gold leaf. The dish was fine. Does anyone really want to eat like this?

The main trouble with 1587 Prime isn't its child-like idea of luxury. It's that it's a steakhouse that doesn't nail the steaks.

On my first visit, I ordered the six-ounce petite filet ($59), one of only three locally sourced steaks on the menu (the others are from Idaho, Australia, and Japan). Although I ordered it medium-rare, the steak arrived a generous medium, with a nice crust but an unpleasantly mealy interior. (Before someone vaults over a banister to tell me my mistake was ordering the filet, I should say: I like a filet, and it is not impossible to cook one well. But I have eaten a better version at a monk-themed novelty steakhouse than at 1587 Prime.)

Perhaps my mistake was ordering it with a "tableside flambé," which you can add to any steak here for an extra $27. After conferring with Debbie about whether this was a good idea, she dispatched a second cart with a second fire-oriented employee.

While he worked, I peppered him with questions. Did he man the flambé cart every night? Yes, by choice. "I've never worked in a kitchen," he said. "I just really like fire." Had he ever singed his shirtsleeves on the cart? "I'm going to tell you guys a little secret," he replied. He leaned over the table and brushed some hair away from his forehead. Most of his eyebrows were missing.

On my second visit, I skipped the flambé and opted for the 16-ounce bone-in strip ($78), which was unusually thin. The crust was flavorful and the steak more tender—but it was still medium, not the requested medium-rare. The "onion jus" ordered alongside was less jus than paste, with the texture of sieved baby food.

Of the three steaks I tried at 1587 Prime, only the 10-ounce hanger from the steak frites ($48)—the cheapest cut on the menu—was actually cooked to temperature. If you'd like ketchup with those frites, you can order the Mahomes Ketchup Flight, which a press release from Noble 33 touted as "a nod to the player's favorite steak pairing featuring a lineup of three unique ketchups made in-house."

The ketchups are not, in fact, made in-house. Two of the three—a truffle ketchup and a spicy ketchup—are *augmented* in-house, but my server confirmed with the kitchen that the base for all three was Heinz. (*Heinz*! This compounded the betrayal. Hunt's would have at least made spiritual sense, given Mahomes's old brand deal.) In one light, this is good news: house-made ketchup is almost universally terrible. In another light, I felt a bit suckered paying $15 for three small ramekins of ketchup, one of which was pure uncut Heinz. A representative for the restaurant tells me the price has since come down to $10.

This is the way of things at 1587, which is ostensibly a mashup of jersey numbers but also a credible restaurant tab. Complaining about the prices at 1587 Prime is like complaining about the wind on Mount Everest: predictable, but hardly the worst part of the experience. All the same, there is no need for anything this mediocre to cost this much.

Some of the best items at 1587 Prime aren't even specific to the restaurant. One of my favorite dishes was the wagyu carpaccio, which had pickled enoki mushrooms, pine nuts, and waxy shards of Parmesan tucked in alongside the black truffle. If you don't live near Kansas City, don't worry—you can also order it at Sparrow Italia, a Noble 33 restaurant in Miami. On the West Coast? You can find 1587 Prime's A5 Tajima Wagyu steak with "whisky barrel-aged soy" and "triple inferno salt" at Noble 33's Casa Madera in West Hollywood.

Even the few local touches feel like cop-outs. The bread at 1587 is from Farm to Market Bread Co., and the desserts are made by McLain's Bakery. These are fine KC businesses, but it's lazy for a restaurant of this caliber and price point to be outsourcing its bread and pastry programs at all. You'd also be forgiven for not knowing any of this as a diner, because nowhere on 1587's dessert menu does it explain that the desserts and ice creams aren't made in-house.

There's one local touch that feels genuine: Almost everyone who works at 1587 Prime is Midwest Nice. The staff are impressively warm and personable for a dining experience that can invite obsequity. If nothing else, 1587 seems to be succeeding as a jobs program for the local service industry and fire-enjoyers. On my visits, there seemed to be an almost 1:1 ratio of employees to diners.

That doesn't mean service is seamless. On one visit, the steaks arrived without steak knives. A bread course that arrived promptly on my first visit was absent the next—when I asked about it, two different food runners were dispatched with two different bread baskets, one of which had been toasted to the consistency of styrofoam. These aren't dramatic service mistakes, but they're basic ones.

Ultimately, 1587 Prime is a parched vision of luxury, simultaneously overreliant on ChatGPT-grade luxury tropes, rehashed ideas from its outside restaurant group, and lazy local outsourcing for stations that a top-tier restaurant should staff. I don't know that it matters. Even now, four months from opening, reservations nearly always show as fully booked. (That said, I put my name on the waitlist on four different occasions while working on this review, and was alerted about an open table all four times.) The restaurant seems to be getting by with the help of a core of jet-setting Noble 33 superfans—who are you? Why?—and a rotating cast of first-time visitors: Chiefs fans, Swifties, curious Kansas Citians.

If you're one of those first-timers, learn from my mistakes. You do not have to order the Heinz ketchup flight. You do not have to buy the Taylor Swift cocktail that tastes like a candle and is garnished with a flaming Brillo pad. You do not have to sacrifice your servers' eyebrows at the altar of the tableside flambé. Above all, you do not have to "come here for the bit." The bit just isn't that interesting.

UPDATE, 1/10/25: An earlier version of this story stated that Betty Rae's supplied ice cream to 1587 Prime. After publication, a representative contacted the author and said that Betty Rae's has not provided ice cream to 1587 Prime since the restaurant's first month of operation, despite the restaurant telling the author as recently as November that it did. The rep said that 1587 Prime continues to list Betty Rae's on its website as one of its local partners despite requests from Betty Rae's to take it down.

LIZ COOK is a Kansas City–based freelance writer and recipe developer. After spending eight years as a restaurant critic, Liz launched the experimental newsletter *Haterade*, where she digs into maligned and misunderstood foods. Her work has appeared in Defector, Serious Eats, *Food & Wine*, *Condé Nast Traveler*, and Eater, among many other publications. Her writing has been anthologized in Best American Food Writing and received awards from the Association of Food Journalists and the Association of Alternative Newsmedia.

Jonathan Martin Finding His Way a Decade After NFL Retirement

ANTHONY OLIVIERI

FROM ESPN • FEBRUARY 12, 2025

Jonathan Martin waits in the wings off stage in a half-full theater in Wilmington, Delaware. He's here to give a TEDx talk, "The Fiat Debt Spiral." It's about Bitcoin, and he's ready to be introduced.

Martin is an accomplished scholar.... An entrepreneur.... He was a professional athlete.... A football player.

He walks into the glare of a spotlight, unable to see his parents' faces looking back from the third row. There's a microphone to his right and a video camera directly in front of him. Dressed in a button-down shirt and dark jeans, his outfit suggests business school mixer. But his 6-foot-6 frame suggests offensive lineman.

A few seconds pass. He takes a deep breath and exhales.

In quick, short sentences, he speaks of inflation and the United States' economic relationship to China, of political polarization and financial freedom. He thinks Bitcoin can level the economic playing field, bridge the gap between the haves and have-nots. He has compared it to the internal combustion engine and the printing press. He sounds like a professor.

He speaks for more than 15 minutes, finishes and leaves to applause.

He doesn't mention football or the Miami Dolphins or what happened a decade ago.

Shortly after his talk, he heads to a conference room. He exhales again.

"I like to present myself," he says, "as I am today."

Martin leans back in his chair.

"All the time I'm recognized as Jonathan Martin from the Miami Dolphins," he says. "That's what people know me for."

His parents are nearby. They flew in from Los Angeles after Martin invited them.

"Football is just something I did," he says. "It wasn't who I am."

On Oct. 28, 2013, the Monday after a Miami loss, Jonathan Martin missed practice. He was in his second season with the Dolphins as an offensive tackle, one of the most important yet anonymous jobs in the NFL. He missed practice again the next day and was listed with an illness on the team's injury report. On Wednesday of that week, Fox Sports reported that Martin had stormed out of the team cafeteria after slamming a tray of food to the ground. The reasons were unclear. ESPN followed, reporting that Martin was the "subject of some ribbing" in the cafeteria. "O-line made fun of him, and he snapped," a source told ESPN. The Dolphins' next game was set for Thursday night, and Martin was listed as doubtful.

At 1 a.m. on that Thursday, a FoxSports.com headline read, "Source: Teammates bullied Martin." The story reported "persistent bullying and teasing" of Martin dating to his rookie season in 2012. Three days later, on Nov. 3, the Dolphins released three separate statements. The first expressed concern for Martin's health and well-being, denied reports that the NFL Players Association was investigating players and added: "The notion of bullying is based on speculation and has not been presented to us as a concern from Jonathan or anyone else internally." The second statement said the Dolphins had received information from Martin's representatives "about allegations of player misconduct." Later that night, the Dolphins said they had indefinitely suspended offensive lineman Richie Incognito for "conduct detrimental to the team."

On Nov. 6—just seven days after the initial news reports—the NFL announced it had retained Ted Wells, a widely known trial lawyer, to investigate and write a report about what had happened in the Dolphins' locker room. National news outlets suddenly appeared outside Martin's parents' home in Los Angeles, training their cameras on the front door.

Wells' report, released Feb. 14, 2014, found that Incognito and two other Dolphins offensive linemen, Mike Pouncey and John Jerry, engaged in a pattern of harassment of Martin—a case that became known as "Bullygate." The report also detailed that Martin had checked himself into a hospital after the cafeteria incident and that his mother had flown across the country to be by his side.

Martin never again played for the Dolphins. On March 11, 2014, he was traded to the San Francisco 49ers. Fifteen games later, after a training camp stint with the Carolina Panthers, he retired from the NFL, citing a back injury that could have kept him out of the 2015 season.

Dec. 28 marked 10 years since Martin's last game. To this day, he does not like to talk about Incognito or "Bullygate." He wants to be known as more than NFL locker room prey.

A legacy can be a living, breathing document. There's a hopefulness in that but also a relentlessness; we're always writing our stories but they're never finished, and we can't fully escape the events of our past.

After years of requests, Martin finally agreed to speak with ESPN. In a series of interviews starting in late 2023, he was determined to emphasize what he's doing now and to communicate that his plans for the future are how he should be judged. His job now might be harder than protecting a quarterback from 300-pound pass rushers.

He edits himself in real time, texting updates and changes to previous comments. He sways from being assertive to being cautious. He describes himself as an alpha and wants to assure you he wasn't a fully formed person in his 20s. He worries over retaining agency of his story.

"I never believed for a second I was being bullied," Martin says now.

He wants the world to forget the only thing it remembers about him.

"It's a story," he says, "that I've been trying to fix for 10 years."

It's December 2023, and Martin is 34 years old and holds a bachelor's degree from Stanford and a master's degree in real estate and finance from Georgetown. In a few weeks, he'll begin his spring semester at The Wharton School, where he's majoring in entrepreneurship and innovation, focusing on monetary policy and emerging alternative currencies. Just over a decade after the Dolphins placed him on the non-football injury list, he walks a brick path on the campus of the University of Pennsylvania. The stones are inscribed with quotes. *Lost time is never found again. Distrust and caution are the parents of security.*

He talks about nearby Steinberg Hall-Dietrich Hall. The building originally was named after a single donor but later was renovated and renamed, new parts added over and around the old ones. He stops to sit at a table.

His passion now is Bitcoin. Some people might hear the word Bitcoin and think of Sam Bankman-Fried and 25-year prison sentences, but Martin is undeterred. "There are fraudulent actors in every industry," he says.

Instead of settling into a post-playing career, he resists being known only as a former football player.

"Life requires intentionality," he says. "No one is coming to save you."

On a youth flag football field in Los Angeles, 11-year-old Jonathan Martin was the new kid on an organized football team for the first time. His shoulders sagged. Every movement was plodding.

His father, Gus Martin, approached from the sideline. Until then, Jonathan's experience with the game was playing catch with his dad at the bus stop—the breath of father and son billowing in the morning light. This was different. It wasn't just for fun. Opposing players were trying to get to him. He had to deal with confrontations.

"I took him aside and said, 'Jonathan, don't let anyone get inside your head. You get inside *their* head,'" Gus says. "And he took that to heart, and he began doing that."

Gus describes how he and his wife, Jane Howard-Martin, arrived with their family in L.A. in January 2001 from Pittsburgh, where Jonathan was born. Gus says that he had gone from nearby Rankin, a steel town 8 miles up the river, to the Ivy League—one of nine members of his family to go to Harvard—and that Jonathan's mother had been the first Black woman partner at a major Pittsburgh law firm.

Gus became a professor at California State University, Dominguez Hills; Jane would take a corporate job where a team of lawyers would report to her. They enrolled Jonathan at The John Thomas Dye School, a private school in Los Angeles' posh Bel Air neighborhood.

At the urging of his grandmother, Jonathan played the violin. For a school project, he and one of his friends, Tarek Tohme, once researched Daniel Pearl, the American journalist from *The Wall Street Journal* who was captured and murdered in Pakistan in 2002. "When I met him, I thought, 'Oh, this kid might go on to become a senator or be a violinist,'" Tohme says.

Jonathan went to the exclusive Harvard-Westlake School for middle and high school. "It was this protective bubble," Tarek says, "...It was an environment that was focused on protecting kids and giving them a safe space to learn and thrive."

Their schools were popular among the children of celebrities. Halle Berry arrived to watch a flag football game. One classmate had the last name Spielberg; another father's first name was Denzel. There were no fistfights, no lunchroom dustups, no confrontation. If anything went wrong, administrators and parents worked in tandem to find resolutions.

Jonathan and Tarek were soft-spoken and, at times, awkward. They also stood out in predominantly white schools. Jonathan was the Black son of a family from Pittsburgh. Tarek, the son of an immigrant from Lebanon, felt comfortable at his home and with his family. Gus' academic expertise was on the Middle East.

Jonathan hit 6 feet tall in middle school, towering above his classmates in crowded hallways.

"[Jonathan's] mom even talks about, when Jonathan was a larger-stature kid, wanting to make sure she protected him from himself in a society where people look at a large Black man as a threat in many ways," Tarek says.

Kids in school sometimes made fun of him, as kids in school do, but Jonathan didn't push back. It seemed to knock him back on his heels. In texts to his mother later described in the Wells report, he said he would "just get sad" and feel like "nobody wanted to be his friend."

When he outgrew it, Jonathan traded in his violin for the viola and, eventually, the viola for football pads. He played tackle football for the first time in eighth grade. His Harvard-Westlake high school coaches told him he had a future.

As players and coaches filtered onto the field after one high school game, an opposing coach approached Martin, the adrenaline of competition still spiking.

"You're a motherf---ing beast," the coach said.

Gus had watched how his son had grown up with football, how he had begun considering it a path for his life. Jonathan played his last high school game on Nov. 23, 2007. Afterward, Gus waited for him to come out of the locker room. Teammates slowly trickled out. The crowd thinned. There still was no sign of Jonathan. Gus opened the door to the locker room and went inside. As he checked on his son, Jonathan's eyes were red. He'd been crying.

In the dining room of Gus and Jane's open-concept home on a quiet street in an upscale neighborhood on the west side of Los Angeles, there are 64 picture frames with photos and documents on the dining room wall. They represent both sides of the family and date back more than 100 years.

There's a college dean and professor.

The first Black federal judge in Baltimore.

A Civil War veteran and early pioneer in the state of Iowa.

A trainer for Duquesne University's basketball, football and hockey teams in the 1930s.

Singers.

A deputy secretary of state under former President Bill Clinton.

"His mom has traced it remarkably," Jonathan's friend, Tarek, said a day earlier. "And that family has achieved incredible success in the face of persecution, in the face of discrimination."

Gus Martin points now at a black-and-white photo of his great-grandparents, who arrived in Pittsburgh from Virginia during the Great Migration. His great-grandfather, who Gus says had red hair and could have passed for a white man, used to belly up to bars in Pennsylvania's working-class Monongahela Valley. When his glass was drained, he'd ask the bartender: "'You don't serve n-----s here, do you?' And they'd say, 'Nah, of course not.' He'd take his glass, [and say] 'You just did.'"

That story stays alive on their wall, not to be erased. There's a framed document, too. It's a family member's emancipation papers. Gus says he doesn't know to whom the papers belong but says his wife's family history traces back to 1619 and the arrival of slaves on North American shores.

"If you read the history books, they say the first Africans arrived, her ancestor was one of them," Gus says. "Ten-year-old girl named Margarida. She was probably Catholic. She was probably Christian. She was taken from Angola, which was a Portuguese area, put on a Portuguese boat going to Mexico to work in the mines that were there. British pirate ships with letters of marque came and took this ship, thinking they'd find gold on there, because the Spanish Main was taking gold. Found these humans in there. So they took the healthiest ones. They needed food. The only English-speaking colony was Jamestown [Virginia]. They offloaded these people in exchange for food."

He stares at the wall.

"Heck of a story," he says.

The house is a collection of Gus and Jane's life experiences. Historical artifacts and mementos from their travels. Photos of Jonathan and family during their happiest moments. They have a Steelers Terrible Towel draped below their television. They kept Jonathan's helmet from Stanford, but there's little else from their son's football career on display.

When Gus and Jane walk to the kitchen to get a snack, to the living room to watch TV, or to the bedroom at night, they walk past the wall.

"There's this line, 'Ancestors are meaningful,'" Gus says, "'family's everything.'"

COACH DAVID SHAW had messages posted around the football facilities at Stanford, including in the locker room, where a sign read "Wring It Dry."

Shaw didn't want his players' experiences confined to the football buildings. In the dorms, they mixed with successful people—often the children of millionaires, billionaires and celebrities—connections that would be useful after they hung up their pads.

"Take advantage of that environment," he says, "and not say, 'I'm just here to play football.'"

Shaw points to former Stanford players such as David DeCastro, who majored in management, science and engineering, and Christian McCaffrey, who was Division I college football's Academic All-American of the Year, or to Andrew Luck, who started a book club in the NFL. Those players' NFL teammates often looked sideways, with a half a grin, as if to say, *Oh, you're a Stanford guy, what are you reading now?*

Martin knew the Stanford environment and fit into it. But when he got to the NFL, the culture was different.

"So many kids will go to a Stanford, Princeton, Harvard and go to the NFL and not have any issues at all with translation," Shaw says. "I could also see being from those types of environments and going to an NFL locker room where there are not a lot of people majoring in what you're majoring in or have your same out-of-sports interests. And the different makeup of that locker room is something to get used to."

Jonathan felt out of place in an NFL locker room and didn't connect with his teammates.

When "Bullygate" broke, Shaw watched from afar. He thought his former player was being mischaracterized, made out to be someone he was not. Shaw had seen controversy before and believed eventually it would blow over.

"It's just that this didn't calm down for a while," he says.

At one point, he reached out to Martin's mother. While recruiting, Shaw had hit it off with Martin's parents. Stanford's recruiting pitch—high-level football and elite academics—had been what Gus and Jane were pushing for Jonathan all along.

Sometime after the story about Martin and Incognito broke, Shaw heard from his former player. "It was mainly me making sure he knew that I was there for him, that I could support him," Shaw says. "And him expressing gratitude for that."

It hurt Shaw to watch what was happening. He knew he couldn't protect Jonathan or stop what was going on. If it had been an on-field issue, he could coach him up. He gave former players advice about their film sometimes. But "Bullygate" was bigger.

"I was not involved in any of the things going on," Shaw says. "But I thought it was important for him to know that I cared about him. That we at Stanford cared about him. And that we were gonna be there for him if he needed us."

Whatever was going on was happening on a different, more public scale than the game. There was no playbook for this.

"You want them to do so well," Shaw says. "You want them to have such a great transition, so when things don't go well, it hurts."

JUST DAYS AFTER a mass shooting at a high school in Parkland, Florida, Gus Martin was at home in Los Angeles when he got a text. It was February 2018, just over three years since his son's last NFL game, and one of Jonathan's friends told him about a post on Jonathan's Instagram account. The post showed a photo of a shotgun with ammunition scattered around it. It tagged the accounts of former Miami teammates Richie Incognito and Mike Pouncey, as well as the accounts of two former high school classmates, and included hashtags for Harvard-Westlake and the Dolphins.

"When you're a bully victim & a coward, your options are suicide, or revenge," the caption on the post read.

His mother was on a business trip at the time. His father headed to Jonathan's condo, worried and concerned for his son. A SWAT team had arrived but left because Jonathan wasn't there. Gus stayed until early morning, but Jonathan had checked himself into a Los Angeles area hospital the same day the post appeared. Jonathan eventually left and returned home.

"And when that happened, gosh, it surprised us," Gus says. "Surprised everybody. But that's when we said, I think we had a fairly healthy response in that we said, 'OK, now we know that he has to receive some sort of medical treatment at that point.'"

Gus said it was good that Jonathan went on his own.

"That's sort of how I think of his personality, that he really didn't mean what he posted," Gus says, "but then he realized he had a real problem, so he went to the hospital."

In August 2015, right after retiring from the NFL, Jonathan posted to Facebook that he suffered from depression and had tried to kill himself on multiple occasions. "Your self-perceived social inadequacy dominates your every waking moment & thought," he wrote. "You're petrified of going to work. You either sleep 12, 14, 16, hours a day when you can, or not at all." He finished his Stanford degree in classics with a concentration in ancient history in January 2016. He had three stops as an intern, in private equity and real estate, over the next two years. Then in 2018, the Instagram post appeared.

Martin was arrested and faced four felony counts in connection with the post. His then-lawyer, Winston McKesson, told *The Los Angeles Times* that the post was "not a threat…it was a cry for help." One count against Martin was dismissed in January 2019, and the others were dismissed in 2021 after he completed a two-year diversion program.

Six years after making that lonely drive to his son's condo, Gus views Jonathan's trying times as woven into his experience: "Like being a quilt," he says. "That we are what we are. We're a tapestry. So, it's certainly a part of him, but it's not all of him."

Martin says he has apologized, privately and publicly, to the people in the Harvard-Westlake community and regrets how his actions in posting to Instagram affected them. Martin says he spent several years lost, confused, and abusing alcohol and other substances. He describes the stages of his life like a book's chapters. One closes and another opens.

"But I will say that it is important for me to say that my actions in 2018 were not what people thought they were," he says. "I don't want to get into more detail than that. But when you have sort of a negative situation like I went through at a young age, you're off-kilter. You're off-balance. And it takes a while to regain your focus."

In late 2019, Martin moved to Austin, Texas, where he started a real estate company with a college teammate before joining another company—all while working on a master's degree from Georgetown. He arrived from New Orleans, where he had spent six months in real estate. It was part of a pattern. He kept starting from the bottom, perpetually seeking the opportunity and the safety of a blank page.

"I think you learn more from your failures than you do from your successes," he says. "And the tabloid media is there to let everyone know about your failures, but they're not there when you graduate from Georgetown or when you start a company in Austin, Texas."

He describes one new version of himself now in a story he tells about a Silicon Valley mentor—"this guy was probably worth nine figures"—who drove a 10-year-old Prius with a front bumper sealed with duct tape. "It was part of his identity," Martin says. "He is blue-collar. And I feel similar, where it's like I want to be a blue-collar businessman. I don't want to be someone with soft, manicured palms. I want to be someone with calluses, with splinters in my hands."

When he arrived in Austin, instead of spending time in an air-conditioned office, Martin says he flipped houses in the heat—"toil, pain, these things are important"—installing vinyl floors, building fences and scraping ceilings even as sciatic pain from a life in football radiated down his leg.

"I don't have reporters in front of my house asking for comments on, 'Hey, you're doing great in life. How's that?'" he says. "It's more so they're showing up when you're not doing great. So, for me, it's an unfortunate reality of media, and the internet, and social media, and everything today, where the internet is forever and perception is reality, right?"

Two summers ago, during a break from Wharton, Martin visited a coffee farm in El Salvador. While there, he got an idea. He had invited a friend with connections to coffee businesses in

Los Angeles to make the trip with him and introduced him to the country's harvest, grown at high altitudes on volcanic soil, making for high-quality flavor. Martin's friend took samples back to Los Angeles, and coffee sommeliers there were impressed. *How would the product be exported to L.A.? What if there were a drought? Could he make a business of it?*

Martin remembers standing in a farm field three hours outside of San Salvador, the country's capital city, and feeling the stare of the locals. "Large Black Americans are kind of rare down there," he says.

His coffee business never got off the ground, but Martin had also been in El Salvador to learn about Bitcoin. El Salvador was the first country to make Bitcoin—a digital currency decentralized from banks—legal tender, and one of his Wharton professors had encouraged Martin to immerse himself there and see how it worked up close. "I was impressed by his initiative," professor Francine McKenna says.

She encouraged him to write for CoinDesk, which covers the cryptocurrency world, while there. In an August 2023 article, Martin wrote: "The core ethos of Bitcoin is to create a fairer and more accessible monetary system for the billions of people worldwide who do not have access to traditional banking services."

Taking up for the underdog became one of Martin's passions. When he dedicated himself to learning about Bitcoin, he also became obsessed with becoming the best in the world at something other than football.

"It took me 10,000 hours to become a 0.1 percenter in football," Martin says. "If you're an NFL starter as an offensive tackle, you're among the 64 best people in the world at your position. I view this journey as probably being similar.

"It's probably going to take me 10,000 hours to become a 0.1 percenter in Bitcoin. But it's a new space, and I enjoy having this feeling of being a frontiersman. It's like being in California during the gold rush."

As he sipped coffee near a volcano in El Salvador, Martin could see the chance to reinvent himself. Confound expectations and defy perceptions.

"I wanted a slight element of danger," he says.

JONATHAN MARTIN PARTICIPATED in the 2014 Wells report. The report found that Richie Incognito, John Jerry and Mike Pouncey harassed Martin, another offensive lineman and a member of the training staff. It described "sexually explicit remarks" about members of his family and said that "at times [Martin was] ridiculed with racial insults and other offensive comments." Five days after the report was published, Dolphins offensive line coach Jim Turner was fired. Incognito, who had been suspended by the team when "Bullygate" broke, did not play in the NFL in 2014.

By phone in March 2024, Martin reflected on the Wells report, saying, "It's my greatest regret of my life to this day is participating in that clown show."

Things happened in that locker room. His teammates called him names and said racist things to his face. They made misogynistic comments. On the spectrum of behavior in football locker rooms, it was extreme, he said. But after "Bullygate" broke, Martin became the martyred face of bullying, a role he says he didn't want to play. He didn't excuse what Incognito and the others did. It angered him. But he saw himself as a football player who had earned his spot on the team. "I was an NFL starter," he said. "I was getting paid millions of dollars." He saw the world of football as intensely competitive, and he saw himself as someone strong enough to be there.

When Martin left the Dolphins' facility on Oct. 28, 2013, reporters started asking questions. At some point after his departure, Martin said during the 2024 call, his mother told a reporter that he was being bullied in Miami, that she "said the word 'bullying.'"

"I had a situation with my teammates that I wasn't super happy about," he said. "But my mother had her own read on the situation."

The word took on a life of its own. The situation went viral.

"I hadn't even told my coaches, hadn't told anyone," Martin said. "And suddenly it's on ESPN, right?"

At the time, he didn't push back.

"I didn't believe any of the stances I was taking, right, where I'm this victim," he said. "I wasn't a victim, right? And, again, it's been a point of consternation."

"His mom and I did strongly intervene," Gus Martin says. "To make sure he was protected."

Jonathan initially had shared with his parents what he hadn't shared with anyone else about what happened in the Miami locker room. Jane Howard-Martin declined to speak for this story, but Jonathan's friend Tarek remembers Martin's parents always trying "to create a safe space for [him] to not have to encounter the same things that they did." It isn't hard to picture them trying to take control during the days of "Bullygate."

"My mother maybe in her mind—I can't read her mind—she thought she was doing the right thing," Jonathan Martin said.

Looking back, Martin said on the call that he understands why his parents would have been overprotective of him.

"She wasn't intentionally trying to hurt me," he said.

He said most people, especially those who didn't play the game, might think what happened to him *was* bullying. But men who sweat and grunt and bang heads for a living often act a certain way when they are around each other. "She's never played football," he said. "She doesn't know what it's like to communicate when you're playing football."

He did need to step away, he said. The environment and pressures took a toll on him. "There's certain things I want to acknowledge—one, I was not well," he said. "I needed some sort of break from football."

Martin said he doesn't view not standing up to Incognito and other players as cowardly: "I was young, and I didn't know how to handle it." The regret now, he said, is how the investigation proceeded and how he responded to the story going public and the resulting fallout. As a result of that, Martin said he no longer could call himself a good teammate at the time.

"I should have stood up to it more," he said. "I should have been like, 'Look, this is wrong.'"

Before hanging up, Martin seemed to replay the moment in his head. He could have told team management his version of the story, he said. He could have put out a statement and made clear to the public what was going on and how he felt about it. He could have countered what his mother had told the reporter.

"It didn't need to be this tit-for-tat on TMZ, right?" he said. "I should have sat down with the owner and head coach of the Dolphins and figured it out."

JOE PHILBIN REMAINED Dolphins head coach until October 2015, nearly two years after Martin last played for him. He was fired after a loss to the New York Jets dropped his team to 1–3.

Philbin has spent four decades in college football and the NFL, most recently as an assistant coach with the Las Vegas Raiders in 2024. Other than four games as interim head coach of the Green Bay Packers in 2018, his only stint in charge came in Miami.

He speaks of Martin and 2013 in broad terms. *Martin worked hard as a member of the Dolphins. He contributed to the success of the team. He is an intelligent guy.*

Whatever conversations he had with Martin during the incident, he won't speak to. "I consider those kind of sacred in the coaching profession with a player," he says. "So I'm going to kind of leave it at that."

Whatever went on in the Miami locker room, he won't revisit. "When you're a coach, you have an obligation to each and every player that you coach, regardless of what level you're at," Philbin says. "And you want all your players to have a great experience playing football. Things happened, some things, but I don't have any feelings about all that stuff.

"That's way in the past."

"Do you want to hear the Richie Incognito voicemail?" Gus Martin asks.

He sits at his office desk at Dominguez in Carson, California. Early afternoon light comes through a window behind him. It's January 2024, and the semester has just begun.

He is a professor in criminal justice administration, and his class on mass shootings and the psychology behind them has just ended.

He keeps the recording in his phone. He places it on the desk and hits play.

It's Incognito's voice, April 6, 2013.

"Hey, wassup, you half-n----- piece of s---. I saw you on Twitter, you been training 10 weeks. I'll s--- in your f---ing mouth. I'm going to slap your f---ing mouth, I'm going to slap your real mother across the face [laughter]. F--- you, you're still a rookie. I'll kill you."

The voicemail ends. Gus picks up his phone, sits back and sighs. The room is quiet.

The next day, he says the relationship between him and Jane and Jonathan has improved. His son calls, and they talk. He believes Jonathan—on the fast track at Wharton, a burgeoning Bitcoiner and businessman—is in a good place.

So why hold on to the tape?

"Firstly, that this happened," he says. "If anyone questions it, if anyone says, 'Oh, it wasn't all that.' It happened. And so I think that's why. In case I have to, oh gosh, remember it myself, which of course I will remember. But in case someone just simply says, 'No, that was all made up.' It wasn't made up at all."

As a lawyer, Gus refers to the tape as evidence. Something time can't erase.

"People sort of remember the past the way they want to," he says. "It's filtered. I always tell my students, 'We're going to look at things as they are, not the way we want them to be.'"

AFTER A PLATE of branzino and Brussels sprouts, Jonathan Martin sinks into a leather couch in a library behind the dining area at a Philadelphia bistro. He's upbeat. He fidgets with pieces on an oversized marble tic-tac-toe board on a table in front of him and describes a crypto hedge fund he and two classmates founded. "It's something that doesn't exist. It's a new product," he says. "It's a new strategy."

Martin is the CEO of the fund but also in charge of investor relations. He meets people, shakes hands, builds rapport. He also works the phones.

"We are all constantly growing and evolving," he says. "I'm not the same person I was 10 years ago. I'm not the same person I was two years ago. So my goal is to always self-improve and then grow."

He wears a T-shirt from his El Salvador Bitcoin trip. He stops shuffling the game pieces and lifts his head.

"There are some similar personalities between the NFL and people in finance and people going to business school," he says. "There's a little bit of you have to really believe in yourself a lot to play on *Monday Night Football* and block someone that's paid $25 million a year to get sacks against the quarterback.

"You've got to really have a lot of confidence in yourself. It's similar when you work in finance with huge dollar amounts, gargantuan dollar amounts. You have to have a lot of confidence in yourself and your abilities. And the way that you build confidence is through practice."

He might make 50 calls in a given day, laying out his belief in the idea. "My real talent is relationships," he says.

Across the room, people come and go.

"The thought of losing is what gets my juices going," he says. "It's not even so much winning. I just don't want to be a loser. I hate losers. I hate losing."

He sounds like an offensive tackle. He speaks deliberately.

"There's some sharp personalities in finance," he says, "and I'll just be like, 'I went to better schools than you. I'm smarter than you. You will respect me. You don't have to like me. You will respect me. When you address me, you will call me Jonathan Martin: Stanford, Georgetown, Wharton graduate.'"

Now he sounds like an Ivy League grad. He talks of using a "multi-sig" cryptocurrency wallet to enhance his security. He inhales books about the debt cycle. He takes notes that outgrow the margins of the pages and spill onto dozens of pieces of paper. This feels like studying tax code, but he does it for fun—and because he is reaching for something else.

"I want to be a master. I want to be the Tyrannosaurus rex. I want to be the lion. I want to be the great white shark," Martin says later. "No peers. Nothing can threaten me, so I put in the work. And that's the goal in torturing myself with homework in my 30s, is to be the apex predator."

MARTIN HASN'T TALKED with Richie Incognito or any of the others linked to the incidents in Miami in the years since.

"But I don't have any hard feelings towards anybody from that situation anymore," he says, "because Richie Incognito and Mike Pouncey already peaked. They've already achieved the most success they're going to achieve in their life. And I'm just getting started."

He pauses.

"John Jerry, too."

Would he consider a conversation with them now?

"No," he says after a long pause.

Why not?

Martin doesn't answer.

How would he handle confrontation differently now?

"I respect everyone. I give everyone a chance," he says. "I'll be nice to you, smile on my face. If you disrespect me, I'll rip your f---ing head off."

By text he reaches out later to clarify his answer: "'Rip your head off' was a metaphor, speaking to competitive fire," he says. "It is not a threat. I am not threatening towards anyone. I follow the rules & I'm polite + respectful."

Reached by phone at home in Arizona, Incognito said he "respectfully declined to comment" for this story. Messages left for Pouncey and Jerry were not returned.

In December, Martin texts to say he went home for Thanksgiving. He spent four days with his parents.

"I do forgive my mother now," he says.

He speaks to a break between what happened then and where he might go now. "Time. And the realization that I'm right where I need to be," he says.

"Dating an amazing girl, and 4 months from finishing my 3rd degree, which football all paid for," he says. "I don't wish I would've played longer even for a second, just wish the ending would have been different."

He texts again three days later: "I also got an interview with my ideal company. So again life has improved recently. Much more optimistic on a job. I'm in a different place than a year ago."

He wants his story to be told fairly, he says. Doesn't want to in any way harm his job prospects. He wants to close a chapter, he says. But he wants to talk again, to make clear *how* things have changed for him since he first agreed to tell his story, to present himself as he is today.

By Zoom in January, from his Philadelphia apartment, Martin says he's looking forward to his graduation from Wharton in May. New stories need blank pages.

He speaks about the crypto hedge fund. *Yes*, he left it in April. *Yes*, he might return to it eventually. "Split amicably," he says.

He talks about Philbin: "I do regret not talking to him man-to-man, eye-to-eye, and explaining the situation, because he would have understood."

He says he didn't know his father still had the Incognito voicemail.

"We know who Incognito is, right?" Martin says. "I have more colorful language I could use, but I'm not going to."

And he talks about his mother, too.

"I can appreciate that my mother loves me and she wanted to protect me," Martin says. "And I am thankful to have both my parents still in my life in my 30s. Not everyone has that. I'm thankful for the time I still have with them. And..."

And then he pauses.

Looking into the future means moving on from the past. Or trying to. Or wishing you can.

"It's a way to move forward," he says one more time.

ESPN researcher John Mastroberardino contributed to this report.

ANTHONY OLIVIERI is a staff writer at ESPN, which he joined as a magazine researcher in 2012. He graduated from Marist University with a degree in communication, concentrating in journalism, in 2005. He lives in Connecticut with his wife, Sylvia, and children, Natalie and Giovanni.

The NBA Integrated 75 Years Ago with the Debuts of Three Black Players

SHAKEIA TAYLOR AND JAMES JACKSON

FROM The Athletic • OCTOBER 31, 2025

Kevin Lloyd leaned forward, his tone marking the seriousness of his point.

"If you [were to] go to my father's house," Lloyd said. "You'd never know he played basketball unless he told you."

Such is the fate of the NBA's pioneers. The NBA debuts 75 years ago of Earl Lloyd, Chuck Cooper and Nat "Sweetwater" Clifton, the league's first Black players didn't garner headlines.

Technically, Wataru "Wat" Misaka, a 5-foot-7 point guard of Japanese descent, broke the NBA's color barrier in November 1947 as a member of the New York Knicks in the Basketball Association of America (BAA). Seven months before Misaka's debut, Jackie Robinson took the field with the Brooklyn Dodgers for the first time.

In 1950, the NBA was still a niche league, and college basketball was more popular. Baseball was still America's pastime. Robinson's presence, coupled with his 1949 MVP award, was bigger news.

Today, Lloyd, Cooper and Clifton are relatively unknown to both the modern fan and the modern player. This season, the

NBA and the National Basketball Players Association (NBPA) will try to change that. They'll be celebrating the 75th anniversary of the NBA's first Black players throughout the 2025–26 season with the first Pioneers Classic game, which will become an annual event, and awarding an NBA Pioneers trophy to highlight the trio's impact.

The journeys of the three men who integrated the NBA may have been overshadowed by the weight of history shifting all at once, but the stories of Lloyd, Cooper and Clifton have been woven into the fabric of the game.

PHILADELPHIA 76ERS ROOKIE guard V.J. Edgecombe had no idea.

At this year's NBA Draft in New York, Edgecombe and other draftees had an opportunity to meet the families of Lloyd, Cooper and Clifton and learn about the early days of three Hall of Famers who helped integrate the NBA, now a multi-billion dollar global enterprise.

"I wasn't familiar with the players' stories prior to meeting their families," Edgecombe said. "Just getting to meet them helped open my mind about the history of the game."

Born and raised in Bimini, in the Bahamas, Edgecombe migrated to America as a 9-year-old before rising up the high-school prospect ranks ahead of his lone collegiate season at Baylor.

"I learned about the first African Americans to play in the NBA and their pain and just the different experiences of life and what they had to go through for future generations, and I'm reaping what they sow," Edgecombe said. "It's just a blessing, though, to be in this position. It helped me cherish the game more and helped my passion grow for the game."

Carter Bryant, selected by the San Antonio Spurs with the 14th overall pick, also wasn't aware of the pioneers' stories before meeting the families, but he said the opportunity made him even more grateful to have joined the NBA's brotherhood.

"It was a dope experience, understanding the heritage and what we've come from before us, the people that laid the path for me to be able to be a professional in the sport I love and always dreamed of," Bryant said. "Because obviously growing up, you don't necessarily see who was the pioneer of it all. You didn't see the first people to break through that barrier. You see the people that reap the benefits, in terms of Michael Jordan, LeBron James, all the guys that we watch play nowadays."

For both Edgecombe and Bryant, the stories of Lloyd, Cooper and Clifton inspired them and reminded them just how far the game they love has come.

On Oct. 31, 1950, when Earl "Big Cat" Lloyd stepped onto the court at Edgerton Park Arena in Rochester, N.Y. as a member of the Washington Capitols, he quietly made basketball history as the first Black player to play in an NBA game.

Lloyd had been a basketball star at West Virginia State College, known now as West Virginia State University. Listed as a guard in his pro debut, he recorded six points, 10 rebounds and five assists in a 78–70 loss to the Rochester Royals. Although his stat line wasn't jaw dropping, Lloyd had changed the NBA forever.

Selected in the NBA Draft's ninth round earlier that year, the lanky 6-5 forward was a two-time All-America selection and conference champion. In the 1947–48 season, Lloyd and the Yellow Jackets went unbeaten throughout the Colored Intercollegiate Athletic Association, now the Central Intercollegiate Athletic Association (CIAA), in regular and postseason play.

"One of my father's biggest accomplishments was [being from] where he came from," Kevin Lloyd said. "He went from dirt poor in Alexandria, Va., into the Hall of Fame. And his main thing was, in order to get to the Hall of Fame, he had a lot of handprints on him that helped him along the way.

"My father never wore fame on his sleeve. He had nothing around the house. He had a closet where he kept everything, even his Hall of Fame trophy. That's how modest he was."

One day after Lloyd's debut, Chuck Cooper, former Duquesne star and the first Black player to be drafted (second round, third pick), made his debut with the Boston Celtics in Fort Wayne, Ind., alongside future Hall of Famers Bob Cousy, "Easy" Ed Macauley and head coach Red Auerbach. Cooper contributed seven points in the season opener.

"He was a barrier breaker," Chuck Cooper III said about his dad. "Beginning at Duquesne University, team captain at a predominantly White college and becoming the second consensus All-American in college basketball history. He played in the college All-American game as co-captain, along with his eventual good friend and teammate, Bob Cousy."

Four days after Lloyd, Nat "Sweetwater" Clifton, a 6-8 center, scored 16 points with 12 rebounds as a member of the New York Knicks against the Tri-Cities Blackhawks. Clifton had played at Xavier University of Louisiana for two years before serving in the United States Army.

"They kicked in the door at the same time," Kevin Lloyd told The Athletic.

Sports across the country were integrating, but acceptance was not a given.

"When our fathers got into the NBA, the league wasn't ready for Black stars," Chuck Cooper III said. "They primarily were brought in to rebound and play defense and on some occasions protect the White stars.

"I think [my father] was more disappointed with not really having the opportunity to fully display his talent. And when you look at all three of the pioneers, my dad, Lloyd and Clifton, all three of them could have been absolute stars in the NBA if they were afforded that opportunity. You're talking about the 1950s before the Civil Rights Act, right? So it was still legal to discriminate.

"This was pre–Emmett Till America."

Because of racial barriers denying full participation, Black players and other non-White athletes were forced to form segregated leagues and barnstorming teams, often playing in environments that were less than desirable.

"[For] Black players, period...Well, there was nowhere else to go," said Louis "Sweet Lou" Dunbar, a former Harlem Globetrotters player and coach and current director of player personnel. "If you wanted to be a professional athlete, you wanted to play the game of basketball, the Harlem Globetrotters was your ticket.

"And where everybody started. I don't think Earl Lloyd ever came to the Globetrotters, but, you know, other than that, everybody else did. And, of course, they had the New York Rens back in the day as well. So, a lot of players played with the Rens, but this was the only avenue—the Harlem Globetrotters."

With teams like the Globetrotters, players were entertainers. There was an element of showmanship to their game. But in a newly integrated league, they often had to suppress their on-court flair.

"My father said that, when he played, they always told him to play down, don't try to be a star," Clifton's daughter Jataun Robinson said. "So he had to stop doing some of the tricks from his time with the Globetrotters.

"But every once in a while he would do some of those things just to get the crowd roaring. And he would like what they gave him. They made him feel wanted. He says he got in trouble, but then they always let it go, because of the crowd."

The growth of sports in post–World War II America mirrored the country's labored progress on racism. The process was often painful.

"[My dad] used to always say out of everything that he went through in his career, he forgave, but never forgets," Kevin Lloyd said of Earl. "Some cities he went through, like Fort Wayne, St Louis, he couldn't stay with the team at the hotel.

"In some cities he went to, he could stay with the team, but he couldn't eat with them. He had to sit in his room until game time. Our parents took a lot of heat for all of today's players."

AMERICAN PROFESSIONAL SPORTS' path to collective integration spanned eight decades, a slow crawl enabled by legalized public separation of people based on race.

Segregation was ingrained into baseball before the NBA (founded in 1946 as Basketball Association of America before the 1949–50 merger with National Basketball League), National Football League (1920) and National Hockey League (1917) were even created.

Although basketball has globalized since Dr. James Naismith invented it in 1891, the sport took its own roundabout route to inclusivity. This season, an NBA record-tying 135 international players represent 43 different countries and territories, but the game's globalization is traced with consistent contributions from Black pioneers across the early 20th century—trailblazers who, by their own hoops-centric spearheading, helped paved the way for Lloyd, Cooper and Clifton to do their parts.

"We're always looking for ways to continue to educate our players on the history of the game," Erika Swilley, executive director of the NBPA Foundation, told The Athletic.

"These guys, at 18-19 [years old], weren't born. They have a context. You know, if you were to ask them who the pioneers are of the game, a lot of them say, like, Bill Russell or, you know, Kareem Abdul-Jabbar, and I don't think they can even fathom that there was a time that the NBA [and basketball] wasn't integrated."

In 1902, an 18-year-old, 150-pound hooper named Harry "Bucky" Lew debuted for the Pawtucketville Athletic Club in Massachusetts, beginning what became a two-decade career, which started not long after the world's first pro hoops league was organized.

Scarce opportunities existed for Black hoopers of the early 20th century. Not only was segregation legal, but formative basketball was hardly organized because players—White, Black or otherwise—were rarely bound by contracts, so it was common for players to switch teams on a day-to-day basis and quit before games.

"I think sports has played a significant role, over time, in breaking down cultural barriers, breaking down race, because, on the court, the beautiful thing about sports is it is a meritocracy," NBA Deputy Commissioner Mark Tatum told The Athletic. "At the end of the day, I think what people realize in sports and in basketball specifically, is that if you could play, you deserved the spot on the team. And it didn't matter what color, what creed you were—if you could play the game of basketball, if you could play at that level, you should be on the team.

"And I think sports has played a significant role over and over in history, in helping to break those different barriers."

Lloyd, Cooper and Clifton very well might have had different fates if not for the NBA. Their reaching the game's highest level—whether direct or roundabout—followed the milestones of Lew, Cumberland Posey (the most dominant hooper of the early 20th century), Edwin B. Henderson (responsible for introducing basketball to Washington D.C.), Robert Douglas (created the New York Renaissance, the first-ever Black professional hoops team) and other pioneers who spent decades contributing to the early growth and mere possibility of integration in basketball's early days.

Lloyd's rookie season lasted only seven games because he was drafted by the U.S. Army to fight in the Korean War. Washington folded in early 1951, shortly before Lloyd started fulfilling his military duty. During his time fighting the Korean War, the Syracuse Nationals picked him up on waivers, beginning a six-year stay that included winning the 1955 NBA championship, when he was one of six Nationals players to average double figures in the postseason.

Once his career finished in 1960, after a two-season stint with the Detroit Pistons, Lloyd spent 10 years as a scout and assistant coach, becoming the Pistons' first Black coach during the 1971–72 season after Butch van Breda Kolff resigned. Unfortunately for Lloyd, the Pistons went only 20–52 the rest of the season, and he was fired seven games into the 1972–73 season. In his post-basketball life, he also spent more than a decade working for the Detroit Board of Education.

Despite Lloyd's array of accomplishments, he never stopped being the person his loved ones knew him as away from basketball.

"I never saw my father as being famous," the younger Lloyd said of his father, who passed away in 2015. "He was just Dad, who happened to coach the Pistons."

Their situations were the result of not only skill and temperament, but chance, and they lived modest, humble lives having felt lucky—grateful—to even have had the experience. Fame in their era looked much different than it does for a professional basketball player today.

"My father wasn't a braggadocious type of person, so he didn't really bring it up," Chuck Cooper III told The Athletic of his Hall of Fame father. "But if asked questions about it, he was willing to share his stories, accomplishments and experiences."

Although Cooper was the youngest of the pioneering trio, he lived a life of distinction before Auerbach brought him aboard Boston's early days preceding its Bill Russell-led dynasty.

As a rookie for the 1950–51 Celtics, Cooper was a key contributor to the first winning season in the franchise's storied history, as Boston went 39–30 and finished second in the Eastern Division during Auerbach's first season at the helm.

Over the first four seasons of Cooper's career, the Celtics' 166 wins trailed only the Minneapolis Lakers (178) and Rochester Royals (170) for the NBA lead from the 1950–51 to the 1953–54 season, during which Cooper was one of Boston's most consistent contributors. During that time, his 1,850 points ranked fourth among Celtics as he trailed only Macauley (2,345) for team lead in rebounds (1,807).

By May 28, 1954, the Celtics sold Cooper's rights to the Milwaukee Hawks, who, after the 1954–55 season, moved to St. Louis. By January 1956, Cooper was a free agent, so he signed with the Fort Wayne Pistons for a 32-game stint to finish the 1955–56 campaign before retiring at the age of 29.

Once his career ended, Cooper enrolled at the University of Minnesota and graduated with a master's degree in social work in 1960. Upon returning to his hometown of Pittsburgh, he served on the city's school board and was its first Black director of parks and recreation. For Cooper—who, during his Duquesne days, became the first Black college player to play below the Mason-Dixon Line—his life and basketball accomplishments were as varied as he was well-traveled. Duquesne's home arena, UPMC Cooper Fieldhouse, is named in his honor.

By the time Clifton stepped into the Association, he was already 27 years old and able to contribute to a title-hungry New York Knicks team for the next seven years.

Few athletes journeyed a path like Clifton, who fought in World War II while serving with the U.S. Army for three years. He joined the Rens upon returning from the war and eventually played for the Globetrotters before playing first base for the Chicago American Giants of Negro Leagues.

By 1950, his Globetrotters contract was purchased by the Knicks, leading to him becoming the second Black player to sign an NBA deal. Harold Hunter holds this distinction after inking a contract with the Washington Capitols on April 26 of that same year. Hunter was cut during training camp and never played for an NBA team.

During the first season of that stint, Clifton was second on the Knicks in rebounds per game (7.6, trailing only fellow future Hall of Famer Harry Gallatin) while ranking fourth on the team in assists (162) and rounding out its top five in points (562).

By Clifton's second NBA season, he and Gallatin became the first Knicks in franchise history to average a double-double. The 1951–52 Knicks went 37–29 and finished third in the Eastern Division before suffering the second of three consecutive NBA Finals losses.

But despite coming up short in the title round, Clifton left what remains an undeniable on-court impact for the Knicks and the NBA, becoming the league's oldest first-time All-Star during the 1956–57 season at 34 years old. New York had the NBA's fourth-highest win percentage during Clifton's seven-season tenure (.557), which included those three finals runs, winning campaigns in each of the first six seasons and two first-place division finishes.

On April 3, 1957, less than a month after his final game with New York, the Knicks traded him, Gallatin and Dick Atha to the Fort Wayne Pistons for Mel Hutchins. Clifton spent one season with the Pistons before retiring from the NBA. He dabbled in basketball and baseball afterward, but he made his retirement permanent at the age of 40 after the American Basketball League folded in 1962. He worked as a cab driver in Chicago, suffering a fatal heart attack on Aug. 31, 1990 at the age of 67.

A man who lived many lives, Clifton made an impact that, combined with Lloyd and Cooper, has been protected by each of their children doing all they can to carry their fathers' collective legacies forward.

To carry any of these legacies forward, it helps to have companionship and support from the league their fathers pioneered.

In February 2018, Kevin, Chuck III and Jataun met for the first time when the Cleveland Cavaliers honored "the First Three" Black players in the NBA along with former Cavs general manager Wayne Embry. Embry, who spent 13 seasons with the Cavs, was the first Black GM and team president in league history when he was named Milwaukee Bucks GM in 1972.

They've since become inseparable through their fathers' shared experience and decided to work together to elevate their fathers' legacy.

"We three are connected at the hip just like our parents were," Kevin Lloyd said.

"I want [people] to understand the struggle," Jataun Robinson said. "It's much easier now, but it was very hard for the first three."

The resilience of these pioneers while dealing with the difficulties of segregation made them cornerstones of the league and helped shape the modern NBA.

Their fathers may not have talked much about their experiences and historic accomplishments, but the game they gave so much to hopes to ensure the names of Lloyd, Cooper and Clifton are more than a passing mention in a game story.

"All of our parents gave Jackie Robinson a tremendous amount of credit," Cooper III said. "But the one thing about Jackie Robinson [is] once they stopped throwing at the great Jackie Robinson, they had to pitch to him. And baseball has enough individual elements to the game that you get a chance to really show your full array of talent."

"So unfortunately, our fathers didn't do that, because in the game of basketball, you need somebody to feed you the rock. If you didn't get the ball, you're not scoring. It was a sacrifice. They sacrificed a lot. They were great ballplayers. They were great men. They were great family men. And as we move forward, the fact that the world is going to finally get an opportunity to understand what they contributed to this great game, we just couldn't be more grateful."

SHAKEIA TAYLOR is an award-winning writer and storyteller whose work focuses on the intersection of history, culture, and sports. She was previously a sports writer and columnist at the *Chicago Tribune*. Taylor is a staff writer at The Athletic where she has covered the NBA since 2024. **JAMES JACKSON** has covered the NBA since 2013 after graduating from Florida A&M University with a bachelor's in political science. He has worked for The Athletic since 2022. There, he's covered cultural basketball stories about the New York Renaissance, Harlem Globetrotters, the *Hoop Dreams* documentary, and more.

The Unforgotten

TOM JUNOD

FROM ESPN • AUGUST 20, 2025

THEY WERE BOTH SO YOUNG.

One would be entering his old age now, with most of a long life behind him. The other would just be entering his senior year in high school, working to fulfill a life of great promise.

A vast gulf of time separates them.

But nobody knows them now except by memory, so time is also what ties them together.

And it is time that tells their story.

They were both so young, are both so young still.

ONE IS JAY Kutner. He is a quarterback. He plays for Holy Trinity Diocesan High School in Hicksville, New York. He is a senior, 17 years old. He wears No. 5. One afternoon, his team, the Titans, is playing a preseason scrimmage against Amityville Memorial, a public school. It is the second week of September, and the day is hot and dry and dusty, and Jay is walking off the field for a drink of water. He is done, like most of the starters. His backup is already stepping behind center. But he hears the whistle blow. The coach is dissatisfied—execution or effort, it hardly matters now. He tells Jay to go back in for one last play. It has been a rough scrimmage, but Jay is wearing a red outer jersey for his protection. He is not supposed to be hit. He barks the signals, the ball is snapped. The play later will be described as "nondescript" or "routine." But mistakes are never routine. There is a problem with the snap. The ball comes loose. The ball is on the ground, and Jay dives for it. So does everyone else. The play is not particularly violent, just crowded. There is a pile, and at the bottom of it, a small voice—"my neck." The whistle blows, and the players peel themselves off of or are pulled from the scrum. They stand up, then they look down. The player at the bottom remains on the ground. The player at the bottom is Jay Kutner, and he does not get up.

The other is Caden Tellier. He is a quarterback. He plays for Morgan Academy, in Selma, Alabama. He is a junior, 16 years old. It is a hot Friday night in August, and he is playing under the lights, first game of the season. Morgan versus Southern. He wears No. 17, in emulation of his hero, Josh Allen of the Buffalo Bills. Most of the people who watched him grow up—the people who know and love him most—have come to the small stadium in the back of the school to watch him play football. His father is here. His mother is here. His sister is here, his girlfriend, his pastor, his coaches, his teachers, his friends. Caden is at home on his home field, with his old Ford truck in the parking lot. He sat out a few games as a sophomore after a shoulder injury. He is healthy now, a rangy kid who is as proud of his legs as he is of his arm. He likes to run. On Morgan's first drive of the second half, he rolls right, toward his own sideline—toward his team, toward his family, toward the home crowd. He sees an opening along the white stripe and is turning upfield when a diving tackler grabs him low and trips him up. *It's a clean tackle* everybody will say. But Caden stretches and sprawls forward, still gathering momentum as he falls. He lands hard, his helmet hitting the turf with a snap. He gets right up, he heads right back to the huddle. But then he takes himself out. He goes to the sideline and takes a knee. He says, "I don't feel good," and slumps over.

It's the last thing Caden Tellier ever says.

You can't miss him. He's good at everything he does—hell, Jay's good at *smiling*. On the pitcher's mound, he throws so hard he wears out the hands of his catchers. On the football field, he stands tall in the pocket and throws a ball his receivers have to either catch or duck. He's 6-foot-2, 185 pounds and still growing, and though his school, Holy Trinity, sits in the middle of Long Island, he has drawn attention from major college scouts as far away as North Carolina, as well as comparisons to Roman Gabriel, the marble statue who quarterbacks the Philadelphia Eagles.

But it's in the halls of Holy Trinity where you see his promise most clearly—where young Jay, with his blue eyes and easygoing and yet purposeful gait, looks like a particularly self-possessed politician, somehow already a handshake away from higher office. It's not just that everyone wants to talk to him; it's that he can talk to everyone, even the grinds in his Latin class. Yes, when the bell rings, he seems to float above the fray, surveying the scurrying underclassmen as if from a great height. But he also sees things—particularly the kids having a hard time. When the yearbook photographer comes to school to shoot senior portraits, Jay pokes his head in the classroom and sees that his friend Tommy Young doesn't have a sport jacket. He gives him his own, an unmistakably loud plaid, along with an assurance that when the yearbooks come out at the end of senior year, there they will be for all of posterity, secret twins stuck in the same jacket. And when he sees one of the biggest and most imposing of his jock buddies roughing up the editor of the school paper after a rowdy basketball game—Brian Clancy has written an editorial condemning the cherished Holy Trinity ritual of under-the-bleachers basketball-game boozing—Jay strides over and taps him on the shoulder. "I don't think this is a good idea," he says. "I know Brian, and Brian's a good guy." His teammate nods, and leaves Brian alone.

Heroism comes naturally to him, but not easily. He's from an enormous Catholic family, one of 11 children, and his father is the unquestioned hero in the house—the war hero. It is a time in American history when many middle-aged men in many suburban neighborhoods fought in World War II. But Harry Kutner flew a B-29 on bombing missions over the Pacific. He is a lawyer who's just about to be appointed judge at the Nassau County Family Court, and to his children he's a judge already, with an inflexible standard of right and wrong and a prickly distaste for the "gray area." Some fight him, some live in fear of him, but Jay—well, one day a kid from the neighborhood shows up at the front door to object to something Jay has done. They all live near a big public park and the kid, Jim Savage, was playing baseball with his friends when Jay came along with his friends and kicked them off the field. Harry Kutner answers the door, with his tall middle son appearing behind him. When Savage finishes his story, the judge turns to Jay and asks, "Did you do this?"

"Yes, Dad," Jay answers.

Without hesitation, Harry slaps his son across the face, hard. Jim Savage is horrified, but what he will remember most vividly, what he will remember forever, is Jay's response. The boy doesn't cry. He doesn't even flinch. He just…takes it, as if endurance has already become his calling and his fate.

THE FATHER AND son, Jamie and Caden Tellier, are also coach and player. They are with each other all the time because Caden wants to be coached all the time—he's *that* kid. A pitcher, he keeps a baseball in his hand no matter where he goes, working on different grips for different pitches even when he's hanging out and watching television. A dual-threat quarterback, he takes pride in studying for games as rigorously as he studies for school, where he can't abide anything less than an A. He likes baseball better than he likes football, but if baseball is his sport, he knows football is his *chance*—his chance to keep playing in college. His chance to leave his mark. Caden has always been a boy with dreams, and Jamie has always been a man dedicated to their realization. He played quarterback himself once; he taught Caden how to play the game in their backyard in Selma, and when Caden became a 15-year-old sophomore starter at the Morgan Academy, Jamie joined the coaching staff as a volunteer. He doesn't have to push Caden because Caden pushes himself. But Caden's dreams keep growing bigger and bigger, and now he has one that he shares not just with his father but also with his closest friends: He wants to see his jersey retired. In the gym at the Morgan Academy, the jersey of Gunnar Henderson, Class of 2019 and now a shortstop for the Baltimore Orioles, hangs from the wall. Caden wants his garnet-and-gold No. 17 to hang right next to it.

But it is not his only goal. He has worked so hard to prepare for Morgan's first game of the 2024 season that he wonders if his worldly ambition is getting in the way of his spiritual one. He has been a professing Christian since he was 4 years old, but he has been spending so much time practicing and studying for football that he has been missing the Wednesday night youth group. His youth pastor, Roxanne Jones, is also his godmother, and he has been telling her that his heart is with her but his head is with football, so she's surprised when he calls one Wednesday night and says he's coming—"Should I bring a pizza?" He arrives late, pizza in hand, and explains to the group that he doesn't know why, but he had to come. Then he becomes impassioned. He's a determinedly soft-spoken kid, but he speaks with such conviction that he causes his pastor to abandon her planned lesson. He might want to see his jersey retired, but what he really wants to see is a spiritual revival of his team. Then he stops himself. "No," he says, "I want to see a revival at *school*..."

Two nights later, he leads his team onto the field for a game against Greensboro, Alabama's Southern Academy, with his father up in the booth calling plays.

THERE SHOULD BE no problem with the snap. The quarterback and the center, Jay Kutner and Richie Callahan, are best of friends, one of them tall and the other so squat he's called "Stumpy." They've practiced the exchange all summer, in preparation for their senior season. Jay has taken hundreds of snaps, until receiving the ball from Stumpy has become second nature to him, just like their friendship. But when preseason begins and the team goes to camp at a nearby seminary, there is a complication. Holy Trinity's head coach, Fred Bruno, has hired a new offensive assistant, an odd, persnickety man with a crewcut and a deep ideological commitment to the University of Delaware's wing-T offense. Crewcut sweats the smallest details, even the snap from center. His center and his quarterback exchange the ball as they have since they started playing football, Richie turning the ball on the upswing so Jay can grab it across the laces. Crewcut tells them they're doing it wrong. He insists on Jay grabbing the ball by the point, a doctrinal choice that's supposed to help the running game but succeeds only in turning what has been routine into a roll of the dice. The quarterback and the center start fumbling. At first, they are just making mistakes; then they do it on purpose, two friends engaged in a secret rebellion. Finally, the coach surrenders and allows them to go back to what was automatic. They don't have to think about the snap again until the day of the scrimmage with the Tide of Amityville High School.

It's Tuesday, the 11th day of September, and it's getting late in the day, a little past 5 o'clock. The scrimmage has been sloppy and short-tempered, the two teams eager for the season to start and the games to count. Coach Bruno blows the whistle, and Richie Callahan heads to the sideline for water. He's done. Most of the starters are done, tired and thirsty and taking off their helmets. Richie figures Jay is done too, but when he turns around he sees Jay still on the field. The coaches are yelling and Jay has gone back under center. Richie wants to put his helmet back on and return to the fray—to his quarterback and his friend. It is a strong feeling, one he remembers. But the Titans need a backup center, and the coaches are auditioning a guard named Mark Pospisil. He snaps the ball exactly as the dogmatic coach has instructed, point up instead of the laces. Tommy Young is playing tight end, and he will remember waiting for Jay to throw him the ball. Kevin Kavanaugh is playing running back and he will remember waiting for Jay to hand it off. Richie Callahan is watching from the sideline, and he will remember exactly that—watching as Jay begins to pivot without the ball in his hands, and wishing he could somehow still go in.

The scrimmage is being played on the grass field where the Holy Trinity Titans play their games on Saturdays. It is a few hundred yards from their locker room, but now it seems a mile. There is nobody in the stands. There is no doctor on hand, and no emergency personnel. There are no cellphones. There is something called 911, but it has just been instituted in Nassau County, and people are still much more accustomed to calling the operator or the fire department in an emergency. They—all of them, the coaches and the players—are suddenly all alone, with no help available and Jay Kutner flat on the field and unable to move. They hear his voice, the fear in it. They have no idea what to do, and they make mistakes. Kavanaugh remains where he stood in the backfield, and he sees Coach Bruno grabbing his quarterback by the belt, as if the wind has been knocked out of him and he's trying to force air back into his lungs. The Amityville players wonder why Jay's helmet is off when he's not moving and he's complaining about his neck. The coaches clear the field, and the teams move away from the fallen player like two armies too exhausted to keep fighting. The Amityville Tide climb back into their yellow school buses and head home. The Holy Trinity Titans, both varsity and JV, gather on the threadbare grass in front of the locker room and stare into the distance at the small knot of desperate men bent over their friend on the playing field. It turns into kind of a vigil if only because they have to wait. Time passes, the sun sinks in the hazy sky. The ambulance finally arrives and drives onto the field, its red light quietly whirling. The father of one of Trinity players is a New York City cop; he watched the scrimmage from the sideline and now he joins Jay in the back of the ambulance. He sees Jay struggling to breathe and he doesn't want him to ride alone, this teenaged boy with a broken neck.

What happens to Caden on Aug. 23 happens right in front of them all. They are so close, in the intimacy of the small stadium they call home; they are so far away, in their inability to change what they see and hear. Caden's father, Jamie, is sitting in the little booth perched at the top of the stands, sending in plays; Caden's mother, Arsella, is a few rows down, sitting where she always sits, next to Pastor Roxanne Jones. When Caden takes himself out of the game, she's immediately worried. "ACL," Roxanne says to her. But when her only son slumps over on the green grass, she turns around and motions her husband to go down to the field. Her gesture—her uncharacteristically urgent gesture—is what lets him know that Caden is in trouble. He rushes down the narrow rickety steps from the booth and then jumps onto the track and then to the sideline. But Arsella reaches Caden first. So does a doctor who was watching from the stands. The game between the Morgan Academy and the Southern Academy somehow continues, somehow persists, until the play-by-play announcer for Morgan sounds an alarm over the booming stadium loudspeakers: "Refs, stop the game—we have a medical emergency!"

The stadium falls into rapt silence interwoven with murmured prayers, and everybody who loves Caden watches as the doctor removes his shoes and prods the soles of his feet with scissors. When an ambulance takes him to the hospital in Selma, the game resumes with a sophomore named Patrick Johnson at quarterback. He doesn't throw the ball very much but Morgan Academy plays inspiring football, the game won on the ground by a team that doesn't know yet that Caden has been flown to Birmingham in a helicopter. His family follows in their car; his teammates return to their homes, and most of them are asleep when, in the early-morning hours, phones begin ringing and their parents begin taking the calls. Amanda Denmark gets a call. Her son, Caine McLaughlin, is a lineman at Morgan and one of Caden's closest friends. She walks into his room and finds him fast asleep, as only a high school boy can be. She wonders if she should wake him but decides not to. Sleep is what he needs and what he's going to need. He's going to have the rest of his life to take in the news that his quarterback is brain-dead.

His name is Tim Timlin. He's a quarterback. He's a junior and he has talent. He was the one waiting to step in during the scrimmage when the coach called Jay back for one more play. He figures that now he'll need to replace Jay as the starter. But there's another scrimmage, this one on the Saturday after Jay broke his neck. It's between the Titans, and it's being played to determine who will lead the team. Timlin has the worst game of his life. He throws three interceptions and the coaches turn to a senior who's one of Jay's closest friends. His name is Bobby DeLorenzo. He's not a quarterback, at least in the way Jay was, and he didn't expect to play quarterback when Jay was starting. He's so nearsighted he has to wear his owlish eyeglasses even when he's on the field. He doesn't have the big arm and, at a shade under 5-10, he doesn't have the stature. He's just a utility player who can do a little of everything and fill in wherever he's needed—"a Swiss Army knife kind of guy," Timlin calls him. But he's perfect for the wing-T, and something happens when he steps in. His teammates respond to him. They would do anything for him. He replaces Jay even as he knows that Jay can't be replaced. And they win.

They win because they find purpose and they find purpose because they win, and after each game they visit Jay in Nassau Hospital. It is not easy for them. It is not easy for him. He broke the two vertebrae, the C-3 and the C-4, high up in his neck. His spine was not severed but his spinal cord swelled, and the swelling did irreversible damage. A tracheotomy saved him when the ambulance brought him in, a ventilator keeps him breathing now. He can barely speak and sometimes he answers questions by blinking his eyes. But those eyes, they're still blue, and that smile, it's still full of mischief. Back when he had a summer job as a crossing guard, his friends used to come by to see him in his uniform, and he would do silly dances for them out in the middle of the crosswalk. Now he tries to crack jokes with his tracheotomy. He does it for them, for his boys, and they in turn do something for him when they play Chaminade 25 days after his injury.

Holy Trinity has been in existence for less than 10 years, and it has never beaten Chaminade, the prestigious all-boys school located in the same Long Island town where Jay is hospitalized. They're behind at halftime, and a priest who has just visited Jay in the hospital comes to the locker room with a message from him: "Win." One of the captains on the team, Gregg Garner, stands up and says, "You hear that? Jay isn't going through all that he's going through just so we can lose to Chaminade!" He begins banging the steel lockers with his helmet and then everybody else does the same and they emerge from the racket and the uproar to defeat their despised rival in the second half. Later that night, they present Jay with the game ball in his hospital room, telling him that they couldn't have done it without him and watching the tears shining in his blue blinking eyes.

Then they leave. For all anyone knows, the victory over Chaminade might hurt Jay as much as it helps him. He might not want a football, given what football has done to him, and when his teammates go home and he's alone again in the hospital, his tears of sparkling joy might turn to tears of hopelessness and sorrow. But maybe he understands that he has done more for them than they can ever do for him, and that's where he finds his comfort. Maybe he told them to win not for himself but for *them*, because he knew they needed to hear it. They are young, 16 and 17 years old, and their lives are in front of them. Most of his life is already behind him, but he changes them, in ways they won't fully grasp for years. A football game sounds like such a paltry thing in comparison to the suffering he has to endure. But what else did they have to offer? He asked them for it, and they gave it to him, and nothing else is ever the same for them, especially Bobby DeLorenzo.

He is the quarterback of his high school football team, glasses and all. He is the first Holy Trinity quarterback to beat

Chaminade, and he leads the Titans to a second-place finish in the Catholic high school league. He winds up dating the girl he will never cease calling the prettiest in the school and then winds up marrying her. He tells himself, always, that he did the impossible after his friend Jay was paralyzed, and so there's no challenge he shies from. It is not until much later that he sees clearly that he had the life Jay should have had. He sees that Jay *gave* him his life, just the sheer opportunity of it. And with both pride and a sadness that still sneaks up on him, he realizes that if you want to know how Jay Kutner might have lived, you might want to look at how Bobby DeLorenzo is still living.

WHEN CADEN WAS 4 years old, Jamie Tellier's father died of cancer. Caden was very close with his grandfather, and his parents worried about how he would respond to the loss. They woke him in the morning after "Pops" died overnight, and when they told him the news they were shocked that he didn't cry, that he appeared unfazed. "Pops has gone to heaven," Jamie said. "Oh, I know," Caden said. "He stopped on his way and told me."

Now 12 years have passed, and it is Caden who is gone. His brain has died, and the body that has been left behind is being sustained by machines in his Birmingham hospital room. His mother and father know what they must do next, because he has told them. He just turned 16 in May, and so he also just got his driver's license. He talked to his parents about his decision when he was checking the required boxes. He was very clear about what he wanted and what God was asking of him. In the event of his death, he wanted to be an organ donor, based on his conviction that somewhere out in the world was a person he was meant to help. Jamie and Arsella were struck by his confidence, by his certainty about an eventuality they could barely bring themselves to contemplate. Now they remember what he had told them as a little boy. He had always behaved as if he were just passing through, with one foot already in heaven. It was what gave him his confidence at 16. It was also what gave him his unearthly confidence at age 4, and it is what gives his parents confidence that Caden is already with Pops in heaven, with just his body in the hospital room.

His mother calls it his "earth suit." And on Sunday, Aug. 25, she and her husband and daughter have to find the strength to let go of it. They have to abide by the wishes printed on Caden's license. They have to allow the doctors to prepare his body for organ removal rather than survival. And they have to say goodbye to their beautiful boy. They are not alone in this. People begin arriving from Selma early in the morning and keep arriving all day. It is a pilgrimage, and as much as they might believe he is already gone, they want to see him, they want to touch him, they want to pray over him, they want to tell him they love him. But the room is closed to all but Jamie and Arsella, the family and Caden's girlfriend and closest friends. So when the doctors come, the nurses come, and when at last Caden is being rolled on a gurney out the door of his room, there are hundreds of people waiting for him. They line one hallway of the hospital, two hallways, three hallways, and Caden rolls past all of them. They are silent, they are softly applauding, they are praying, they are sobbing, they are waving goodbye, until at last another set of doors opens and closes, and he is gone—gone to do good, for good.

Back in the summer , before the onset of football practice, Jay went with some of his friends to visit a classmate in the hospital. She was, in many ways, his counterpart—an accomplished gymnast, a captain of the cheerleaders, a leader of her class. She had suffered a spinal injury during a gymnastics camp. Jay visited her at the Rusk Institute of Rehabilitation in New York City, where she was already demonstrating the resolve that sustains her to this very day. But Jay was shaken. On the drive home, he said to the friends jammed into an old Mercury Comet something they will not forget: "I don't know if I could do it. I don't know if I could live like that. I think I'd rather be dead."

He has a friend, Tom Casey, at Trinity. Tom's mother, Janet, is a nurse. She's the supervising nurse at Nassau Hospital. She likes to stay late at the hospital and visit her son's friend Jay Kutner. She likes talking to him, because they have something in common. They both have a secret. Jay's is that he's terrified of what's to come. Janet's is that she's a Catholic woman who's planning to leave her husband. Jay can't go home. Janet doesn't want to, so she stays with him. Maybe she tells him it's OK to be afraid.

One day, she meets one of her student volunteers, Nancy Fischer. Nancy is a sophomore at Holy Trinity. Janet tells her to visit Jay. Nancy is 15, tall, and a little awkward. She knows who Jay Kutner is, of course—everybody does. But she doesn't know him. She's not friends with him. In truth, she's embarrassed, because she doesn't think she's worthy of him—what can she do for Jay Kutner? And she's also scared by the sight of him in his bed, helpless among the machines. But Janet is her boss, and she's not giving Nancy a choice. She starts visiting him every week, sitting by his bedside. She talks about school, mostly—the things that happen throughout the day. He doesn't say much. He can't. So he just listens. She wishes she could say something profound instead of hearing herself prattle on about this and that. But he smiles when he sees her walk into the room, and one day, when he smiles, she realizes he's withering away.

Jay doesn't stay at Nassau Hospital, in Mineola. He is a chronic case, so he moves to Goldwater Memorial Hospital, on Roosevelt Island in New York City, in the middle of the East River. There was once a penitentiary on that island. The smallpox hospital and the almshouse and the asylum used to be on that island. And it is on that island, and in that hospital, that fear really takes hold. He still has visitors; his mother, Virginia, even with all the children at home, visits every day, and Bobby D and the boys drive 45 minutes to the city whenever they can. But whoever visits Jay at Goldwater Memorial Hospital will talk about Goldwater Memorial Hospital and have bad dreams about Goldwater Memorial Hospital for a long time—the men in the iron lungs, the brusque nurses, the coughing, the groaning, the hopelessness, the isolation, the sodality of lost causes. There are people who visit once and never again, and there is Sister Amelia who taught Jay at Trinity and now teaches in Manhattan. She tries to visit him every week, and once, when she is sitting next to him, she hears him struggling to speak. It is hard for him, but she can hear him well enough, and she'll never forget what he says: "What should I think about God?"

"If you're angry at him, you should tell him," Sister Amelia says. "Have that conversation. Because if you speak to him honestly, that will be your prayer."

It is hard to be a helpless hero. The people who have invested their hopes in Jay have little choice but to keep doing so. They want Jay to be brave, and he is brave. They want Jay to hold fast to his will to live, and he holds on for as long as he possibly can. But he is dying. He is susceptible to infections and fevers. He burns, there in his bed at Goldwater, and at the end of April, around seven months after he fell on the field at Holy Trinity, he is transferred to another hospital, this time Bellevue, on the East Side of Manhattan. Not long after, his friend Georgie Wich hears from his father, a New York City cop. Do you want to go see him, he asks. Dad, it's late, George says. Do you want to go see him, his father asks again.

George and his father go to Bellevue in the middle of the night. He spends time with his friend, and on the next day, May 23, the Feast of the Ascension, Jay dies of a bladder infection. A few weeks later, the yearbook that honors his graduating class is published. There, among the black and white senior portraits, are Jay Kutner and Thomas Young, wearing the same loud plaid blazer. It belonged to Jay; he shared it with Tom when Tom didn't have one. Now Jay is gone, and Tom is the only one who knows, who remembers, what Jay did for him.

THERE IS A worship service on Wednesday, three days after well-wishers crowded the hallways at the hospital. It's at The

Cathedral of Christ the King, the church downtown where the Telliers worship. Seven hundred people come, so many that the crowd overflows the chapel. Most are from Selma, but not all. The story of Caden Tellier's short life and precipitous death has made the national news over the weekend, to the extent that Jamie Tellier, on Monday morning, opens his phone only to read the news once again that Caden is gone. People have traveled from all over Alabama to be part of the service, including a family from around Greensboro. The player from Southern Academy who made the fatal tackle just five nights ago has come to pray, along with his parents. The Telliers embrace them in the absolute conviction that Caden wants them to—not that he would want them to; that he wants them to, now, from his place in heaven.

Two nights before his injury, Caden told his youth group that he wanted to see a revival—a spiritual gathering of sorts—on his football team and at Morgan Academy. This night, at Christ the King, is the beginning of it. But what is a revival at a school that was chartered in 1965 in response to the Civil Rights Act, that was named after a senator who doubled as a grand wizard in the KKK, and that admitted its first Black student in 2008? What is a revival on a team that plays a sport predicated on pointed, intentional and occasionally lethal violence? There are problems in our schools and in our sports that sometimes feel nearly as old as original sin and nearly as resistant to change. The convulsions of grief that shake Selma in the wake of Caden's death do not transform Selma; they allow people to pray for the power of pardon, to forgive and to be forgiven.

Grief might sometimes tell stories, grief might speak through the imagination, grief might find its way into our dreams as well as our prayers. But stories do something real if they help us survive. Imagination speaks the truth if it helps us stay alive. And dreams are gifts of mercy if they give us the strength to offer ourselves to others when we have lost everything. The Telliers have lost Caden. Morgan Academy has lost Caden. The people of Selma have lost Caden. They all tell stories about him—triumphant stories. He died for a reason, they say, he died for a cause, he died as part of a plan, he died for us. Some people believe those stories; some people don't. But it's because of those stories that the Telliers have the astonishing strength to accompany Caden's body as he is rolled out of the hospital room. It's because of those stories that Caden's teammates call the boy from Greensboro who tackled Caden along the sideline and is still grieving himself. They take him out for dinner, and then take him out hunting, so that he knows they don't blame him, they're not mad at him, it was an accident, it was not intentional, it was a good clean hit, he was only doing his job, it was not his fault, it's nobody's fault, these things happen, and God is always good.

There are stories told by grief and time about Jay, too. Fred Bruno is the coach who called Jay back for one more play, one more snap. It turns out to be his last season at Trinity. He resigns and begins coaching at a public high school in Suffolk County. His coaching colleagues say he made the move for better pay. But he never wins a championship, and the death of Jay Kutner always follows him around. When he quits coaching, he becomes a pastor at a Christian church in East Meadow, just a few miles from Holy Trinity.

Kevin Kavanaugh holds Coach Bruno accountable for Jay—the way he picked him up by the belt. He was right there, the running back waiting for Jay to hand him the ball. Jay never got there, and Kevin, a few years later, feels as if he's still waiting. He's 24 years old and his life has yet to begin. Then his life almost ends. He eats something he shouldn't eat. He has no idea he's allergic to it, but he finds out his susceptibility by going into anaphylaxis. His throat closes. He can't breathe. He's dying, and then suddenly he's dead—his heart has stopped. A doctor is working on him, telling him, "Don't go, don't go, don't go," but he's leaving, all the voices coming to him now from a great distance. And then he sees two faces. One belongs to an aunt who died when he was a little boy. The other belongs to Jay Kutner. They say, "Go back, you're not ready yet," and that's when Kevin takes a breath and speaks to the doctor. "I'm not going anywhere," he says.

Tommy Joyce is another of the Titans' running backs. He blames himself for failing Jay. He visits Jay, but he can't shake the fear he sees in Jay's eyes when he sits with him in those hopeless hospital rooms. He wants to say something to take the fear away but doesn't know what it could be. He spends his life searching for those words and he finds them when he gives his life to God. Tommy becomes the man he always wanted to be, a graduate of Annapolis, a decorated fighter pilot, a husband, a father, and a captain with an office in the Pentagon, where he sits on the morning of Sept. 11, 2001. He is 45 years old. He's thinking of Jay, because it has been 28 years to the day since Tommy saw Jay break his neck diving for a fumble. Then an explosion knocks him to the ground, and when he looks out his window, he sees an enormous billowing fireball. A plane has hit the Pentagon, and he begins moving immediately to get people out. That fear he saw in Jay's face so long ago—he sees it again. This time he knows what to do, and he becomes one of the many heroes of 9/11, taking people out of the burning building, saving lives.

Jay Kutner died more than 51 years ago, on May 23, 1974. He was 18 years old. According to National Center for Catastrophic Sport Injury Research (NCCSIR) statistics, in 1974, a total of 10 middle school and high school football players died of the traumatic injuries they incurred from playing. In 1975, 13. In 1976, 12. In 1977, seven. In 1978, nine. In 1979, three. In 1980, nine. In 1981, five. In 1982, seven. In 1983, four. In 1984, four. In 1985, four. In 1986, 11. In 1987, four. In 1988, seven. In 1989, four. In 1990, zero. In 1991, three. In 1992, two. In 1993, three. In 1994, zero. In 1995, four. In 1996, five. In 1997, six. In 1998, six. In 1999, four. In 2000, three. In 2001, eight. In 2002, three. In 2003, two. In 2004, four. In 2005, two. In 2006, one. In 2007, three. In 2008, seven. In 2009, two. In 2010, two. in 2011, three. In 2012, one. In 2013, eight. In 2014, five. In 2015, seven. In 2016, two. In 2017, two. In 2018, two. In 2019, four. In 2020, the pandemic year, zero. In 2021, four. In 2022, three. In 2023, two. In 2024, three, including Caden Tellier, who, before he died at age 16, chose to donate his organs.

I WAS JUST a boy. And I was there.

I was there on Sept. 22, 1972, when Jay Kutner threw a 73-yard-touchdown pass against Syosset. I was a freshman at Holy Trinity, 14 years old. It was the first high school football game I ever attended. The Holy Trinity Titans wore the green-and-white of my favorite team, the New York Jets. They were losing when junior quarterback Jay Kutner stepped in. He wore No. 5. He was tall. He faded back in the pocket and threw the ball 50 yards downfield. The ball landed in the outstretched hands of a receiver named Barry Pannell who never broke stride. It was beyond beautiful—it was everything I ever wanted, in a spiral, in the arc of communication between quarterback and receiver. And it changed everything for me. I was a slow split end on a freshman team I barely made. But suddenly I wanted to do *that*. I wanted to be a quarterback. I wanted to be like Jay Kutner.

I was there a year later, on Tuesday, Sept. 11. I was a JV quarterback. Jay in his kindness, told me during training camp that I threw "a nice ball." We scrimmaged against Amityville alongside the varsity, on the same field. Then the coaches ushered us off and herded us back to the locker room. Coaches and players were running around, with a terrible harried look in their eyes, as if dogs had set upon them. We gathered in the bristly grass out in front of the locker room and waited in the dust, stared out in the distance, and tried to understand what it meant, what we were hearing, that Jay Kutner was badly hurt. It was a long time ago. But I remember the futility and the panic and the wait. I remember the ambulance and fire truck drove right onto the field, so late that they seemed to bring darkness with them.

I was there on the day set aside to mourn his death. It was late spring, the school year almost over. There was a memorial Mass in the big chapel across from the entrance to the locker room. Jay's teammates assisted, as altar boys. Kids trying to look brave, kids trying to look solemn, little knots of kids everywhere, sobbing, the way rainstorms break out, simultaneously across a hodgepodge of clouds. I wandered around and came upon two girls from my class, crying so hard they were shaking, they were embracing each other, they were one broken person. I had never seen anything like it, and I wondered: What must it have been like to be loved like that? What must it have been like to be Jay Kutner? And what might Jay Kutner have become?

JAMIE TELLIER HAS a decision to make. He has already made the decision to speak at Caden's funeral, because he wanted to testify to Caden's love of the Lord. That was his decision as a father. But now he has another kind of decision to make: a decision of a father who is also a coach. He has to decide whether to return to football.

It is entirely up to him. Certainly no one would blame him if he simply said, I can't. The Morgan Academy Senators have a new head coach this year, Jacob Webb, and he has already been told by the school's headmaster that this season is not about wins and losses but rather about making sure his players take care of each other. Coach Webb has told Jamie he should do what he feels is right for him and his family. *Everybody* has told Jamie he should do what is right for him and his family. But what is right for him and his family? And he asks himself, what is right for Caden?

He saw it, from the booth—he saw the tackle, and he saw Caden take himself out and then slump down. And, of course, he still sees it, every second; he can't stop seeing it, eyes open or closed. He agrees that it was a good tackle, a clean play; he calls his son's injury "the accident." The question he has to answer is whether he can see it again, any of it, another tackle, another hit, another boy slow to get up, more football. He has time; the game scheduled the week after Caden's death has been canceled and the following week is a bye. He wouldn't be able even to consider walking on the field otherwise. But can he consider it now? The game on Sept. 13 is against Monroe Academy. Three weeks have passed since the tackle, the accident, the loss, the walk down through the hospital halls. But Jamie Tellier doesn't make his decision until two hours before game time.

THEY ARE ALL survivors. There were 11 of them, to start with. But Jay played football. Rosemary Kutner was born with Down syndrome and died in an institution at age 4. Matthew was born with a congenital heart condition and into a childhood of multiple surgeries; he dreamed of playing hockey, and when he was 19 his doctor approved him to do so. His heart gave out and he collapsed in his brother Kenny's arms playing in a street hockey league; he was pronounced dead at the hospital. Stephen lived to a saintly adulthood, but when he died of cancer in 2018, he was the fourth child Virginia Kutner buried before her own death two years later. There are seven of them now. And yet as they all meet with me around a conference table in a law office in Garden City, New York, they project neither fragility nor diminished numbers—anything but.

There are three brothers, Harry and Chris and Kenny, all of them lawyers; there are two sisters, Bernie and Marybeth; there are a brother and a sister, Raymond and Ann Marie, attending on Zoom, along with Harry's son, John Joseph Kutner II; and there is Harry's wife, Barbara, who keeps her husband in line and hence everyone else. They are in their 50s and 60s and 70s. Their hair is mostly gray and white, but the men all wear sharp suits, the women have all dressed for the occasion, and, en masse, the Kutners are blessed with the electricity of big sprawling families, the eternal youth of their eternal jostling. With their quips and their complaints and comebacks, they pride themselves on being a tough crowd, and even with all of their losses, they do not seem like a tragic family but, rather, a family that has endured tragedy. And yet there is something that they've never done, never had the time to do nor the inclination: They've never sat in one place, all together, and talked about Jay.

They're doing it now, and so they're crying, one at a time, two at a time, sometimes as they're speaking and sometimes after they've spoken, reflected on some moment, told some story. The bad news of Jay's injury; the horrible news of how very bad it was; the hope that dwindled away; the individual isolation of the big booming household; the loneliness caused by Virginia's faithful vigil at her son's bedside; the pitiless education they received from the sight and sound of the iron lungs on Roosevelt Island; their unspoken prayers, at Bellevue, for the mercy of an ending. They talk for hours, and what they come to at last is not simply a reckoning with grief, but also with the man who bore up under it. "Tell me about your father," I say, remembering what one of Jay's friends told me about Judge Harry Kutner and the slap. "Aw Jesus, now you've done it," his namesake Harry Jr. says, drumming his fingers and rolling his eyes. They each have different versions of the old man. But they agree that he softened at the end of his life, learning how to lend an ear, becoming a father the kids could bring their troubles to because he had troubles of his own. The war hero, the B-29 pilot, the NYC cop who learned the law at night school, the man of unyielding rectitude who turned out to be born for the bench—he couldn't forgive himself about Jay. He couldn't forgive himself for not visiting Jay in the hospital more often. He had gone, sure, but not enough, never enough. He died at 94, still regretting. The kids would tell him don't be silly, he had 10 mouths to feed and a wife who visited her son every single day, no matter what. But the Judge would wave them off. A hero must follow his own example.

"Did your father have any heroes of his own?" I ask.

"Jay was my father's hero," Harry says, and for once all of them, all those squabbling, surviving Kutners, don't have to add anything. They just nod in solemn agreement. Yes.

His name is Patrick Johnson. He is a fledgling quarterback because he's a fledgling football player. He's "double-sided" about football, he acknowledges—playing the game mainly because his friends play. He's a sophomore at Morgan, and he's satisfied to be Caden Tellier's backup. He goes to practice, but he's happy to be on the sideline during the games, and he pushes neither Caden nor himself. It is, in fact, Caden who pushes *him*, Caden who makes sure that Patrick gets his reps, Caden who tells Patrick of his potential, Caden who instructs Patrick to go out there and don't try to be anyone but himself. On Aug. 23, 2024, Patrick is on the sideline when Caden appears to break loose on a running play before he's tripped up and spills forward. He watches Caden take himself out; he hears Caden complain that he doesn't feel well. He wonders if Caden has a concussion and can't help but wonder how many games he might sit out, how many games Patrick will have to…

Three days later, Patrick goes on Facebook and writes a long tribute to the late Caden Tellier. He writes about all of it—his uncertainty about his role, the game that resumed after Caden went to the hospital, the tough victory Morgan Academy dedicated to its quarterback, the celebration afterward, the news that Caden had a brain bleed, the tears that his parents shed telling him that next morning that Caden was brain-dead, Patrick's decision to do what he feared most and stand in the hallway of the hospital and watch Caden being wheeled away. It's a beautiful post because of its honesty, and also because, implicit in those words is the story Patrick is telling not just about Caden but about himself. He's 15 years old, and he's the quarterback now. He wants to honor Caden's legacy, but the only way he can do that is to do what Caden will never have the chance to—grow up, be himself, live a life, be a leader, become a man. "Why him, why not me, why did he deserve it of anyone in the world," he asks. Then, in the end, he addresses his friend: "God sent us an angel for 16 years that we didn't deserve. Satan tried to get this to tear our school apart but all it has done is make us stronger. No matter what, I will always consider myself QB2 because you will always be my Quarterback. I love you #17 and I will never forget the impact you had on my life."

It's a post that, despite the youth of its author, raises powerful questions about character and God and fate. What it never does—what none of the many tributes to Caden ever do—is raise questions about football.

We have made a kind of uneasy peace with the pain. It is, of course, a defining and inescapable feature of the game. We cannot watch our favorite teams play without also watching some of our favorite players being carried off the field. We cannot avoid becoming witnesses to injury and sometimes agony. Why do we keep watching? Because to us, the game is worth it. Because pain makes football feel authentic. If players put themselves at physical risk to play it, we will put ourselves at moral risk to watch it. And that is the pact that has made football America's national sport.

But we have not made peace with another aspect of football that has been part of the game since its inception. In the first decade of the 20th century, when it was a fledgling sport of rising popularity, it was also a sport in which people died. It had a fan in President Theodore Roosevelt in those days. He thought its brutality could preserve American manliness and help his country win wars. "I believe in rough games and in rough, manly sports," he said in a 1903 speech. "I do not feel any particular sympathy for the person who gets battered about a good deal so long as it is not fatal." But eight young men were killed playing football in 1904 and 18 the year after that. In 1909, 26 players perished.

Newspaper editorials and university presidents called for the game's abolition. Roosevelt helped institute the modern system of down and distance and pushed for the legalization of the forward pass so that fewer players would be stampeded. Fatality became the line that football approached but hoped not to cross, the line that a sport of breathtaking "roughness" came to live by.

Players have died playing lacrosse. Players have died playing hockey. Boxers not only die, they are literally beaten to death. But no other team sport has the record of on-field mortality that football does. According to statistics compiled by the NCCSIR, nearly 2,000 football players have died while playing since 1931, the causes of death divided evenly between "traumatic injury" and "exertional" events such as heat stroke and cardiac arrest. The incidence of fatal injuries peaked in the years when football displaced baseball as America's national sport and the numbers of people playing it surged: between 1966 and 1986, 306 football players died of "traumatic injury." And there is further heartbreak implicit in the mute testimony of the statistics. Since 1966, 370 players in high school and middle school have died of "traumatic injury" playing football. One of the three players who died in 2024 was a 13-year-old who suffered a brain injury making a tackle during practice. There are a number of theories that attempt to explain why immaturity and mortality are linked. The brain keeps developing through adolescence, making it more vulnerable than a mature brain to the kind of trauma football inflicts. But even without explanation the numbers are terribly clear: Most of the players who die playing football are young men and boys.

Jay Kutner and Caden Tellier were in many ways the same kind of boy—what used to be called "All-American." They were popular, handsome, talented, kind-hearted, leaders less by virtue of the position they each played than by the character they each developed. They played in different decades, in different parts of the country. But how they lived is intertwined with how they're remembered, and how they're remembered is intertwined with the game they played. People admired them. People followed them. People loved them, and football was and still is central to that. There was something beautiful about how they lived, because football can be beautiful; there was something unbearable about how their lives ended, because football can be unbearable. Teddy Roosevelt was right: Football can make men out of boys. But Jay and Caden were boys who never had the chance to become men.

He cries. He's just a boy, and he thinks he shouldn't. But his aunts and uncles are crying, so he figures he can cry without shame. He is standing with them on a field being dedicated to the memory of their brother, an uncle he never met. They talk about him sometimes—Uncle Jay. It's 1994; he died 20 years ago from a broken neck he suffered in this very place, on this very football field. But there's his name, spelled out on a big sign on the back of the bleachers, visible from the main road. You can't drive past Holy Trinity High School without seeing it: John Kutner Memorial Field. People called him Jay. People call the boy John or JJ, but his name is the same. He is named after his uncle. He is John Joseph Kutner II.

He does not go to Holy Trinity when he's old enough for high school. He goes to Garden City High. But the name follows him around, because people see it whenever they drive on Newbridge Road in Hicksville. "Is that *you*?" they ask, oblivious to its meaning. He shakes his head. "No, that's my uncle. He died." But in a way, he's a walking memorial—he plays baseball and basketball and lacrosse, and he excels in all of them. Once he finds out the number his uncle wore, he wears No. 5.

There is, however, one sport JJ Kutner wishes he could play, but can't. He can't play football. His lacrosse coach wants him to play football, wants to toughen him up. JJ wants to play football, wants to prove he's tough enough. But he's not allowed to. His father, Harry, won't let him. Harry has inherited some of Judge Kutner's vehemence, and so he doesn't have to say it more than once—"You're not playing football. There's no discussion." The coaches might want JJ to play football, but they know better than to try appealing Harry's edict. So does JJ. He's a Kutner, part of a big and endlessly competitive family. He has 31 cousins. Only one of them braves the family prohibition against playing football.

JJ plays college lacrosse, enduring a series of knee injuries to become more of a star in his sport than even his Uncle Jay was in his. His name, over time, becomes less of a burden to him, and more of a point not only of pride but of meaning. He might not have known the first John Joseph Kutner, but he knew his Uncle Matthew, and one of his earliest memories is attending Uncle Matthew's funeral after he suffered a heart attack playing street hockey. He was 19, Uncle Matthew. JJ is in his 40s now, a man with a wife and child, and therefore a decision he has to make. I meet him in the fall, at a hotel where children are running around on the grass and his family is enjoying the soft waning sunlight. He knows why his dad forbade him to play the sport he wanted to play most of all—it's...*dangerous*. People call what happened to his uncle an accident because it was unintentional. But people get into accidents by driving too fast. They get into accidents driving drunk. Jay Kutner didn't do any of that. He was innocent. He was just playing a game. And yet the game...

JJ still feels that he missed out. He missed out on meeting Uncle Jay. He missed out growing up with Uncle Matthew. But he missed out on football too, and so neither he nor his wife is definitive on the subject. Their little boy is running around on the green grass, with long blond hair, beautiful and wild. Football or no football? JJ can't imagine making the choice for him the way his father did. He suspects he'll let his son make a choice for himself. The little boy drifts back to the table, and this time John Joseph Kutner II grabs him and makes the introduction.

"Say hello," his father tells him.

"Hello," the boy says.

"Hello," I say to John Joseph Kutner III.

I CRASH THE reunion. Holy Trinity High School, Hicksville, New York, Class of 1974. They're easy enough to spot at a big chain sports bar on Route 110, the white hair, the pink faces, the vestigial beer-drinking postures of Catholic school magically preserved. And they're all there, Bobby DeLorenzo, Kevin Kavanaugh, Brian Clancy, Georgie Wich, some of the Tommys. They're all welcoming to the interloper in their midst because they have a story to tell about two people who are *not* there and whose absence has always fused this particular graduating class together. It still sounds unbelievable in the telling—two of their classmates suffered spinal injuries within a few weeks of the onset of their senior year. One, the gymnast, managed to thrive; she has a husband, two children, a career, and a talent for art. The other, the quarterback, wasn't even supposed to be in there; it was the end of the scrimmage, they were done, it was the last play, the last snap, the coach called him in for one more exchange with the center and it proved fatal.

I spot the center right away. The football team grieved for Jay Kutner, but it also celebrated itself for what it accomplished that year—the seven games it won against all odds, including the landmark victory against Chaminade—and it is still celebrating itself at the reunion. The players had all been through something and come out the other side, and the chemistry between them endures 50 years after the fact. But one of them operates on the periphery, and wears a tentative, sometimes pained expression. Jay's youngest sister, Marybeth Kutner Marchand, has also come to the reunion to find out more about what happened to her brother on Sept. 11, and when she introduces herself to him, he shakes her hand and responds immediately: "I'm Mark Pospisil. I snapped the ball."

For years, people thought it was Richie Callahan. Even most of his teammates thought that he was playing center when Jay Kutner fumbled; they didn't ask him about it because they thought he wouldn't want to talk about it. And Richie did feel bad about it, he did feel guilty about it, just not for the reasons they thought. He didn't snap the ball. He wasn't playing center when the ball came loose. He had taken himself out, believing the scrimmage was over. He went for water. He watched. There was a fumble. He has never stopped thinking he should have gone back in when he saw Jay go back in; he has never stopped thinking that he let his friend down.

Mark Pospisil wasn't even a center. He was a guard. The coaches put him in to try him out. He was just doing what he was supposed to be doing, the counterintuitive snap one of the coaches favored. He was blocking when Jay fumbled. He was playing line, enveloped in the scrum, the tussle. The fumble happened behind him. He didn't see. He heard about it later, when his teammates started talking about it—and then he got scared. He heard about it in school and then, a few weeks later, the coaches called him into their office. The office was a scary place, a big plate-glass window between the office and the locker room, which allowed the coaches to see out and the players to see in. They asked him questions. They were concerned about liability. What did he remember, did Jay Kutner have his helmet on or off when Mark left the field and headed to the locker room? Harry Kutner Sr. was suing the school, suing the Catholic diocese for not having a doctor on hand and leaving his son to the ministrations of the coaching staff, a suit later settled out of court. But the questions stuck with Mark. He thought of them as the decades went by, asking himself about his level of responsibility. He didn't play center again at Holy Trinity. But he played center for life.

Richie and Mark. They're in their late 60s now. Jay Kutner fumbled the snap and didn't make it past 18. They both spent 50 years wondering if it was their fault, the death of their quarterback.

But there's something they need to know.

It's something people say, when players die of injuries they sustain playing football.

It's a violent sport, and so, by definition, they die violently. Someone hits them, someone delivers the fatal blow. The terrible consequence is not intended, but the violence is, an intrinsic part of the game.

And yet what can the death be called but an accident? It sometimes even comes by accident, as the result of a mistake, a freak happenstance—a loose ball, a player laying himself out for a first down.

And so, what Richie and Mark need to know is what the Telliers said and what the players from Morgan Academy said to give comfort to the boy who took Caden down by a shoestring.

It wasn't their fault, it's not their fault, it was nobody's fault.

It was football.

Jamie Tellier finally makes his decision on game day, three weeks after Caden's fatal injury. He will not go back to the booth perched on top of the stands. He will not return to the place where he watched his son's last run, both too close and too far away. He instead goes down to the field and does his coaching from the sideline. He will be as close to his players as possible. If one of them gets hurt, Jamie is going to be present, right there, in the fray.

Now two months have passed, and it's the last game of the regular season, first day of November 2024. Jamie is on the sideline, with a headset framing his hair and his beard touched silver, and Caden…well, Caden is everywhere. His No. 17 is on Jamie's shirt. The No. 17 adorns the T-shirts the entire Morgan team wears for warmups and all of their helmets. It's on a circle on the 17-yard line of the field and on the game clock—17 seconds left—until kickoff. Students are wearing buttons emblazoned with photos of his face, and they can be heard, in the stands, espousing their determination to "Live like Caden." Listen closely: *Live like Caden*. He was just a boy. But he wanted—asked for—two things before he died: to have his jersey retired and to start a culture of religious revival at Morgan Academy. He has accomplished—though not lived to see—both.

It has become part of his story, the belief that Caden died young but did not die until he did exactly what God put him on Earth to do. The story that his life was short but remarkably and even enviably complete. And yet there is another story being told when Morgan takes the field against Lowndes Academy, and it also has the power to last. Lowndes is bigger, stronger and faster than Morgan, and Patrick Johnson, the sophomore starting quarterback, struggles along with the rest of his team. On the sideline, he seeks the counsel of his quarterbacks coach, Jamie Tellier, who puts his arm around his shoulder and talks to him with a solicitude that is unmistakable even from the stands. He has lost his son, but he is sure that his son would have wanted him to keep coaching Patrick and to keep coaching at Morgan until Patrick is no longer there. And so that's what he'll do. He'll take care of him. They'll take care of each other. They talk for a while, the coach and his quarterback, and it is such a human moment, such a loving and protective moment, that it almost comes as a surprise when the whistle blows and Jamie sends Patrick back onto the field.

I SAW THE signs for years, every time I drove by my old school and passed John Kutner Memorial Field. I thought of Jay, with his New Frontier smile, and wondered who else remembered him. I decided to ask. I sought them out, his teammates and classmates. I asked them to go back in time, back 50 years, and in response they made me wish that I could go with them—wish that I had known Jay better.

I never saw him again after he broke his neck. I never visited him in the hospital. I was a scrub and didn't think I had the rank to pay him a visit. What I remembered most, after the panic and desperation of his injury, was what I witnessed a few days after he died. The memorial. Those two girls in my class embracing each other, shaking and sobbing. Jay Kutner was gone; he had suffered, died and was buried. I still wanted to be him.

I decide to call one of those girls, Joanne Cappuccio Lopilato. I haven't talked to her in decades; we might as well be strangers. But when I ask her if she remembers the day of the memorial Mass, she answers instantly.

"I remember," she says. "And I remember the day he was hurt. I was *waiting* for him, back at the school. I was waiting for him to get out of practice. Oh, I had such a crush on him. Everybody did. He was the Big Man on Campus. But we used to talk. He was so kind. And do you know what? He still is. He'll never age. He'll always be that happy, smiling face. He'll never change…to *us*."

It's when I begin talking about Jay—about the permanence of Jay—that I hear the news about Caden Tellier, down in Alabama.

I hear that he's in heaven, I hear that he's in God's hands. I picture them on the same field. I see them linked. I even imagine that some people who read this story will believe that Jay Kutner and Caden Tellier are friends now, protected by a spiral of angels. And I know people for whom that will be enough, will be everything.

I don't know any of that. I can't say I know. But there is something I can say. I went back into the past for a glimpse of the future. I talked to people about something that happened 50 years ago to be certain about what could happen 50 years from now.

Jay Kutner died in 1974. Caden Tellier died in 2024. A year later, just before football season began, some 200 players in Dallas County, Alabama—from every school with a football team—gathered for a dinner hosted by the Caden Tellier Foundation. They broke bread together and listened to pastors pray for their protection. Jamie saw the night as another fulfillment of Caden's dream.

Amen.

Nobody knows what's going to happen in the 2025 football season. No one can say if our prayers for protection will be answered. But Jay Kutner's family and friends can tell the Telliers what happens 50 years from now.

They can offer this assurance, this comfort: that Caden, like Jay, will be remembered.

That even *100* years apart, the boys who suffered the same fate will share the same fate.

The fate of the unforgotten.

TOM JUNOD is a senior writer for ESPN, where his work has won an Emmy and the Dan Jenkins Medal for Excellence in Sportswriting. He is a two-time winner of the National Magazine Award for Feature Writing and a winner of the James Beard Award for essay writing. Previously, he was a staff writer at *GQ* and *Esquire*. The film *A Beautiful Day in the Neighborhood* was based on his article in Esquire. His memoir, *In the Days of My Youth I Was Told What It Means to Be a Man*, was published in 2026. He lives in Atlanta with his wife and daughter.

Go Ebaide

NOA AVISHAG SCHNALL

FROM *Esses* • OCTOBER 2025

Ebaide Joy Udoh has traversed 20 African countries on her 250cc motorcycle, and she's barely been riding two years. In that time, the 33-year-old Nigerian has butted heads with Guinness World Records in her bid to achieve the woman's title for "Longest solo motorcycle journey in Africa." From four wheels, to three, and now two, her vocal fanbase has followed her odyssey and consistently grown. Now, with her next ride looming, the Naija girl is gunning for the title and taking the continent along for the ride.

The world of adventure riding, known as ADV among enthusiasts, is less about speed and precision and more about longtrail durability, the endurance of your machine, and where your rig can take you: road or off-road, muddy climbs, rocky terrain, through forests, jungles, or snow. When Ebaide first picked up a bike, she knew none of this. All she wanted to do was "explore the Earth, you get?"

Ebaide didn't know how to ride a motorcycle—let alone a bicycle—when she purchased *Aurora*, the Power Tekken 250cc that would carry her across the continent. But it satisfied both her need for light travel and agility. What might deter most, a motorcyclist's exposure—the lack of protection at high speeds—is exactly what draws her in. The thrill of riding, starting each day aware of the danger and being fully present in it, fuels her adrenaline. "It's so therapeutic because I know I might not live, and that's what makes it the most interesting," says Ebaide.

From the road, she tells the sort of stories that invite doubt, except Ebaide has documented much of her life via a 360° camera mounted to her bike. Nearly attacked by a black mamba? There's video evidence. Asked for grease money by countless police and at several border crossings? Plenty of footage. Crashed into the dirt? You know it.

She tackles each encounter head on. We see Ebaide get upset, argue, cry, and stand up for herself. It's this unapologetic vulnerability, rare in this era of tightly edited, highly produced content in front-facing format, that differentiates her in the motorsports field—and as an influencer more broadly. She has the bravery to learn new skills on camera while narrating her failures along the way. And it doesn't hurt that she is a tall, charming beauty with a bright smile and sharp wit.

When clad in motorcycle gear, with her cowrie-shell adorned dreadlocks tucked into her jacket, and helmet visor down, she's indistinguishable from the men riding their motorcycles. That camouflage is useful for remaining unbothered on the road, and has led to a few surprising reveals—usually for gas station attendants and checkpoint officers—when the helmet comes off. No matter the reaction, Ebaide takes it all in stride, with a laugh and a bit of banter.

"Whether or not people are close-minded is none of my business," she said on Lagos-based podcast *Lahor Talk* this June. "People always try to box [you] in, especially [us] African women. It doesn't matter—if you want to do it, you can do anything."

Like many, I was moved by the raw emotion pouring out of the woman on my screen. The video was fed to me by an algorithm that inherently thrives on controversy, and is attuned to my interests in travel, overlanding, and culture stories on the continent. There she was, seated on a motorcycle, describing her treatment at the hands of Guinness World Records. The Naija syncopation spoken through tears caught my ear immediately. Down the Ebaide Joy rabbit hole I went.

There is a heaviness to Ebaide's story, but you would never guess it upon meeting her. She was all laughs, relishing the retelling of her road-bound mistakes. Motorcycling may be a solo pursuit, but adventure riding the way Ebaide does it seems to be all about the encounters: Being fêted by a biker club in Niger Republic, lifted off the ground in Abuja by exuberant rider Mandu, given a Beninoise history lesson and a meal by biker Yasmina, or crossing paths with biker Aisha "Iron Butt" for a mid-road dance-off. The videos offer insight into someone unafraid to lean on others, ask for help, and embody her middle name: Joy.

Her storytelling style—360° road edits spliced with front-facing monologues, vulnerability woven with humor and healthy skepticism—is mesmerizing. That skepticism, no doubt, has been the key to her safety while traversing 20 countries. "My fear," she says, "keeps me alive."

The preternatural ability to adapt and figure things out along the way is Ebaide's M.O. "All my vehicles—I bought them before I learned how to ride." Ebaide went from driving a used Toyota Camry in Nigeria to buying a 1987 Nissan Vanette in Kenya and spending the next several months converting it to a camper. Her mechanic taught her to drive stick which, of course, she documented on her channels. It was with "Daddy," the van she painted copper-orange, that she first gained a prominent profile among adventurers in Kenya, and then wider audiences. She is sure she was among the first African women publicly living van life on the continent.

Throughout 2023, Ebaide began vehicle swapping as if she was testing the comfort of various chairs. Daddy was too big for her traveling needs, so she acquired a keke—the common term for a tuk-tuk in Nigeria—which she learned to drive via YouTube. After living out of the three-wheeler for several months, using a tarpaulin to cover her electronics in the back, she decided it wasn't the right fit for her travels either.

So, Ebaide decided to further condense—two wheels and even less baggage. She considered a Kibo, a brand of motorcycles assembled in Kenya, but a friend who had helped with her van customization recommended the Power Tekken 250cc as a better fit for her height. She bought the bike brand new, and the following month attempted her first ride at Tiwi Beach. With no prior experience, the ride ended disastrously, "in the water and in the bush," says Ebaide deadpan, pausing, and then laughing at herself.

She realized this was not a skill she could teach herself. She enrolled in a week-long motorcycle course with an instructor in Nairobi. Despite her instructor's protests, she decided that her fledgling skills were no impediment to planning a multi-destination international journey. "He's like, 'Are you crazy? Nobody travels when they don't even know how to ride!'" But after a second week of training in Mombasa, and an additional twelve hours off-roading the notorious Shimba Hills route in south Kenya without a single fall, the instructor deemed Ebaide ready.

So, in March 2024, with less than 1,200 miles on her new bike's odometer, Ebaide set off on her first pan-African journey through Kenya, Uganda, Rwanda, Tanzania, Zambia, Angola, Republic of Congo, Cameroon, and a return to her native Nigeria. Of course, simply listing countries doesn't do justice to her travails. But with the hundreds of videos shot en route, she brought followers along in her virtual sidecar. Several hours from the finish line in Lagos, Ebaide arrived in Ibadan, the city that raised her. She was welcomed with a homecoming party of fellow bikers and icons of Nigerian culture.

By October of the same year, she began the second leg of her journey where the first had left off, in Nigeria, and continued west through Niger Republic, Benin, Togo, Ghana, Ivory Coast, Liberia, Sierra Leone, Guinea, Guinea-Bissau, Senegal, The Gambia, and back into Senegal. Though Ebaide procured the visa for her final destination, Morocco, she was prevented from reaching it via the penultimate country, Mauritania. To this day, she says the embassy never responded to her visa request. Ebaide returned to Nigeria with Mauritania and Morocco untraversed.

This is the point at which I've met her, between legs two and three of her long-distance endeavor, in the limbo of logistics, press, and the unease that comes with being a traveler between travels. Some people are meant for a life on the road; for them, the in-between time breeds restless energy. Toward the end of our week together, spent between Lagos and Ibadan, and with a particularly exhausting day under our belts, we sit in a small, darkened restaurant bathed in a neon blue glow, finding relief in our drinks. Ebaide has just finished detailing her dizzying feats when she leans in to recount the episode with Guinness. "Okay," she says. "Now this is the real story."

Ebaide first applied for a title with Guinness World Records (GWR) during the second leg of her travels, submitting the route she intended to complete. GWR denied her application. After an exchange of messages, Ebaide was told to reapply under their commercial service, rather than the standard route, for a fee of £10,000. When she protested, Ebaide claims her application was deleted. She publicly contested the decision, and sparked an outcry. The process left her feeling "dismissed and cheated. And I don't like being cheated." The story went viral, and her video garnered over 5.7 million views, 751k likes, and 23k comments on TikTok alone.

GWR was forced to respond. They refunded her original Priority Application service fee and accepted her application under the title "Longest journey by motorcycle in Africa (female)," the status of which is now "pending evidence."

The current record stands at 30,000 km across 27 countries—"held by a non-African," Ebaide is quick to point out. She says she has already completed around 24,000 kms across 20 countries and hopes to complete the necessary mileage and country count on the upcoming leg of her journey, beginning this September. The planned route will take her from South Africa to Kenya, through Namibia, Botswana, back into South Africa to the enclaves of Lesotho and Eswatini, then onto Mozambique, Zimbabwe, Zambia, Malawi, Tanzania, Burundi, looping back into Tanzania, and finishing in Kenya. She expects the journey to take approximately three months. Returning to the starting point of her overall journey is a requirement of GWR, as is using the same motorcycle throughout. Ebaide has already visited three of the countries included in this next trip; so her total country count when completed will be 29, two more than the current record. Leg 3 will add approximately 11,000 kms to her tally, bringing the total distance to approximately 34,000 kms on her grand tour of Africa.

GWR doesn't have the same recollection of events. A Guinness World Records spokesperson refuted the claim that Ebaide's application was deleted, and added that the refund was granted on account of GWR being "unable to meet the response timeframe outlined in that [Priority] service's terms." From their perspective, it was suggested that she go the commercial route, citing that "Ebaide's journey is a significant undertaking, with multiple countries and long-term logistics involved," and suggesting, not requiring, the consideration of the "additional support, such as access to a dedicated account manager, guidance around the complexities of record verification for extended or mobile attempts, and potential licensing opportunities to help promote the journey."

Though the outlines of the interaction align, the tenor differs greatly. On Ebaide's end, and by extension, among her fanbase, emotions ran high. She credits her supporters for GWR's reversal, admitting that her individual efforts proved powerless. "I don't *think* it's because of people. I *know* it's because of people." Below the Instagram video first explaining Ebaide's upset with GWR, one commenter—himself a Nigerian creator with over 400k followers—wrote, "You don't need your colonizers to validate your achievements." Fans revolted in the comments section, their ire directed at the British institution (with Irish roots) that they felt would not legitimize her journey across her own continent. The racist overtones were unavoidable.

Woven into her travel content are Ebaide's Pan-Africanist beliefs in the value of a unified continent. "It's absurd that we need multiple visas to travel within Africa, yet one visa grants us access to [all of] Europe!" She also addresses the political, social, and financial incentives of a unified space, and the message has clearly resonated. Scroll through the comments of any one of her posts or videos, and her impact is palpable. Both her journeys and her vision inspire not just fellow Nigerians, but others across the continent, and throughout the diaspora. After her experience with GWR, Ebaide was motivated to create the African People's Records, an entity for archiving the records of other Africans, celebrating and encouraging African achievement instead of waiting on Western recognition. "Records are not necessarily for validation as people think they are," she says. "Records are to keep your name in history, for representation."

Ebaide's own history is a painful one. Though she'd emphasized the Guinness episode as the moment that brought a new virality to her online presence, she was already social-media famous on the continent. And the more time I spend with her, the less central the recent intercontinental fame is to her "real story."

Born in Edo State, where she lived for three years before moving to Ibadan, she became what she calls "half orphan" at five, following her father's passing, and "full orphan" at 13. Though never officially diagnosed, Ebaide believes her mother struggled with severe mental health issues, which exposed both her and her brother to abuse and neglect at a young age. Reflecting on the traumatic, formative period, she says, "long before I lost both parents, I didn't have both parents." An all-girls secondary school provided the structure and inspiration she needed to survive.

Ebaide focused on the conventional path, pursuing higher education and work in radio and television. When that didn't feel like the right fit, she even tried driving for ride-hailing apps. "I bashed the hell out of that car," laughs Ebaide. "[It] saw way better days before it met me." But once she realized she wanted something more, she made a vow to herself to seek adventure on the road. From that point, everything became about how. She began saving money to travel. "Right then I started planning my escape," says Ebaide.

Ebaide's travels started "small," she says, with backpacking trips across West Africa—Nigeria to Liberia—sometimes with friends and other groups of adventuring women, and other times solo. But now, with the success of her platform, Ebaide has been able to focus full-time on ADV life and the various related projects by hiring a support team. Manager Kayode "Promo Masta" Adepoju has been by Ebaide's side for three years, and helps with her Afrobeats career—Ebaide also sings, has accompanying music videos, and has been featured on the radio. When her profile surged with the Guinness affair, Ebaide took on Ifeoluwa "Ife" Ayo Vaughan and Tinuola Akinsete to help balance her calendar and social media presence.

Now, three years since her first Instagram post, Ebaide has made a life of adventure into a public career. Unfortunately, though predictably, she faces misogyny online and in her day-to-day. In interviews, she's often asked, "Are you married?" The answer is sometimes met with sucked teeth or followed by "Why not?" But much more commonly Ebaide finds rousing support, even stopped on the street by fans. In the two instances this writer witnessed, both fans were men—one looked to be in his mid-twenties, the other in his late fifties—beaming with excitement and pride to meet the African adventurer whose exploits they'd been following on their screens.

That effect she evokes has made her a marketable figure as well. Hero MotoCorp, a hugely popular Indian manufacturer of motorcycles and scooters, recently offered Ebaide some free gear and a bike. On the Tuesday I'm in town, she rides their Hunter model, a light 100cc, from Lagos Island to Ibadan, where the company has set up a banner at St. Anne's Girls School, her former secondary school, which traces its history back to 1869.

At the outdoor assembly organized in her honor, she stands before around 75 students who are still outfitted in the lavender and houndstooth uniform and green beret Ebaide once wore. Now sporting her new motorcycle jacket, Ebaide calls to them, "This is the school that created me." There is a slight tremble in her voice, quickly steadied; her usual audience is digital and on a few hours delay. "I was like you at one time," she tells them, "and whatever today is, it doesn't define your life. What you do with your life eventually is what defines it." She leads them in a spirited call and response, "Up school!" "Up St. Anne's!"

Ebaide is deeply candid with the girls. She speaks openly about her orphanhood, and acknowledges the challenges they may be facing, whether some girls may have walked long distances to reach school or others may have arrived on empty stomachs. When one student asks how Ebaide managed to keep going without giving up, she responds, "I still struggle." Ebaide briefly pauses as she begins to tear up. "But, I know my life has a huge meaning. I know I am making huge impact with my life. So nothing else matters."

It is just past sunset and we have settled into a small upstairs restaurant in the Ojaja Mall, midway between Lagos Lagoon and the Gulf of Guinea. We're about an hour into decompressing from our day, and share my plate of suya because Ebaide's chicken and chips has yet to arrive. "I'll pack it," she says. Over the past week we've spent together, she's mentioned that she doesn't eat out much anymore; she thrives in solitude. While Ebaide enjoys sharing her life with the world, she prefers—maybe needs—the buffer that a screen affords.

And that system works for her. The adventure rider, who uses an iteration of "Go Ebaide" on all platforms, has amassed legions of followers: nearly 300k on TikTok, nearly 290k on Instagram, 62k on Facebook, and 41k on YouTube.

There is something in Ebaide's journey and the way that she portrays it that sparks this Pan-African pride, inviting others to partake and engage with her journey. On a TikTok video from April of this year, the first handful of comments come from Senegal, The Gambia, Canada, Burkina Faso, the U.S., South

Africa, and an unspecified Congo. They take the form of cheers, wishes for Ebaide's safety, and requests for visits to respective countries: "When are you coming to Gambia?"; "You are really making moves and great strives [sic]"; "Good job [thumbs up emoji] God shall continue to grant you[r] journey mercies." While there is the usual smattering of detractors, for the overwhelming majority, it seems that her victory is theirs to share. So when she felt cheated, and shared that sentiment online, it's no surprise that her community did too. Perhaps the only surprise was the depth and reach of their response.

Currently, in the caption of her most popular post, Ebaide writes: "When I ride, I carry Africa on my back, but I know you carry me on yours."

Now, we get ready to leave. But before we do, I ask her something I've been wondering from the start. If the Guinness situation is settled, and she finishes the trip and claims the record for herself, what comes next? What's the next grand achievement? Ebaide is not someone who can sit still.

The normally rapid-fire Ebaide eases to a stop. When considering the future she draws a clear distinction between what she can see and what the universe has in store for her. "Projecting what I'll be is like telling the universe to limit my greatness," she says, grinning.

So, no, she won't venture a guess as to what comes next. How could she considering all she has achieved in such a short span?

"I do not want to know," she says, "because it's beyond my imagination. It's unbelievable."

NOA AVISHAG SCHNALL is an author, journalist, and photographer whose work focuses on stories of justice, resistance, and cultural celebration. She holds a master's degree in Indigenous Journalism, and her studies continue to inform her commitment to decolonial approaches to storytelling and collective liberation. Her first book, *Homebound: A Memoir Traversing Oman*, was published in 2025. She has also reported aboard two flotillas to Gaza.

All Eyes Are on the NFL's Most Atypical Owner. Where Will Her Curiosity Lead Her Next?

JOURDAN RODRIGUE

FROM The Athletic • DECEMBER 20, 2025

INDIANAPOLIS—The clocks in the most important rooms throughout the Indianapolis Colts' training facility are all identical. Large and rectangular, they hang inside the general manager's office, the team meeting room and a brightly lit conference room on the other side of the building. Their LED numbers tick toward and away from the large and small moments of the franchise and the family that owns it.

A game planning session; a special teams meeting; a signature charity event. A quarterback signing. A Sunday of football. A funeral.

In early December, a quote Carlie Irsay-Gordon had written on a whiteboard underneath the clock in the conference room particularly stood out: "The things which hurt, instruct." She drew a box around the words in hopes that nobody would erase them while wiping away various meeting notes.

At that time, the locals grumbled about the first sticking snow of the season and worried about quarterback Daniel Jones' fractured left fibula. They had no idea that the team was just days from the tipping point of its season.

The Colts had won eight of their first 10 games. It was a burst of joy for a mourning franchise and city still in shock over the May death of Jim Irsay, the former owner and the father of the 45-year-old Irsay-Gordon and her sisters and co-owners, Kalen Jackson and Casey Foyt.

But that Sunday, Jones tore his right Achilles. The Colts went on to lose six consecutive games and by late December were out of postseason contention.

The franchise now faces its most significant offseason in years. It's Irsay-Gordon's first at the helm. Crucial and potentially painful decisions include whether to extend Jones, who has a long recovery ahead and would otherwise be a free agent. She will have to consider the futures of Chris Ballard, the Colts general manager for nine seasons who has just one playoff win, and head coach Shane Steichen, who is 25–25 in his first three seasons. Irsay-Gordon has strong relationships with both Ballard and Steichen, who have staunchly supported her during the personal and professional strain of the team's transition following Irsay's death.

All eyes are on Irsay-Gordon—but they have been for months.

"Most people don't like change," she said then, a few days before that fateful Week 14 loss at Jacksonville. "I think there's something wrong with me, but I feel like it is the one thing that is a guarantee. I think it can be exciting."

Irsay-Gordon leaned comfortably in a thickly padded chair in the Colts' team meeting room as she spoke. She sat still but for her hands, which moved through the air as she talked, and the light caught little flashes of the diamond rings on her fingers. Her large blue-green eyes were sharply intense and probing, though she spoke warmly.

The room was once an indoor racquetball court that Jim Irsay used to play on several times a week with friends. Irsay-Gordon had it refurbished a few years ago. It's been years since the renovation, but she and other longtime employees sometimes think they can still hear the *thwack* of the ball hitting the walls.

Jim Irsay never pushed Irsay-Gordon or her sisters into football, but Irsay-Gordon, like her father famously did before her, worked in nearly every department in the organization for years, even while pursuing other interests, including an undergrad degree in religious studies and geoscience from Skidmore College, and work toward a doctorate in psychology.

In her teens and early 20s, she interned all over the organization, from ticket sales to marketing to internal media and management before she eventually moved into a fuller football operations role. She has represented the Colts at the NFL's annual meeting for over two decades.

But the ownership transition in the spring coupled with the team's early success this fall inspired new and viral interest in the NFL's youngest ownership group—especially Irsay-Gordon, who had been captured by cameras on the sideline during an early-season game wearing a headset like a coach and scribbling down notes between plays.

"Well, why wouldn't I be?" Irsay-Gordon said, chuckling softly. Many in the Colts' building—from players to coaches to members of the front office—were also bewildered by the greater public's fixation on that detail. Irsay-Gordon has worn the headset on the sideline for years, and before that was stationed up in the booth with the scouts and executive team. She never speaks into it, but writes down what she hears people say, charts every play and additionally notes sideline observations and interactions throughout the game.

She has sat daily in the back rows of team and position group meetings for even longer, taking detailed notes and often pulling aside coaches or players for questions about what they just studied. She's at every walkthrough and practice. She's been on the road with scouts. She's in the draft meetings and has a place in the draft room. She keeps the same hours as the coaches, arriving early and staying long after dark.

"I don't know if I've ever been around a more process-driven person than her," Ballard said.

Irsay-Gordon was a curious, individualistic child. Pete Ward, the Colts COO and a 45-year employee of the team as well as one of Jim Irsay's best friends, has known Irsay-Gordon since infancy. "She definitely was her own person very young, you know," he said. "[At] like 6 or 7, the thing that stands out the most is she would wear these kind of eclectic outfits, you know? And I asked her mom, 'So who picks out her attire?' And she said, 'I let her pick out what she wants to wear. I want her to develop her own tastes.' She's always been that way. She marches to her own drummer."

Along came kind Casey, then spirited Kalen—nicknamed "Piper" as a child by Jim Irsay, after the airplane. In her sisters, Irsay-Gordon found fellow independent adventurers, all encouraged by their father to pursue what interested them, even if it wasn't football. "Go be weird," he used to tell Irsay-Gordon. "It's cool to be weird."

"He really liked the different people, if you will, and like the imperfect people," said Kalen Jackson. "Those are the people who interested him the most.... Having two parents that were like that, I think naturally made us very curious about the world, very curious about what makes people tick."

As children, the three daughters looked with great interest at the world around them and it did so right back. Jackson referred to the Indianapolis of her youth as a "little-big town" because everywhere they went, Irsay either knew somebody—or was about to make a friend. The family's open-book relationship with the city grew deeper as the Colts started regularly winning, including Super Bowl XLI in February 2007.

"Growing up, everyone always recognized my dad no matter where we went," Jackson said. "...We grew up in a world where we always had to share him with everyone else, but not in a bad way. It was a beautiful thing."

It was also, at times, complicated. Irsay was a man cherished by the city for his eccentricity and outsized heart but also his honesty about his longtime struggles with mental health and addiction. Irsay eventually had to publicly address multiple overdoses. (After his death, *The Washington Post* reported that there had been additional undisclosed overdoses in the final years of his life.) Irsay-Gordon and Jackson both said they'd been in therapy since early childhood and speak openly about the pain of watching a beloved parent suffer.

Over time, Jim Irsay became a passionate public speaker about his own ongoing demons, and gave time and resources to help others dealing with similar struggles. The Colts launched Kicking the Stigma in 2020 to help fight the mental health crisis in Indiana. Now spearheaded by Jackson (also the organization's chief brand officer), the initiative has committed tens of millions to funding research on and treatment for mental health issues and organizations providing resources and support, and in raising awareness nationwide.

All the while, Irsay prepared his daughters to lead. If they were curious about how something in the organization worked, he opened the door for them to go learn all about it.

When Irsay-Gordon decided to take on a larger role with the Colts in 2008 instead of pursuing a career in clinical psychology, she knew she had to be all-in. Unlike many other owners, she wanted to be immersed in every part of the building every day. Irsay-Gordon hates titles, and she didn't want others to think of her position first when they talked with her. She wanted to be a student. She understood that more involvement with the team required a deeper education in football and football operations, so she sought out teachers in the equipment, video and film, data, salary cap and scouting departments, and especially among coaches and players.

Irsay-Gordon prefers to study how a decision got made versus its result. It is why she is especially drawn to position meetings, where specific strategies are taught or concepts installed and there is an explanation of why the team is using them that week. She maps out questions to bring into weekly Monday meetings with Steichen and Ballard. She loves asking players about their techniques and how they do their job; a particularly memorable response came from veteran defensive lineman Grover Stewart.

"Carlie, my job is to be physical," he said in his pleasant drawl, "I get in my little car, and I just go."

Ballard said Irsay-Gordon is not judgmental, nor does she rush to conclusions.

"She lets you work," he said. "She's gonna ask great questions...she's gonna challenge your thinking...but she does it out of curiosity, not in a way where she's judging your decisions."

Ballard, who became the Colts general manager in 2017, has a reputation for being unfiltered. Watching a Colts game anywhere in his vicinity is a ride on a profanity-laced, emotional roller coaster. After a particularly tough loss to Kansas City some years ago, Irsay-Gordon and Ballard were text messaging back and forth when he snapped, typing out paragraphs of mostly curse words before pressing send. "It was not kind," he remembered.

The next day, Irsay-Gordon walked into his office. Ballard was surprised—"she could have gone to her dad and said, 'hey, f— this guy,' but she didn't; she came to me"—but mostly he was embarrassed and sheepish. He told her she should fire him. "No," she replied, "that's what you felt. I don't want you to ever hold back when you feel something." The exchange altered their work relationship forever. Ballard never holds back his opinion from his boss. Irsay-Gordon treats him the same whether or not she agrees with it.

"I think when people have that connection and you have those relationships, then you don't get people pointing fingers as much," she said. "Or, if you get people pointing fingers, someone else stands up and says 'no—what good is blaming someone gonna do if we don't focus on finding the solution?' That's where you develop learning mindsets; growth mindsets. People not afraid to be curious."

Irsay-Gordon likes to say that studying psychology actually gave her eight years of "studying to be neutral." She believes decision-making should be based on a series of facts without emotion, with discipline and process—and few exceptions.

Irsay-Gordon is as invested in the strategy and function of the football team as she is in the franchise's culture. For decades, she and her sisters watched Jim Irsay act with personal attention and care beyond a typical owner toward the members of the organization, from the star player to the mailroom intern. Irsay was the rare owner chosen to present multiple former players into the Hall of Fame.

Similarly, there is a dynamic between Irsay-Gordon and players that must be seen and felt to be understood. She has the pulse of the locker room in a way only some beloved coaches do.

It's not just that she is in position group meetings; by now she is expected there. Players are frequently called into her office for check-ins. These conversations have led to changes over the years, from improved nutrition to the quality of equipment to significant investment in mental health programming for players and staff. Sometimes they're simply called into her office because it's their birthday and she brought them cupcakes.

"Guys are like, 'the owner really came to me and asked, 'Is there anything [I] can do?''" said Stewart. "Other owners, they're like, 'Whatever I do, I do.' That's a big thing for the guys on the team and the chemistry around the building."

Tyquan Lewis, another veteran defensive lineman, refers to Irsay-Gordon as one of his best friends. They often exchange Lego-building strategies—Irsay-Gordon and her two kids love the kits, as does Lewis' younger daughter, Tyla. Recently Irsay-Gordon gifted Tyla a set, the ice castle from *Frozen*.

Irsay-Gordon and Stewart, an avid landscape artist at his large Georgia property, frequently talk about gardening. They each tried to grow hydrangeas, but Stewart lamented he didn't have the right fertilizer or soil for the picky flower. His didn't make it, and Irsay-Gordon gave him hell for it (hers thrived). Stewart compares Irsay-Gordon to an oak tree because of her enduring stability.

When photos of Irsay-Gordon wearing a headset, notebook in hand, started going viral over the summer, it seemed like everybody had an opinion. Relatively few women are on NFL sidelines, and even fewer wear a coaching headset. The Colts received pictures from fans of their young daughters or sisters dressed up like Irsay-Gordon for Halloween. Other reactions ranged from genuine curiosity to derision.

Many in the organization found ways to show their support. Some players wore T-shirts featuring her viral images; others reminded inquisitive outside media members how many years Irsay-Gordon had been on the sidelines.

Ballard has generally taken a colorful approach. He said an opposing team called him to complain about Irsay-Gordon being on the sideline three years ago, asking if Ballard planned to speak with her about it.

"Absolutely f—— not," he replied, "I don't have a problem with it." He said that team could call Irsay-Gordon directly. No call was ever made. Irsay-Gordon was amused when Ballard mentioned it to her.

"Well, I'm not leaving the sideline," she said calmly.

"Well, I'm not asking you to!" he shot back.

Irsay-Gordon didn't need anybody to stick up for her; she is the principal owner of the team, a billionaire and a businesswoman, and just as individualistic as she was as a child. It's clear throughout the football building that nobody was protective of Irsay-Gordon in a way that patronized or softened her. They did it because she is one of them, and their standard is to look after one another.

"She's earned that because of her work ethic, because of how she treats others, because she's so inquisitive and gets to know people," Ballard said. "She has put in the time and earned her way."

Irsay-Gordon often refers to the organization as "an organism," each part requiring its own specific care. Employees of any level are allowed to eat the same healthy meals and snacks provided to players and coaching staff. With Jackson's support, the Colts brought in a counselor who players and employees have access to if they need help.

"Everyone sees it, how much she cares," Steichen said. "...It's refreshing to have an owner that cares so deeply about the people. Like, '*how can I help you? What do you need?*'"

The Colts display their Lombardi trophy in a glass case at the end of one long hallway inside the practice facility. All football teams want to win a championship—obviously, said Irsay-Gordon.

"[But] what makes a *team*?" she asked. "I think, essentially, it's the connection and the relationships you have with the people here."

Can a little-big team from the little-big town keep its soul while once again competing among the heavy hitters in the most brutally competitive sport in the world? It's a concept Irsay-Gordon is eager to test.

"It's not change just to change," she said, adding: "We have to compete with other teams. We have to look outside and define meaningfully what is going on outside and how do we need to pivot inside in order to remain relevant, in order to remain competitive?"

Between the hours of time invested and energy spent, between the wins and the losses, it's almost easy to forget Irsay-Gordon and her sisters are still grieving the loss of their father. Football continues even when life is happening, and football people are wired to do the same—to push through, no matter the pain.

"They've handled it with grace," said linebacker Zaire Franklin, who is close with Irsay-Gordon.

"People go through things and you kind of forget, man, this is the first Thanksgiving without their dad. This is their first Christmas without their dad. Those type of things really hit you. Those type of things really hurt."

The team paid tribute to Irsay all season. The former owner was deeply passionate about music, so Steichen had a guitar built with the Colts logo and the phrase "Win for Jim" printed on its face. A different player carried the guitar into the stadium on game days each week. Irsay-Gordon posed with her sisters and star running back Jonathan Taylor for a media promotion and they brought the guitar. They looked like an all-female rock band. Frontwomen. Irsay would have loved it.

Memories of him are all over the building. Ward's office alone has become a kind of holding place for piles of photos, paintings, tokens from well-wishers, awards and more. Other enlarged photographs of moments in the team's history—in Irsay's life—hang on the walls. The business of the organization continues, but it carries with it the weight of loss.

So does Irsay-Gordon. She rarely reveals it, but those who know her well notice when small flashes of grief peek through: When she and Jackson play Irsay's famously long voice memos, every one of them still saved in their phones, just to hear him. When they turn to each other mid-conversation and say, "Oh you just know how Dad would respond to this."

As Irsay's health declined in the years leading up to his death at 65, the family and many in the organization recognized that they had to plan for what might come next. They wondered how Irsay-Gordon might lead, but they knew she'd be ready. For all of the energy and openness Irsay dedicated to preparing Irsay-Gordon and her sisters to take over, the painful truth was that he did so understanding that if they ever did it would be because he wouldn't be there to see it.

The Colts' last-effort swings to make the postseason, including coaxing future Hall of Fame quarterback Philip Rivers out of retirement, became a story of their own in a year that started in grief, crescendoed into bittersweetly tinged joy and ended in disappointment.

But NFL teams are built in the offseason. It begins in one week. Only months after taking over as principal owner, Irsay-Gordon has franchise-altering decisions to make. Many of them will be difficult. As always, she will look squarely at them, without judgment, and with her own blend of honesty and curiosity.

The clocks move onward. *The things which hurt, instruct.*

JOURDAN RODRIGUE is a senior NFL writer for The Athletic. Previously, she covered the Los Angeles Rams for The Athletic, the Carolina Panthers for The Athletic and *The Charlotte Observer*, and Penn State football for the *Centre Daily Times*. She is an ASU grad, a recipient of the PFWA's Terez A. Paylor Emerging Writer award (2021), and the creator of "The Playcallers" and "Finding Rams" series.

After L.A. Fires, a Local Run Club Helps Pick Up the Pieces

MICHAEL A. FLETCHER

FROM ESPN • JUNE 5, 2025

ALTADENA, Calif.—Nearly five months after the Eaton fire reduced his rented home to ashes, Carl Walton still lives mostly out of his car. Walton, 42, stashes most of his belongings in a storage unit more than an hour from his former home, and he sometimes showers at the gym. His workout gear and other necessities are stuffed in duffel bags he keeps in his burgundy-colored Jeep Compass.

One for martial arts and boxing. One for yoga. And yet another, along with his portable table, for massages. There was a bag he used for his job loading trucks at UPS until he was laid off in March. There is also a bag for running, something he started taking more seriously two years ago when he joined the Pasadena Run Club.

Before the fire, running had become a way for Walton to recalibrate and to stay in shape for his other athletic pursuits. What started as a way to keep his body tuned gradually became something more. The club gave him community. And in the disoriented months since the fire, it gave him something close to salvation.

In the uneasy days that followed the blaze, the club was suddenly doing more than logging miles. It raised more than $1,000 and split the money among several members who had lost their homes. The gesture was modest, but meaningful.

"It's a little drop in the bucket," said Lidia Garcia, the club's founder and a clinical social worker. "Half of it is keeping your chin up, keeping your spirit up. Obviously, you can't rebuild a house with one thousand dollars. But maybe now they can get some shoes so they can go back to running without feeling like they're breaking the bank."

The gift mattered. But so did the message: You are not alone. In the immediate aftermath of the disaster, club members mobilized. They partnered with other local running groups to distribute food, spread word about emergency housing and direct survivors to counselors and aid. They gathered leads and made calls. Since then, the club has only expanded its reach.

In partnership with The Langham Huntington, the historic Pasadena hotel that once hosted presidents and film stars, it is organizing a charity run set for June 22. The proceeds will go toward restoring recreational areas damaged by the fire.

Some went further. "I was part of a group of 20 people looking like a flash mob running around with chain saws," said Jason Seto, a data science manager who has been with the club for three years. "People were out there with garden hoses and weed whackers, and axes, just cutting down trees and trying to get things clear so cars and ambulances and other emergency vehicles can get by."

They cleared roads. They checked on each other and dug through the ash. But members of the Pasadena Run Club know the work that comes next is less visible. The backbreaking labor of recovery is one thing. The difficult process of healing is something else entirely.

THE EATON FIRE ignited in the foothills above Altadena on the evening of Jan. 7. At the time, Walton was taking a nap, preparing for his night shift at UPS. "My roommate came in the house and was like, 'There's a fire out there.'" Walton looked at the orange glow in the distance and dismissed it as an ominous yet manageable spectacle. "I was like, shoot, that's Echo Mountain," Walton said.

Knowing the mountain was a couple of miles away, he wasn't too concerned as he prepared for work. He told his roommate to let him know if the situation changed. "I said 'text me if we have to evacuate,'" he said.

Before long, the fire surged. Driven by powerful Santa Ana winds, it scaled canyon walls and raced downhill into Altadena and nearby communities that had always existed with the threat of wildfire but never experienced this type of inferno. Entire blocks caught fire, destroying almost everything. The intense heat blistered asphalt and caused trees to burst into flames. "In the middle of the night I got that text," Walton said. "I said, 'I got to go,' and they let me leave."

Walton was redirected by first responders who had blocked off his neighborhood before he could finish the 20-minute drive home. Walton retreated to an evacuation center in nearby Pasadena, where he connected with his roommate. Once the sun rose a few hours later, the two of them tried again.

"It was like World War III going up there," Walton said. "Everything was on fire on both sides of the street. Power lines were down. Plus, we had to get around the roadblocks."

By the time Walton reached the house, its roof was ablaze. He wrapped a cloth around his mouth and darted through the front door. But the heat was too much, the air too thick. He barely made it inside before the fire pushed him back.

Moments earlier, he had owned things. Not many, but enough to stake a small claim on a future. A brand-new massage table and chair—purchased that day—were meant to mark the start of something new. Training gear, his martial arts instructor's certification, a passport, a laptop, the fragile frameworks of his life. All of it now smoldering ash. Just a month earlier, he had moved into the modest house in Altadena after years of rented rooms and sad apartments. Now the place was gone, and with it, any illusion of permanence. He had no insurance, no real fallback, just the echo of a life paused once again.

"The only thing I had were the clothes on my back," Walton said. The fire was not his first. Decades earlier, in a childhood apartment in Long Beach, another blaze had consumed everything his family owned. It had left behind only a sobering clarity: Stability is a promise easily broken. Ever since, he had been chasing something more solid. He thought he had found it here. Walton spoke in a low, measured voice of someone trying to hold things together, even as the pieces kept slipping.

"I've spent a long time moving from place to place, renting bedroom after bedroom," he said. "There, I thought I had a two-year plan. Maybe I could get some money together. Maybe even buy a property. But that's knocked off right now."

Since the fire, his life has become a zigzag path of temporary shelter. There have been hotel rooms and Airbnbs, short-term solutions provided by relief agencies that often solved one problem while creating another. Two of the places required him to share a bathroom with five strangers, an uncomfortable return to the instability he had been trying to escape. Another, he said, had three aggressive dogs roaming the property.

Most nights now, he crashes on the couch in his aunt's small apartment in Long Beach, the same city where he grew up. Still, he clings to hope, knowing things could be worse. "I'm grateful, because I'm here and I still have my car," Walton said. Then he paused, as if weighing whether gratitude was enough. "But there are a lot of kinks to work through right now. You know what I mean?"

BY THE TIME the Eaton fire was declared fully contained on Jan. 31, it had consumed more than 14,000 acres across the San Gabriel Valley, destroying at least 9,400 structures. The fire incinerated homes, businesses, schools, churches and cars, reducing entire neighborhoods to a hellscape of toxic ash and scorched rubble.

Eighteen people were confirmed killed in the blaze, and more than 100,000 others were forced to evacuate. The fire was among 18 that ignited across greater Los Angeles in January, burning nearly 51,000 acres. By the time the fires were contained, at least 30 people were dead, dozens more were injured, and entire communities were destroyed. One estimate put the economic toll as high as $131 billion.

In Altadena, many places looked like a bomb had gone off. Steel mailbox poles leaned at impossible angles. Front steps led to nowhere. Brick fireplaces stood sentry over the charred ruins. In most spots the landscape was burned beyond recognition.

"The mountains were my backyard," said Ron Ferraz, who helps lead the run club with his partner, Garcia. "I rode there every day. I'd seen fires before—they'd flare up, the helicopters would come, drop water and it'd be over. This time was different. It just kept going. It didn't stop."

He still rides, but not through the same terrain.

"You can't recognize it," he said. "The climb up doesn't look like anything I've seen before. And I was there all the time."

The fire didn't just take homes and businesses. It also took away the ground that some club members ran on. Several trails that runners used for hill work are closed at least until the end of the year for repairs, and to allow for the recovery of charred land.

Garcia founded the Pasadena Run Club in 2021 as a modest effort to connect people to one another through the sport. Shaped by Garcia's belief in wellness as a social practice, which members say is unusual among the more than 100 running clubs in the Los Angeles area, it has attracted serious runners, as well as beginners. Its mailing list has more than 1,000 names, ranging in age from 13 to the mid-70s.

The club does not focus on pushing the pace. Instead, it extends an open invitation: meet each Wednesday evening at the Lululemon store in Old Town Pasadena and move at your own rate, and someone will be there to encourage you. The club offers a 2.5-mile walk, or 3- and 5-mile run options through the streets of Pasadena, and even now as many as 150 people take part each week—about the same number as before the fire.

The more serious runners spend the rest of the week following their own routes, some that once wound through the now devastated communities like Altadena and the mountain trails overlooking the area.

"People do their own thing," Garcia said. "It's not like a competitive group where everybody has a training schedule, even though there are those who do. And we have had certain races that we wanted people to do throughout the year just to feel like they were working towards something. But the fires kind of threw a big monkey wrench into what that would look like."

The fire left ultrafine particulates, carcinogenic ash and other poisons in the air. The public health advisories were urgent: Stay inside, don't exert yourself and wear a N95 or P100 mask if you must go out.

The club was forced to adapt. Unable to train along their usual city routes, the runners moved indoors for seven weeks, organizing treadmill sessions at a local fitness studio. Others fled the smoke entirely. "Some of us who were training for races were driving to places where the air was a little bit safer," said Seto, who was preparing for a half-marathon in the weeks following the fire. "I've been driving down to Newport Beach, which is about an hour south of here to do my run. I couldn't run around here because of the mixture of the air quality. And I think mentally it was just too difficult."

Agencies from the federal, state and county governments moved swiftly through the initial phases of cleanup: removing toxic debris, household chemicals and unstable remnants. The next step, clearing what's left, will take months. The U.S. Army Corps of Engineers and Los Angeles County say that 88% of the debris in Altadena—1.3 million tons—had been removed be the end of May.

TIANA HILL HADN'T grown up with fire seasons, having moved to California from Arizona four years ago. She's 49, an associate mental health therapist and a regular presence at the Pasadena Run Club, where for the past two years she's found a running routine and a circle of friends.

"When I moved here, I didn't have a community, so I was like, I really want to join one of those," said Hill, who said she previously found running to be punishing. "I walked on down to our local club in Old Pasadena and found these lovely people, and I just quickly became part of the community."

On the morning of Jan. 7, she and her fiancé, Joseph Brumfield, sat in front of their television watching live news coverage of a brush fire creeping through Pacific Palisades, 35 miles west. They felt sympathy, distant but real, for the multimillion-dollar homes under threat. "We were feeling so bad for those people in that community," Hill remembered.

Later in the day, there was more news: A second fire had sparked in Eaton Canyon. It was close to home. "That's right down the street from where Joseph grew up," Hill said. "His whole family still lives in Altadena."

That evening, they kept an eye on their phones, checking in with Brumfield's family members—including his daughter, sister, nieces and ex-wife—who lived in three houses clustered in Altadena, which for the past half-century has boasted one of Southern California's most racially diverse communities.

Thanks to the relatively affordable prices and the Fair Housing Act of 1968, Altadena became a rare stronghold for Black homeownership in the decades that followed. Unlike other communities, where desegregation provoked white flight, Altadena held firm, welcoming an influx of Black families. By 1980, African Americans made up 43% of the population. In more recent years, Latino and Asian American families have settled in.

"That night we were watching it get closer and closer," Hill said. "We finally told the family to call us if anything changes. We tried to sleep." The call came at 3:30 a.m. Police with bullhorns were moving through the streets telling people to evacuate immediately. Hill and Brumfield still clung to hope that the evacuation was precautionary. They soon learned it wasn't. By dawn, the flames had taken everything. Later that morning, they were driving toward Altadena through a world they no longer recognized. Ash fell like snow. Trees lay across roads. Smoke blocked out the sun and intense heat radiated off the pavement. "Everything was on fire," Hill said. "You could feel the heat in the car."

When they reached the site where Brumfield's sister's home had stood just hours earlier, there was not much left to identify it. "I was like, 'How do you know?'" Hill said. "It was complete rubble."

So was Pasadena Rosebud Academy.

Brumfield, who is currently the VP of business development at ride-sharing company HopSkipDrive, helped co-found the public charter school 17 years ago with the dream of creating something his community could call its own.

Serving about 175 Black and Latino students, the school had become a beacon in Altadena, with a reputation for being nurturing, rigorous and grounded in culture. Just weeks before the fire, the school had received a seven-year renewal of its charter, a validation of its success and stability. Then, hours later, the school building was gone.

There was no saving the classrooms, no salvaging the library books or student projects. Just disfigured playground equipment, blackened signs and scorched concrete. Today, its students attend classes six and a half miles away, sharing space on an elementary school campus in central Pasadena. It's a temporary arrangement, but no one knows how long temporary might last. When asked what it was like to lose so much—the family homes, the school, the neighborhood—Brumfield paused before answering. "It's just tough," he said.

He had spent the morning with his 21-year-old daughter, Sydney, at the ruins of the home she lived in with his ex-wife.

She had once been a standout basketball player and is a black belt in karate. Now she was sifting through ashes, searching for remnants of her former life. "She was looking for trophies, for her belts. Anything," he said. "We didn't find anything."

The flames had their own logic as they moved through Altadena, destroying some homes entirely while inexplicably skipping others. But in the aftermath, no one was spared the disruption.

Power was out for two weeks after the fire was brought under control, and some sections of Altadena went four months without potable water running from the taps.

Altadena's Super King Market, a grocery store on the community's west side, reopened in late January. Grocery Outlet, located closer to the heart of the 8.5-square-mile unincorporated town, didn't fare as well. Smoke damage forced the store to shut down for weeks, and it wasn't until mid-February that its owners were able to clean up, restock and welcome customers back.

Still, the broader picture remains bleak. Fewer than one-third of the 746 businesses affected by the Eaton fire have reopened, according to local officials. "They are either lost to the fire or they're still waiting for their landlords to settle with insurance companies so they can remediate and reopen," said Victoria Knapp, chair of the Altadena Town Council.

Fair Oaks Burger, a family-run spot that had been serving the neighborhood for years, was the last structure left intact on its block. In the months since, the restaurant became a hub for the community. Working with World Central Kitchen, the nonprofit known for showing up in disaster zones with hot meals and human connection, the restaurant served free food out of its parking lot.

Now, after months of cleanup, the restaurant is set to fully reopen in mid-June. "Those are the kinds of announcements I love to hear," said Los Angeles County supervisor Kathryn Barger, whose district includes Altadena. "Because it is a step closer to recovery."

Still, the road back is winding and slow.

Burned lots hide invisible danger like lead in the soil from old house paint, and the ash from scorched electronics. Businesses that escaped the flames now face the threat posed by a shortage of customers. Also, many homeowners remain locked in battles to wring justice from insurance companies.

Even before the Eaton fire wiped them out, residents here were already living in the shadow of another slow-moving crisis.

Insurance companies, spooked by the growing frequency of wildfires and other climate-fueled disasters, had begun pulling out, leaving homeowners scrambling for coverage. Many were pushed onto California's FAIR Plan, the state-run insurer of last resort. However, this safety net is beginning to show signs of strain under the weight of the latest catastrophe.

Barger reports that her office has received numerous complaints from policyholders who believed they were adequately covered only to discover that their FAIR Plan policies fell short of providing full compensation. "This fire actually shed a bright light on just how dysfunctional the insurance industry is in the state," Barger said. "When I talk to some people who have the state plan, I find out they have been paying these exorbitant premiums but getting inadequate coverage. They probably never thought they would have to use it but now they're frustrated."

Overall, Barger said a return to something resembling normalcy in Altadena remains years away. "I will feel like we're definitely on the right track when we get to 1,500 homes that have been rebuilt," she said, adding that 10 permits to rebuild homes in Altadena have been issued so far.

"If all goes well, I see that happening in two to three years."

Many people are worried that the cherished character and racial diversity of their community, a rare stronghold of African American economic power in Southern California, will be lost in the rebuild. Some of the burned out lots in Altadena have already been sold, snapped up by investors.

For some longtime residents, the insurance ran out too fast. For others, the thought of rebuilding was too much, or the offers for the land too lucrative to pass up. Black residents comprise 18% of Altadena, and their presence is anchored by home ownership, which stands at 81.5%. That stands in stark contrast to neighboring Pasadena, where Black residents make up 7.7% of the population and have a homeownership rate of 35.4%. Across Los Angeles County, where Black residents account for 9% of the population, Black homeownership rate is 33.5%.

The Eaton fire has left that hard-earned legacy of prosperity in jeopardy. As Altadena turns its focus toward rebuilding, the question hanging over the recovery isn't just how to replace what was lost, but how to ensure that legacy homeowners, so central to the community's identity, are not left behind. "There are signs up saying "Altadena's not for sale,"" Brumfield said. "But the harder thing to see is who is going to stay to rebuild."

IN THE UNSETTLED months since the Eaton fire devastated their community, its victims have begun to reckon with the true contours of the loss of homes, businesses and the familiar rhythms of their lives. Walton has navigated his path to recovery in fits and starts. He lost everything in the fire. But he did not lose everyone.

The members of the Pasadena Run Club, the group that first drew him in with its easy camaraderie, refused to let him fall away. They called. They showed up. They made sure that even if he stumbled, he would not be alone. Now Walton trains when he can, his running schedule shaped by the demands of a life he is still piecing back together.

He is back to offering mobile massage therapy, the work he was doing before everything changed. Between clients, he drives for Uber and Lyft. His GoFundMe has raised more than $11,000—enough to buy some breathing room. Through it all, the run club remains a constant, helping him move forward. The group has turned its focus outward, raising money, organizing events, looking for ways to be of use in a community still staggering from loss.

"Part of our culture is that nobody runs alone," Garcia said. "We don't leave people behind."

The fire destroyed buildings, trails and comfort, but as far as Walton is concerned, it also revealed something else: a community willing to go the distance for one other. "People's support has meant a lot to me," Walton said. "The people in the club were pretty cool from the beginning. And after the fire, they've been here for me. Right on standby."

MICHAEL A. FLETCHER is a senior writer with ESPN's enterprise and investigative team. Before that, he wrote for ESPN's The Undefeated, focusing on politics, criminal justice, and social issues. He spent 21 years at *The Washington Post*, where his beats included the national economy, the White House, and race relations.

The Best Player in the W.N.B.A. Now Has Her Own Shoe. It Took a Long Time.

TANIA GANGULI

FROM *The New York Times* • MAY 9, 2025

A'ja Wilson, a center for the Las Vegas Aces, is widely acknowledged as the best player in the Women's National Basketball Association. She is something like the league's on-court answer to LeBron James or Michael Jordan.

"I don't shy away from having conversations with her about being the greatest to ever play," said Becky Hammon, who has coached the Aces since 2022.

Ms. Wilson was the W.N.B.A.'s Rookie of the Year in 2018, won its Most Valuable Player Award in 2020 and 2022 and won a championship in 2022. But while she racked up achievement after achievement, one marker of basketball stardom eluded her: the shoe.

If Ms. Wilson were playing in the National Basketball Association, she would have long ago gotten a signature shoe, the on-court footwear designed with and for a player. More than two dozen N.B.A. players have them.

For years, marketers largely ignored the women's game. But Ms. Wilson's star has risen alongside that of the league she plays in, and in early 2023, Nike finally told her that it planned to create a signature shoe for her.

"I probably cried for a couple of days," she said.

The plan remained secret, and her fans got angry as Ms. Wilson continued to dominate on the court—winning another championship in 2023—without any news of a shoe. Fans were happy last May, however, when Nike announced that it would release her signature shoe, the A'One, this month, alongside an apparel collection.

(The year in between gave them even more reasons to be happy: Ms. Wilson became the first player in W.N.B.A. history to score 1,000 points in a season, won a third M.V.P. Award, was named one of *TIME* magazine's women of the year and had her jersey retired by the University of South Carolina.)

The A'One went on sale on Tuesday, with a "Pink Aura" version, making Ms. Wilson the first Black W.N.B.A. player to have a signature shoe since 2011.

"It's time for people to have a shoe and see a shoe from someone like me, considering it hasn't been done in a long, long time and it comes from a Black female athlete in this world," she said. "I'm grateful."

The 28-year-old was speaking in the Saint-Germain-des-Prés neighborhood of Paris, at a hotel suite overlooking Le Bon Marché, the famous department store. Her 6-foot-4 frame was dressed in the athletes' off-court uniform of sweats, with jewelry in her ears and on both sides of her nose. She was there on behalf of Nike. It was men's fashion week, so outside the hotel, photographers waited behind a rope in case celebrities emerged.

The Rise of the W.N.B.A.

W.N.B.A. players are bigger stars now than they ever were before, arguably with more cultural impact than they had even in the league's heady early days in the 1990s, when players like Lisa Leslie and Sheryl Swoopes became household names. Last season, interest in the league spiked, buoyed by the popularity of the rookies Caitlin Clark and Angel Reese. Brands rushed to play catch-up.

That resurgence has happened in the shoe industry, too, where brands have struggled to monetize products connected to female athletes.

The first W.N.B.A. player to have a signature shoe made for her was Ms. Swoopes in 1995. Nike's Air Swoopes had a tab on the back that made it easy to put on with the long fingernails she liked to sport. Nike made seven editions of it, the most it has made for any female player to date.

Eight other W.N.B.A. players released signature shoes between 1995 and 2001, according to a database kept by ESPN. In 2005 and 2006, Nike made shoes for Diana Taurasi, who starred at the University of Connecticut, for the U.S. women's national team and for the Phoenix Mercury. After her shoe, Nike didn't make another signature shoe with a women's basketball player until 2023.

Nike wasn't alone in its hiatus. Between 2011, when Adidas released a product with Candace Parker, and 2022, there were no W.N.B.A. signature shoes, according to ESPN's database. There just wasn't much of a market, industry observers say.

Women's models make up a small portion of the basketball shoe business, said Matt Powell, a retail analyst with BCE Consulting, in part because many female basketball players prefer wearing a men's shoe.

"It costs a tremendous amount of money to develop a shoe and then to build that shoe," Mr. Powell said. "If sales are not going to be huge, and that is the history of what we've seen, any brand is like, 'How much of an investment can we make here?'"

That all started to change when women's college basketball became more popular. Social media allowed players to create personal brands, and in 2021 the National Collegiate Athletic Association shifted its rules to allow athletes to capitalize on name, image and likeness (N.I.L.) deals, increasing their visibility with commercials and other advertisements.

Broadcast channels helped, too: ESPN began televising the N.C.A.A. women's tournament in 1996 but did not air the championship game on its broadcast network, ABC, until 2023. Ms. Reese's Louisiana State team defeated Ms. Clark's Iowa for that title, drawing nearly 10 million viewers.

The 2024 championship game drew 18.9 million viewers, beating the men's championship game by about four million, according to Nielsen. That interest has trickled up into the W.N.B.A. as the players moved there, too.

In July 2023, Nielsen reported a rise in interest generally in women's sports. It also said surveyed viewers were frustrated by a lack of access to live women's sports and a lack of media coverage.

"Sneaker companies are always reactive to the public, and they're always responsive to what they perceive as popular at a given time," said Brandon Wallace, an assistant professor at Indiana University who has studied the industry.

Sabrina Ionescu's shoe came out in 2023, her fourth W.N.B.A. season, all with the New York Liberty. It was Nike's first unisex shoe and is one of the most popular shoes for N.B.A. players to wear during games. Players have said they like its look, which includes intricate embroidery and customizable colors, and how it feels on their feet. The structure is similar to Kobe Bryant's shoe, which revolutionized the industry.

Nick DePaula, a journalist who covers the sneaker industry, said he expected Ms. Wilson's to be popular among the men as well. In part because of its design—he cited "the grip and the support and the lightweight element"—and in part out of solidarity.

"She's worn LeBrons for years and supported his line," Mr. DePaula said, referring to the Los Angeles Lakers superstar, who also has a deal with Nike. "There's an element of players excited for her personally."

Bam Adebayo of the Miami Heat, who has been romantically connected to Ms. Wilson, has already worn her shoe in a game, before its release.

Mr. Powell, the industry analyst, also said he believed that Ms. Wilson's shoe would do well among women's basketball shoes, in part because of the heightened interest in the W.N.B.A. and in part because of its relatively low price. Adult sizes are $110 and children's $90, compared with $190 for Mr. James's signature shoes or $130 for the Sabrina 2.

The Caitlin Clark Comparison Game

The launch of Ms. Wilson's shoe has not come without controversy.

In April 2024, when news broke that Nike was planning a signature shoe for Ms. Clark, then heading into her rookie season with the Indiana Fever, it set off a firestorm.

The news of Ms. Wilson's shoe wasn't public yet. Her fans wondered if racism played a part in giving Ms. Clark, who is white, a shoe before the much more professionally accomplished Ms. Wilson, especially since the only other active players with signature shoes—Ms. Ionescu and Breanna Stewart, a two-time M.V.P.—are both white.

Others noted Ms. Clark's exceptional popularity: She was selling out arenas and causing opponents to move their games to bigger venues. Games she played in set viewership records.

Strangers debated Ms. Wilson's merits. Some said that her personality wasn't charming enough, or that her style of play lacked charisma. Frontcourt players are sometimes thought to be less marketable because their style of play is often less flashy.

"It was very hard for me to navigate, only because in the back of my mind I'm like, 'Yes, I know a shoe's coming, but I really have nothing to share,'" Ms. Wilson said. "And to constantly be in those conversations and constantly having my name dragged through the mud and having my résumé dragged through the mud is really hard."

When the shoe was announced, Nike leaned into the controversy: Ms. Wilson wore a sweatshirt that had "Of Course I Have A Shoe Dot Com" written on it.

Now some writers and fans are wondering why Ms. Clark isn't getting her shoe alongside Ms. Wilson.

A prominent Substack sports columnist, Ethan Strauss, suggested that Nike was delaying Ms. Clark's shoe because of Ms. Wilson's coming product, calling it "corporate malpractice" to not cash in on Ms. Clark's popularity.

Tanya Hvizdak, Nike's vice president of global sports marketing, said Nike was not delaying Ms. Clark's shoe for Ms. Wilson. She said creating a signature shoe took time and disagreed with the characterization that it had taken too long for Ms. Wilson to be awarded a shoe.

"What I would say is we've been supporting our women's basketball athletes for 40 years," Ms. Hvizdak said.

Mr. Powell, the analyst, said Nike's recent struggles as a business and its overhaul last year were instructive as well.

With Nike's stock price falling and cultural relevance slipping, its board announced the abrupt retirement of its chief executive, John Donahue, in September and said Elliott Hill would replace him. Mr. Hill had spent 32 years with the company before retiring in 2020.

"I think we would have seen the Caitlin shoe a lot faster if Elliott had been at the helm," Mr. Powell said. "His predecessor just did not appreciate product and the value of endorsement."

Nike is expected to announce a shoe soon with Paige Bueckers, the first pick in this year's W.N.B.A. draft. Ms. Reese, who plays for the Chicago Sky, has a shoe in the works with Reebok and has already released lifestyle shoes for day-to-day wear.

A Move Into Fashion

It confuses the people close to Ms. Wilson that marketing opportunities have come more slowly than her basketball accolades.

"She's a supportive person," said Sydney Colson, a teammate for the last three seasons and one of Ms. Wilson's closest friends. "And not even just superstars, but people like that are just rare to come by."

Ms. Wilson decorates the lockers of her teammates for their birthdays and buys a cake celebrating Pride for her gay teammates each year. Last year's Pride cake was pink with disco balls, rainbow frosting and lettering that spelled, cheekily, "Hooray you gay."

Ms. Wilson is also outspoken. When Mr. James signed a $154 million contract with the Lakers during her rookie year, she posted a tweet saying the W.N.B.A.'s best were hoping just to reach $1 million. At the time, the league's top players made salaries of $115,500. Ms. Wilson will make $200,000 this season, which opens on May 16.

Nike and Ms. Wilson declined to comment on the size of their overall deal, but *The Wall Street Journal* and The Athletic have reported that Ms. Clark's Nike deal is worth $28 million over eight years.

Ms. Wilson has not shied away from discussing the impact of race on why she is sometimes called not marketable.

"It's 100 percent about race," she said. "And it's one of those things where we can sit there and say that all the time, but there's going to always be someone that's like, 'Well, no you're just making it about race.'"

As new opportunities have come her way Ms. Wilson has used them to cultivate her image. She has especially leaned into the fashion world's recent embrace of her; *Vogue* and *GQ*, for instance, featured her last month in a spread related to the Met Gala.

The collection with Nike includes single-leg leggings like the ones that Ms. Wilson popularized in the W.N.B.A., made in hot pink, and a hot pink sweatshirt with satin-lined hood (because her mother got tired of seeing her wearing a bonnet at the airport, Ms. Wilson said).

When she went on tour last year for her book, *Dear Black Girls*, her team approached the designer Sergio Hudson, who has dressed Michelle Obama, former Vice President Kamala Harris, Beyoncé, Rihanna and Jennifer Lopez, to outfit her.

He knew Ms. Wilson was stylish, and he liked the idea of supporting a W.N.B.A. player, especially one from his home state, South Carolina.

"When I saw her walk out in the first outfit we made for her, I was like, 'This girl is a star,'" Mr. Hudson said.

"At that time it wasn't how it is now," he said. "It wasn't that long ago, but it's like overnight things have shifted and the W.N.B.A. girls are prime celebrities, and everybody wants to dress them."

TANIA GANGULI is a business reporter at *The New York Times* and has spent most of her career writing about professional sports. She has a bachelor's degree from Northwestern University. After nearly 15 years in the industry, ending with covering the NBA Bubble during the Covid-19 pandemic, she took a break to get a master's degree in mass communication from the University of Minnesota, where she studied the relationship between marginalized communities and media coverage. She lives in Brooklyn, New York, with her husband, son, and dog.

Fifty Years After History's Most Brutal Boxing Match

VANN R. NEWKIRK II

FROM *The Atlantic* • OCTOBER 2025

It was oven-hot inside the arena, and that was before the fight began. The building's air-conditioning had already lost the undercard against the tropical sun, and the air was thick with humidity. Still, almost 30,000 people waited with sweat soaking their shirts, standing on tiptoe to get a glimpse of the men walking toward the center of the arena. From one side, draped in a dark-blue robe and flanked by an entourage in matching work shirts, Joe Frazier walked slowly through the crowd, stern and granite-jawed. A ripple of applause passed through the arena.

From the other side of the arena, dressed in a white satin robe with his name embroidered on the back, walked Muhammad Ali. Even at age 33, approaching the twilight of his career, Ali was electromagnetic, drawing the crowd to its feet and polarizing its constituents all at once. The noise was raucous. When match officials placed a more-than-three-foot-tall trophy in the middle of the ring, Ali grabbed it and feigned running away with it. In the ring, after his name was announced, he pantomimed heartbreak as boos overcame the adulation. Frazier, whose ring demeanor generally toggled between glowering and frowning, glowered.

This was the third bout between Frazier and Ali. Held on October 1, 1975, in the Philippine Coliseum, the fight is remembered by many who attended as the best heavyweight contest in history, and possibly the pinnacle of the sport. The match was the first ever broadcast live overseas by satellite, and hundreds of millions of people watched from abroad.

It was not the most dazzling display of pugilism as an art. There were no knockdowns, no calls from commentators that now live on as sound bites. The significance of the fight was more narrative than technical, and its appeal was elemental: a bitter test of wills and an exploration of the outer limits of human endurance. The final contest between Ali and Frazier was the culmination of a relationship that had begun in friendship but curdled into deep enmity, the decisive battle in a war that had become larger than the two men in the ring. The match was filled with contradictions. It had been pitched as an announcement of the arrival of the postcolonial Third World—but staged in part to help cover up the abuses of an autocratic regime supported by the U.S. government. It would be a showcase for all of the beauty and ugliness of boxing, a sport that made the world smaller by making tall tales of men. Looking back now, 50 years later, the event reveals—perhaps more than any other since—the ways that sport can be a mirror to society and the soul.

Ali and Frazier faced each other as the bell rang. And so began the Thrilla in Manila.

THE TWO FIGHTERS advanced, Ali jogging enthusiastically and Frazier plodding, cautious. They put up their guards and began to maneuver and dance, keeping their feet moving as they surveyed each other. Ali kept his hands high while Frazier reached out, almost gently, with a shot to the abdomen. Ali hit back with light left jabs as Frazier probed further, gauging Ali's reaction time as he shifted his guard.

Their measurements taken, the fighters increased their intensity. Ali aimed to knock Frazier out early, at times holding the shorter man off by extending his left fist straight out, like a football stiff-arm, while he waited for openings to strike with his coiled right. Frazier, though, was relentless, seeking a way inside Ali's reach, driving blows into Ali's ribs but moving too fast to get caught by the night-ender Ali had planned.

Ali had spent much of the previous month telling any reporter who would listen how slow and tired the 31-year-old Frazier was, but it was immediately clear that the two were evenly matched. The crowd roared when they exchanged combinations, when Ali jawed at Frazier, and when Frazier yelled back. When the bell rang at the end of the first round, Frazier tapped Ali on the butt, almost playfully, as if to let him know: I'm here.

Jerry Izenberg used his walker to prop open the door of his ranch-style house and beckoned me inside. "I used to be a lot faster," he said. We were in Henderson, Nevada, a suburb of Las Vegas in the foothills of the McCullough Range. His house bears all the hallmarks of a Vegas retirement refuge—a rock garden, a brilliant-green turf lawn, a view of the Strip across the Mojave Desert. But Izenberg is not retired. In his mid-90s, he still writes columns for the *Newark Star-Ledger* in New Jersey, making him likely the oldest working sports journalist in America. (Dave Goren, the executive director of the National Sports Media Association, told *The Atlantic* that "if there's an active sports journalist older than Jerry, I have no idea who it might be.") His book about the heyday of heavyweight boxers, *Once There Were Giants*, was released in 2017.

As he talked about his 74 years of sportswriting, the ease with which Izenberg recalled the fights he covered decades ago, and even the scorecards of specific rounds, astonished me. But he reached a different level of clarity when we talked about Ali and Frazier's final fight. Izenberg leaned closer, recounting the entire match, blow by blow, and quoting the two fighters as they spoke to each other in the ring. It was the greatest match he'd ever seen in person.

In late September 1975, Izenberg landed in Manila. The flight from San Francisco had been packed with sports reporters, and they were all transported to the Bayview Plaza, where the promoter Don King had arranged accommodations for journalists. The hotel, famed for its views of the sunset over Manila Bay, had been well stocked for the incoming brigade of thirsty men. They flocked to the bar for Joe's Knuckle Punch, a drink made with lambanog, a local palm liquor that supposedly wouldn't come with a hangover. The reporters drank for lunch and for dinner, and some stayed up late, talking politics over cocktails.

By the time Izenberg arrived, Ali and Frazier had been in Manila for days in order to acclimate to the heat and prepare for the fight. Frazier had gotten there first, landing at the airport at dawn. He was greeted on the tarmac by security guards and taken to his hotel.

Ali's arrival was more of a spectacle. His team had delayed the plane's departure from Honolulu so that instead of getting to Manila before dawn, Ali would arrive just after 6 a.m., which provided enough light for television cameras—and also coincided with the news hour back in the States. Hundreds of people crowded the runway to greet Ali, pushing against a cordon of soldiers armed with truncheons. As Ali stopped to address the crowd and the cameras, a disturbance broke out between the jostling spectators and the soldiers. "I don't want any fighting here," Ali said. He praised Ferdinand and Imelda Marcos, the president and first lady of the country, and bantered with the crowd, then launched into a poem he'd workshopped back home: "It will be a killa', chilla', thrilla' / when I get that gorilla in Manila." The rapturous arrival struck a chord with President Marcos, who aspired to build his own cult of personality in the Philippines. "I'd have to kill him," he allegedly later said about Ali, "if he was a Filipino." It was a joke, but only halfway.

Staged in a former U.S. colony just five months after the fall of Saigon, the fight was billed as a showcase for a new postcolonial era. With no evident sense of irony, Ali had likened his role as an international figure to that of a "Black Kissinger," a statesman for the Third World. Ali had recently taken huge purses, negotiated by King, for the "Rumble in the Jungle" in Kinshasa, Zaire, and a title defense in Kuala Lumpur, Malaysia. But in Zaire, he had been the guest of the kleptocratic dictator Mobutu Sese Seko, who'd paid handsomely for the good press. Marcos hoped to receive similarly favorable publicity.

Under Marcos's rule—which was propped up publicly by U.S. military aid and secretly by CIA assistance—the Philippines had been transformed into a police state. In 1972, in the name of fighting communism and terrorism, Marcos had declared martial law, granting himself supreme power. Three years into his regime, it had become commonplace for Filipinos to have family members who'd been disappeared, or to encounter the mutilated bodies of the president's political opponents, left on the streets as warnings.

One way that the Marcoses managed their reputation at home and abroad was through glitzy events that projected the Philippines as a booming, modernized state. The fight—for which they paid millions in purse money, promotion, and setup—was among the boldest examples. Nobody who knew the country was ever really fooled, and even Kissinger—the white one—warned President Richard Nixon that he thought Ferdinand Marcos was a self-serving tyrant. But boy, could he put on a show.

It was always unclear whether Ali's wide-eyed embrace of authoritarian regimes was a product of naivete or something more calculated. As with all things Ali, the boundaries between theater and reality were purposefully vague. But he readily availed himself of the Marcoses' hospitality, taking members of his entourage to parties and events. When Ali's mistress appeared at a state reception in Manila, Ali's wife, Khalilah, flew to the Philippines in a fury. Asked by the press about the fight, she responded tersely, "I'm going to root for the best man to win tonight—whomever that turns out to be."

In many ways, the extracurriculars—the women, the parties, the junkets—were all standard Ali fare by this point. A week before the match, Izenberg wrote that when it came to time, "he never has as much as he would like because there are so many things he wants to say and do before the bell rings. Some of them even concern the fight."

But Ali's antics in Manila had a more vicious edge. He leaned into his portrayal of the darker-skinned Frazier as more animal than human, even going so far as to wear a shirt imprinted with the image of a gorilla to the weigh-in. He had brought a toy gorilla to a press conference announcing the fight and pretended his sparring partners were gorillas. During one of Frazier's training sessions in Manila, Ali taunted him from the rafters. One night, Frazier heard shouting from outside his hotel window. He looked down from his balcony and saw Ali pointing a pistol at him. Ali and his team would later say that the pistol was a toy, but the truth has never been determined.

Frazier's time in Manila was less remarkable. During press conferences, he always called Ali by his last name at birth—a growled, clipped "Clay," as if even that one word was too much acknowledgment. He spent downtime at a villa in the mountainous outskirts of Manila, passing hours in monk-like silence. Cutting an image that contrasted with Ali's more libertine act, Frazier traveled with his family, including his teenage son, Marvis, an aspiring boxer himself. Marvis had greeted Ali at the airport when he arrived in Manila, and was on hand to witness his delivery of the "gorilla" rhyme in front of the crowd.

When reporters asked Frazier about Ali's abuse, he would point to his children and ask how he could be an animal with such beautiful kids. He brushed off most of the taunts. But inside, as he later wrote in his autobiography, Frazier seethed. He wanted to kill Ali, or die trying.

FRAZIER WAS MAKING his point early. Ali had assumed he was slow, creaky, and dangerous only with his left hand. But Frazier was a new man in Manila. Ali was scoring plenty with jabs and flurries, but his attempts to land big punches mostly fell flat.

By the third round, the temperature in the arena may have reached 120 degrees. Ali gave up trying for a quick knockout blow and instead allowed Frazier to push him back into a corner, hoping to employ the "rope a dope" strategy he'd used so effectively against George Foreman in Kinshasa. Ali covered his face and tried to absorb Frazier's metronomic body blows, aiming to tire him. Twice, Ali taunted Frazier, beckoning him to hit him. Frazier obliged, surprising Ali with a cross and an uppercut from his supposedly weak right arm.

Ali began trying to clinch Frazier, putting his gloves behind the shorter man's head and seeking to weigh him down. The two-man dance became a triad as the referee, Carlos "Sonny" Padilla Jr., repeatedly pulled the men apart and scolded Ali.

Ali had often ridiculed Frazier for turning fights into slogs. Now he was in the mud himself. Despite it all, he managed his usual jabs to the chin and eyes, but Frazier seemed unfazed. Realizing the shift in rhythm, during the fifth round, Ali snarled at Frazier: "You ain't got no right hand! What are you doing?"

IZENBERG FIRST MET Cassius Clay in Rome, while covering the 1960 Olympics. Clay was an 18-year-old amateur then, the Louisville golden boy who'd already captured eight regional Golden Gloves and two nationals. He was a dyslexic kid who'd chafed at the indignities of growing up Black in a visibly segregated city, and for whom the lynching of Emmett Till in 1955 was deeply traumatic. Precocious, loud, and ambitious, he was discovered early by local trainers and promoters, and proved to be a boxing prodigy. He knew early that the sport would be his way out.

At the Olympics, he was skinnier than you probably remember him, and the warrior-poet braggadocio that later defined him was still embryonic. His surprising gold medal in the light-heavyweight division, over a Polish champion seven years his senior, made Clay something of a household name in the States.

Izenberg didn't actually watch Clay fight in the Olympics, but remembers him cracking jokes in the Olympic Village. "Athletes are walking by," Izenberg told me. Many didn't speak English, but something about Clay captivated them, especially the women. They "walked past him, turned around, walked back a few feet to take a look at him," Izenberg said. Later, Izenberg got in touch with the young champion, who begged him to come watch a fight. The two struck up a friendship that lasted for the rest of Ali's life.

Joe Frazier, two years younger than Ali, arrived at stardom on a Greyhound bus. He was born to a Gullah sharecropping family in South Carolina's Sea Islands. The shack where he and 12 siblings lived had been built by his father out of scrap lumber; luxuries such as plumbing belonged to another world. Like most sharecropping children, Frazier started working on the farm early. In his flickers of leisure time, at 8 years old, he made his own heavy bag, stuffed with moss, and tried to train himself to be the next Joe Louis. But a hard life made its mark. One day, he fell and seriously injured his left arm while trying to wrangle the family's 300-pound hog. The family had no money for doctors, and the arm healed crooked, forever limiting his reach and range of motion. But, as Frazier liked to say, the arm's awkward angle kept it "permanently cocked" for a left hook, which would become his signature punch.

At 15, Frazier joined the Great Migration, taking a bus north to New York and then settling in Philadelphia, where he landed work at a slaughterhouse. He was 18 before he finally received his first formal boxing training, at a Police Athletic League gym in Philly. He worked out obsessively, carrying his own record player to the gym late at night and training solo to the soundtrack of Otis Redding and Sam Cooke. The hard-nosed, straightforward style that he developed suited his adopted city, and would later provide a contrast to Ali's finesse. He made the 1964 Tokyo

Olympics as an alternate after another American boxer was injured, keeping to himself in the Olympic Village and focusing on training. Improbably, he kept winning his bouts. In the heavyweight semifinal, he broke his thumb, but he won that fight too, then hid the injury in order to compete in the final. He won the gold over the older, more experienced German fighter Hans Huber, only to be fired from his job in the slaughterhouse because his hand was in a cast.

It seems only natural in retrospect that Ali's and Frazier's lives would become intertwined: the dyslexic boy who found purpose—and a refuge from racism—in boxing, and the young sharecropper dropout who escaped his own inner-city blues in the ring; the would-be heirs of the Brown Bomber, Joe Louis. And for a time, they were friends. Ali would turn pro shortly after his Olympic coming-out party, and within four years, at the age of 22, he claimed a heavyweight title by beating Sonny Liston. The same year, he joined the Nation of Islam and changed his name. He cultivated both fame and infamy with his outspoken Black radicalism, and with his denunciations of the war in Vietnam. When he refused the draft in 1967, citing his faith, he was convicted for draft evasion and sentenced to five years in prison, and then stripped of his boxing licenses, passport, and heavyweight title. Before public opinion turned against the war, Ali was likely the most despised man in America. In the boxing world, Frazier was among the few people who didn't cut ties.

Frazier had come up in Ali's shadow. With Ali no longer eclipsing him, his career took off. In 1968, he fought Buster Mathis for the New York State Athletic Commission's heavyweight title, one component of the unified world heavyweight title. After the fight, a reporter asked, slyly, if Frazier considered himself a champion. According to the *New York Daily News*, Frazier glowered.

The promoter Butch Lewis later said that when the two met, Frazier continued to call Ali "champ," even after taking part of his title. Ali moved to Philadelphia while waiting for his appeal to work its way through federal courts, and the two often crossed paths. In an interview he gave later in his life, Frazier would say that Ali popped into Frazier's gym to talk about their inevitable fight, and asked Frazier for help with getting his license back. Frazier said he obliged. In 2011, many obituaries of Frazier mentioned that he said he'd lobbied President Nixon for Ali's reinstatement.

During his time away from boxing, which would end up lasting some three years, Ali supported himself with speaking engagements and appearance fees. According to Frazier, Ali liked to characterize the duo as generals in two different theaters. "Just keep whuppin' those guys in the ring and I'll keep fighting Uncle Sam. And one day we'll make a lot of money together," he told Frazier. Ali decided to write an autobiography, *The Greatest*. In it, he said he admired Frazier. "Of all the people in my profession I would like to have had as a friend," Ali wrote, "he was the one."

On a summer day in 1970, according to that book, when the two men both had appointments in New York City, Frazier, flush from his earnings as the newly crowned heavyweight champion, picked Ali up in Philadelphia in his gold Cadillac and drove him to New York. Frazier told Ali about his aspirations as a soul singer, and Ali sang a ditty he'd composed, "Mighty Whitey." They talked about race in America, and Frazier told Ali about having to fight his way through the Jim Crow Deep South.

Sitting side by side, the two often returned to rhapsodizing about how their future fight might play out. There was no shortage of playful insults, but Ali told Frazier in earnest that with his fighting income dried up, he needed a job. He wanted to be Frazier's sparring partner, and asked for money. Near the end of their trip, Frazier loaned Ali a hundred bucks. He let the top down on the gold Cadillac and they cruised. But when it came time for Frazier to drop off Ali, the men agreed that they shouldn't be seen as friendly in public. Nobody pays to see two friends fighting.

SHORTLY AFTER THE sixth round began in Manila, the dynamite in Frazier's left hand finally exploded. He connected with a thunderous hook, stretching his arm and body as far as he could reach to snap Ali's head back. A few seconds later, Frazier hit him again with the same punch. Ali stumbled, throwing a feeble, off-balance uppercut to the space where Frazier had just stood. The crowd, which had favored Frazier—for his Christian faith, it was said, and out of a national affinity for underdogs—erupted in cheers. Now it was Frazier who jogged and Ali who lumbered. Three more times in the round, Frazier's left found Ali's face cleanly. For the first time in the match, Frazier was the clear winner of a round.

But after his exile from boxing, Ali had discovered something useful, and something terrible. Stripped of the preternatural speed of his prime, he realized, quite simply, that he could sustain more damage than most fighters could deliver. In the seventh round, Ali shook off the punishment and for a time found some of his younger self, beginning to dance in the middle of the ring again. Frazier kept pounding Ali's body. But now, as Frazier advanced, Ali peppered his face with starch-stiff jabs and two-punch counters. His fist kept finding Frazier's right eye.

THE GENESIS OF the Frazier-Ali feud all depends on who's telling the story. Long after Frazier's retirement from boxing, after his hatred of Ali had solidified into a defining part of his life, he denied in his autobiography that they'd ever really been friends. And *The Greatest*, Ali's autobiography written with Richard Durham, a renowned Black journalist and former editor of a newspaper for the Nation of Islam, may not be entirely reliable in its characterization of Ali's sentiments. It was published in 1975, just two months after the Manila fight, with a mandate from Ali's handlers to scrub unsavory elements of his life. It's possible that the book's praise for Frazier was a real-time revision of the ugliness Ali had recently unleashed in the Philippines.

But the balance of the evidence suggests that the two men did share a bond. Frazier had looked up to Ali, and is said to have asked for his autograph when they'd first met, hoping they would one day fight. The question of when that might happen was postponed for a long time as Ali appealed his case. A match planned in Florida fell through, and rumors of bouts in Mississippi, Canada, and Australia never materialized.

Ali had always made a habit of taunting his opponents, many of whom took it as funny and gave back as good as they got. That's boxing. But over the course of his exile, Ali's barbs and stunts against Frazier grew into something more venomous.

During his sojourn in Philadelphia, Ali constantly challenged Frazier to unsanctioned fights. On a September day in 1969, he showed up at the Police Athletic League gym, demanding a fight with Frazier right there. According to a local report, more than 1,000 people who'd gotten wind of the challenge also arrived, and police soon broke up the crowd. Outside, Ali stood on top of a car and stoked the nascent mob, promising them a fight at a rec center a few miles away. He led a mass of people across the city to the supposed fight location, where as many as 10,000 people eventually gathered. Ali urged them to form a ring, and led them in chants calling out Frazier, who never showed.

These spectacles might have all been excused as Ali doing what he did best: promoting. But ultimately, there was never room enough, in town or in boxing, for both men. It was not a given that Ali would ever fight again; that he could avoid jail time and be vindicated; that he'd reclaim the title. And all the while, Ali felt that Frazier was a counterfeit champ who wasn't his equal in the ring, the face of all that had been taken from him. In the other corner, Frazier constantly had to prove himself as a deserving victor, even though his style and persona never quite captured audiences the way Ali's did. And years of continual needling is apt to get under anyone's skin.

The growing fissure became a permanent rift when one day Frazier heard Ali doing a radio interview. Ali boasted about how easily he would beat Frazier, calling him a coward, as he'd often done. But this time, Ali added something new: He called Frazier an Uncle Tom.

After repeated provocations, Frazier grew so incensed that he drove to Ali's residence, where Ali began a frustrating game he would play with Frazier for the rest of their lives. He insisted that he hadn't meant anything by the insults, that he was just trying to gin up attention for their eventual fight. Frazier was being too sensitive, he said; he needed to loosen up. But Frazier wasn't having it. He'd told Ali about how he'd had to scrap with racists who meant him physical harm just to make it out of the South. Being called an Uncle Tom was a betrayal.

They finally fought in 1971, at Madison Square Garden, a few months before the Supreme Court ruled that Ali had been improperly denied status as a conscientious objector and overturned his conviction for draft dodging. The "Fight of the Century," as it was dubbed, was marked as much by personal animosity as by the unique excitement of having—by virtue of Ali's forced hiatus—two undefeated champions face off in a title fight. In the months before the $5 million match, Ali turned up the invective, calling Frazier dumb, mocking his dark skin, and painting him as a lackey for his white handlers.

Frazier didn't hide his anger, raging in prefight interviews about how badly he would hurt Ali. He'd never called Ali by his chosen name, but now Frazier's insistence on calling him Clay was tied to a larger rejection of the Nation of Islam, and his contention that the group was using Ali.

Ali countered, saying that Frazier was himself being used by his management group, a collection of white businessmen in Philadelphia. He said that rooting for Frazier made a Black person a traitor, and that Frazier fought for Nixon. (According to a member of Frazier's entourage, Dave Wolf, Ali also said that Frazier fought for Klansmen.) As a result, Frazier received anonymous death threats, and his children feared for his life. Winning the fight would not be enough for Ali; he evidently needed to erase the idea of Frazier as an equal, both in and out of the ring.

The "Fight of the Century" lived up to the billing. Ali came out aggressively, with rapid-fire punches in the first few rounds. But he was slower than he'd been before his hiatus, and as he got tired, Frazier's constant, precise body work took hold. Frazier was more John Henry than Joe Louis, driving steel over and over again into the core of his opponent. The fight went the distance, a full 15 rounds, but the outcome was clear. In the 11th, Frazier uncorked a left hook that made Ali wobble. In the 15th, he delivered another that knocked Ali down.

The scorecards were unanimous, although Ali and his team disputed the decision and demanded another fight. After the match, Frazier said that he'd reached back home to "the country" for some of the blows he'd landed. In a match that was, in a sense, a referendum on Frazier's Blackness, the arm that had been permanently marked by Jim Crow had forced a judgment.

BY THE 10TH round in Manila, Ali and Frazier both knew that this fight would take something from them, something they hadn't had to give before. Sweat poured off them, and between rounds they sank onto their stools and gasped. This was a test of endurance, against each other and against the hellish conditions in the ring.

A beleaguered Ali had gained momentum in the eighth, launching a barrage of punches that momentarily hurt Frazier, and began to swell his face. But Frazier was inexorable. He kept Ali on his back foot, driving him into the corners and delivering vicious shots to the head, blows that—had they been delivered by a slightly younger Frazier—might have knocked men out cold. Ali shook it all off. He was a blanket, still trying to clinch Frazier and hold him down. The two boxers teetered against each other, exhausted, until Padilla stepped in again, pulling Ali's gloves off the back of Frazier's neck. They raised their arms, almost unwillingly, and resumed slugging.

WHEN CARLOS PADILLA Jr. had woken up on the morning of the Ali-Frazier match, he was not the chosen referee. Amid all the acrimony between the Ali and Frazier camps, they hadn't agreed on who would stand in the ring between the two men. Their second fight, in which Ali had thoroughly avenged his defeat in the "Fight of the Century," had been marred by controversy over the officiating. That bout, also held in Madison Square Garden, was less a boxing match than a hugging match. According to Frazier's trainer, Eddie Futch, Ali had clinched more than 100 times, often pulling Frazier's neck down in order to tire him. Both corners had criticized the referee, Tony Perez—Frazier's side for not stopping the clinching, and Ali's for a key moment in which Perez had accidentally ended a round too soon, after Ali had stunned Frazier with a right hand and might have been able to go for a knockout. Even on the eve of the fight, Ali's and Frazier's teams and the boxing authorities could not agree on which of the candidates who'd been brought to Manila would be in the ring.

There was a uniquely Marcosian way of breaking the deadlock. According to Izenberg, when the parties met that night to finally settle the issue, one of the omnipresent Filipino military men placed a .45-caliber pistol on the bargaining table between the two sides and suggested that the referee be Filipino. The leading candidate was Padilla. At dawn on the day of the fight, the commission called Padilla's home to let him know he'd be the referee. But he had already left for the Coliseum to report for the undercard fights. After he arrived, he told me recently, an official said to get a move on; reporters were waiting for him. Confused, Padilla asked why. "Don't you know you're going to referee the Ali-Frazier fight?" was the answer.

He had never refereed a fight above the 135-pound weight class, and most of his experience had come in amateur gyms and converted cockfighting rings, which were small compared with a regulation heavyweight ring. "I said, 'Goddamn, it's big!'" Padilla recalled. He'd never had to give instructions to fighters in English, and his English wasn't so great. Trying to separate two

200-plus-pound men would be difficult for anybody, and at 5 foot 8, Padilla was diminutive next to Ali and Frazier.

I met Padilla at his home in Las Vegas, not far from Izenberg's. He's 91, still spry, and still wearing the same thick mustache that made him stand out in the ring. Padilla is fiery and prone to a "goddamn," a favorite expression. He was eager to show me a Facebook video, taken the year before, of him working a speed bag, sending it flying with a steady rhythm until it became a blur.

We talked in his living room, which was crowded with photographs and Catholic figurines. On the wall and in frames propped up behind me were pictures of Padilla's refereeing career, and of boxers who'd been in his orbit. In the middle were the highlights: photographs of Ali and Frazier squaring up in Manila, with Padilla looking on.

Long before that fight, boxing had been a prominent part of life in the Philippines. After America seized control of the archipelago from Spain in 1898, then brutally suppressed Indigenous rebellions, it exported American culture in the name of "civilization"—part of the "white man's burden," as Rudyard Kipling put it in 1899. As was true of colonialism's other exports, the intended subjects quickly made the art of boxing their own, subverting the original intentions. The legendary Pancho Villa won the world flyweight championship in 1923. In the 1960s, Gabriel "Flash" Elorde held the world super-featherweight title for seven years. Also trained in eskrima, the national martial art of the Philippines, Elorde embraced a boxing style—of "dancing" and maintaining distance while landing quick strikes—that influenced a young Muhammad Ali. When Ali floated like a butterfly and stung like a bee, he was likely channeling Elorde.

Padilla happily recounts his role in all of this history to anyone who'll listen. The morning of the match, he was nervous: He had never officiated anything with anywhere close to this level of attention. Then again, nobody had. The fight was held at 10 a.m. local time, in order to accommodate an expected global audience of hundreds of millions; it was likely one of the most-watched television events in history at that point. Many people who watched the match live paid to do so in movie theaters or arenas equipped with closed-circuit projectors. But nearly half a million viewers in the United States watched it live via satellite on a new network, HBO.

If Padilla got anything wrong, the error would be indelible. Just about every person in the Philippines would be watching. Hundreds had traveled to Manila just to be close to the action, even if they couldn't get into the arena. "They slept around the outside of the Coliseum," Padilla told me. "For boxing, Filipinos pause everything in life," Jay Gonzalez, a Manila-born boxing coach and academic, told me. He was 11 years old in 1975, and watched the fight in class on a television his teacher rolled in. He and his classmates were excited to watch two Black champions, feeling an affinity as people of color. It didn't hurt that the referee was Filipino.

Padilla endeavored to make his mark early. With the Marcoses looking on—seated in high-backed thrones that Padilla believes were bulletproofed to foil assassination attempts—he barked at both fighters, trying to project authority. It was almost unheard-of for a referee to disqualify a fighter in a heavyweight championship, and Filipino officials warned Padilla not to make history. But he was never demure. He told Ali that he would penalize him for illegal holds, and gave a warning to Frazier early on for a low blow. Padilla kept the fight brisk, a welcome change from the wrestling match that had transpired during the previous Ali-Frazier fight.

ALI COULDN'T HAVE known that Frazier was fighting one-eyed—that he had been fighting one-eyed for years, having lost most of his sight on his left side because of a cataract. He had made it past physicals by memorizing eye-test charts and tricking fight doctors, just as he'd shrugged off other injuries and ailments that would have sidelined other men. But now his right eye—the good one—was failing him.

After taking Frazier's punishment to his body and skull for the better part of 10 rounds, Ali started landing power punches more frequently around Frazier's face and right eye. Inflammation on each side of the socket met in the middle and began to shut it.

In the 13th round, with the eye swelling and bleeding, and with blood pouring from his mouth, an exhausted Frazier willed himself out of his corner, throwing blows that even a gassed Ali could avoid or ignore. Frazier could not see clearly, and his entire head seemed swollen, and Ali kept landing punches. He knocked Frazier's mouthpiece into the crowd, but somehow, miraculously, Frazier still stood.

ON A SWELTERING April night, I hailed a GrabCar and sped from the Manila airport to my hotel in Quezon City, one of the cities that make up the megalopolis of greater Manila and the site of the Ali-Frazier fight. Everywhere I looked, armed security guards crowded street corners and building entrances. The country's midterm elections were approaching, and violence around elections was not uncommon. Still, as guards and a bomb-sniffing dog checked the trunk for explosives outside my hotel, I sensed a bit of theater in all the security. The legitimacy of the government, now led by Ferdinand "Bongbong" Marcos Jr., the son of the two famed kleptocrats, still seems to rely on the appearance of safety more than anything else.

The next morning, I ducked into the cool refuge of the Araneta Coliseum, which had been temporarily renamed the Philippine Coliseum in 1975 before it hosted Ali-Frazier III. The white-domed arena, now gray with age and grime, didn't resemble its namesake so much as a spaceship, a Starship Enterprise plopped amid high-rises. Inside, the place that had been so hot as to be nearly unbearable on that morning 50 years ago was mostly empty, and the air-conditioning was cranked high enough to give me goose bumps. If I was looking for traces of Ali and Frazier, they might have been covered from my view: The venue was being prepared for a live show by performers from *RuPaul's Drag Race* the following night.

I left the Coliseum and walked around the corner to Ali Mall—built in honor of its namesake in 1976—and then to Gateway Tower, where I met Jorge Araneta, the leader of the empire that had built the Coliseum and the business district around it. He was 89 years old, still svelte and sharp in a patterned blue resort shirt, and still wearing the easy, confident air of authority. We sat at a round wooden table in his office and he picked up a stack of photo albums, all filled with snapshots taken during Ali's time in the Philippines. Araneta found a picture of two smiling men attending the dedication ceremony of the mall I had just visited. One was quite obviously Muhammad Ali. It took me a moment to place the young face of Araneta himself.

The Araneta clan had grown prosperous as sugar planters during Spanish rule, he told me. After their home was destroyed during World War II, his father took a trip to Rome and, upon seeing the Colosseum, had a spark of inspiration. "He said: 'I'm going to build the same,'" Araneta told me.

At the time of its completion, in 1960, the Araneta Coliseum was the largest building of its kind in the world. Its inaugural event was the super-featherweight title fight between Flash Elorde and Harold Gomes, when Elorde became the first Filipino in decades to capture a title.

When Marcos declared martial law in 1972, the elder Araneta, a prominent backer of the opposing Liberal Party, fled to New York. Jorge stayed behind and ran the business. When Marcos's regime needed a venue for what would be the biggest sporting event in the history of the Philippines, there was just one real choice. The regime's sole imposition was the temporary renaming of the building. In his office, Araneta laughed. "At least they gave it back," he said. "Some people would have kept it."

The Coliseum today has hosted everything from Boyz II Men concerts to the Miss World Philippines pageant, but it still carries a special association with combat sports: boxing, kickboxing, mixed martial arts. The Filipino boxing legend Manny Pacquiao, who recently returned to the ring after a four-year retirement, is planning an event commemorating Ali-Frazier at the Coliseum, fueling speculation that he might himself fight there. The arena is also home to an annual tournament billed as "the biggest cock-fighting event in the world." Blood still regularly stains the floors of the Coliseum's rings.

This is a fulfillment of the elder Araneta's vision. Inside the first Colosseum, the masses of Rome watched slaves and animals butcher one another. Brutality, coercion, and terror were always elemental parts of the entertainment. But there were also moments of transcendence mixed in with the gore—the beauty and creativity of martial arts, the thrill of the contest, the inquiry into human limits and potential. And there was always the chance that some fighter might one day, through repeated victories, win freedom from the fight.

Perhaps the importance of the Ali-Frazier match derives from the extremity of those blood-sport contradictions. Ali—or Richard Durham channeling Ali—would write just months after the fight that some part of him had always rebelled against the primal allure of his sport. "Like in the old slave days on the plantations," he wrote, "with two of us big black slaves fighting, almost on the verge of annihilating each other while the masters are smoking big cigars, screaming and urging us on, looking for the blood." But he, the race man's race man, had needed so badly to prove something in that ring that he'd tried to turn the entire Black community against someone he might otherwise call brother.

Frazier had needed to prove something too. In this, his last big bout, he had the opportunity to fight for a kind of freedom—freedom from torment and from constant comparison to his nemesis. But part of the reason the crowd was so rapt was the silent speculation—dreadful and giddy, and building in the final rounds—that he might face a gladiator's end.

FRAZIER CAME OUT of his corner in the 14th all but blind, rocking on unsteady legs. A knot on his forehead was growing by the second, and his mouth and both eyes were badly swollen. Ali went forward stiffly, his trunk and hips deeply bruised from Frazier's body blows. He seemed to struggle to lift his arms. Whatever well from which he'd drawn energy had gone dry.

Frazier couldn't defend himself, but he kept throwing wild, delirious punches. A few left hooks landed, but they didn't have much power anymore. Frazier kept tapping his own face, either to will himself on or simply to try to clear his limited vision. He almost entirely abandoned his guard. Ali threw wide, slow blows that arrived on Frazier's skull by telegraph. It was like he was punching underwater. But the punches kept finding home.

When they went back to their corners, Futch, Frazier's trainer, asked Frazier why he couldn't avoid Ali's winding punches. Frazier told Futch that he could no longer see Ali's right hand. Frazier was determined to finish the fight. But Futch had seen boxers die in the ring. Against Frazier's murderous protestations, he told Padilla to stop the fight.

After Padilla raised Ali's arm and declared him the victor, the champion collapsed in a heap. The crowd roared, launching into chants of "Ali! Ali! Ali!" His team helped him push himself up to sit slumped on his stool, his arms dragging toward the floor as if his fists were too heavy to carry, his head bowed between his knees. When it came time to talk to reporters, Ali wobbled, barely able to steady himself or hoist the trophy. He told Izenberg that this was the closest to death he'd ever been. In his recap of the fight, Ali mostly eschewed his usual bravado: "I was surprised Joe had so much stamina," he told a reporter. "He is the greatest fighter of all times, next to me."

"Except for you," the reporter replied.

"Except for me."

AS THE REFEREE, Padilla was one of the three people who submitted an official scorecard for the fight. All three had Ali up by a healthy amount going into the 15th round. Padilla said that even if Futch hadn't told him to do so, he probably would have called the fight. "Because Frazier was no more."

The unofficial scorecards from journalists were more favorable to Frazier. The Associated Press scored the fight even going into the final round. *The New York Times* gave Frazier eight of the first 11 rounds. "Going into the 15th round, I had Ali ahead by one point," Izenberg told me.

The general consensus is that Ali won the beginning of the fight and dominated the end, and that Frazier owned the middle. Frazier always maintained that Ali was too exhausted to fight the 15th, and that he could've won by a knockout if he'd just been allowed to fight.

After it was over, the Marcoses invited Ali to one of their many homes for the evening. They'd been pleased by the fight. In the Philippines, citizens rejoiced in it, and particularly in Padilla's presence. "President Marcos wanted a showcase to the world," Araneta told me. "What better show can you present than Muhammad Ali?" But the source of the regime's good fortune sat in silence at dinner in the palace, seemingly unable to eat.

Araneta hosted Ali at his home for lunch shortly after the fight. "He was very somber" and could "hardly walk," Araneta told me. "I wanted to uplift his spirits, and I said, 'Muhammad, I'm going to name a building after you.'" That woke Ali up, he said. The next year, Ali would come back for the opening of Ali Mall.

The mall was one small testament to what Ali meant in Manila and in other corners of the subaltern world. He wasn't all pageantry and promotion; people were genuinely inspired by his presence, his idealism, and his earned status as a symbol of resistance against empire. Even in the Philippines, where he dined with a butcher and entered the ring disfavored against Frazier, he is now revered—all part of the contradictions of the man. As President Barack Obama would say on the occasion of his death, Ali was "a name as familiar to the downtrodden in the slums of

Southeast Asia and the villages of Africa as it was to cheering crowds in Madison Square Garden."

Frazier didn't attend the Marcoses' after-party. He was too hurt to go, and probably too prideful. He sat in his dressing room, his face battered into a new shape. His son hugged him, and Frazier grumbled with his team about what might have been. "I was there, wasn't I?" he said.

Ask anyone what makes a human human, and they'll likely mention something to do with our brains. Maybe they'll say we stand alone in our capacity for language, or reason, or self-awareness, not knowing that science has chipped away at each of these presumptions. We suspect now that whales can talk; that crows can reason; that octopuses may be self-aware. But one thing that seems to be truly unique to Homo sapiens is this: We are the only animal with fists.

Perhaps the fist evolved as an anatomical accident, a by-product of the lengthened fingers and opposable thumbs that gave humans their unparalleled tool-grabbing dexterity. That's one theory. But compelling evidence suggests that the exact shape of the human fist evolved at least in part for punching. The theory would place the duality of human nature quite literally in our hands. On the one side, we have our instruments for the written word and our tools for daily diplomacy—for shaking hands or putting our palms up in peace. On the other side, we carry our most primal weapons.

In Jerry Izenberg's home, there is a shrine to the human arsenal: a case holding a single, cherry-red boxing glove. On the thumb of the glove, Muhammad Ali's famous, compact signature, scribbled in black marker. On the body of the glove, Frazier's larger, swooping signature. The souvenir, which Izenberg thinks was signed after Frazier's and Ali's retirements, might suggest a thawing of relations between the men. But there's some deception at play. According to Izenberg, the autograph seeker who'd first owned the glove had Ali sign first and then took it to Frazier, holding it so as to obscure Ali's mark while Frazier signed.

In the waning years of Ali's and Frazier's lives, friends and media figures tried to patch things up between the rivals. But they never really reconciled, and both men's lives were too abbreviated to let time do its healing. Like many of their peers in the pantheon of Black heavyweight boxing, they died relatively early, facing serious health and financial trouble.

Shuffling and diabetic, Frazier died broke in 2011, at the age of 67. As he had in Manila, Ali outlasted him, but again in Pyrrhic fashion. Parkinson's disease hollowed him out in front of the world's eyes, and he died at 74, in 2016, his own fortune having been diminished by friends and hangers-on.

There had been promising statements and portents—charity matches and television appearances—that made it seem like Ali and Frazier might finally rekindle their friendship, but all were false starts. Invariably, Ali would renege on his apologies.

In 2000, when Izenberg was working on a 25th-anniversary retrospective for the *Star-Ledger*, he interviewed his friend Ali by phone. "And he said, 'I don't know why he doesn't like me,'" Izenberg told me. "I said, 'Yes, you do.'" He reminded Ali about Frazier's children, who would come home from school crying when other kids teased them about their father being a gorilla or an Uncle Tom. "If Laila came home crying—'Daddy, they think you're a gorilla; you're an animal'—how would you feel about that?" he asked Ali, referring to Ali's daughter. Ali responded that he hadn't meant to hurt Frazier's family—again pleading that he hadn't quite understood the impact of his own words.

Izenberg later called Frazier to relay Ali's regrets. "Well, first of all, let him come and say that to me," Frazier told him. It was something of a cruel jab toward Ali, who by that point struggled to get around on his own, and to speak. Frazier, despite his own infirmities, took pride in the idea that his blows in Manila had contributed to Ali's Parkinson's—or even caused it—going so far as to gloat about the possibility on the outgoing voicemail message for his cellphone. "But secondly," he continued on the phone with Izenberg, "I ain't accepting no apology. You hurt my boy, and that's all there is to it."

There's a lifetime of what-ifs between the two signatures on the glove, of parallel realities where the two men did find common ground, and with it, a measure of peace. I envisioned how the glove might look if I squeezed it together, so that Ali's and Frazier's names finally found themselves side by side. But I realized that to do so would be to reconfigure the imaginary hand bearing the glove. It would disfigure the fist, our one uniquely human trait, and diminish that which makes us us.

VANN R. NEWKIRK II is a senior editor at *The Atlantic*, and the host and co-creator of the Peabody-award-winning podcast *Floodlines*. In 2024, Newkirk was named Journalist of the Year by the Washington Association of Black Journalists. He lives in Maryland with his wife, Kerone, and their two children, but will always be a Tar Heel.

For Black British Women Footballers, Hair Is a Matter of Pride and Precision

TAMERRA GRIFFIN

FROM *The Athletic* • OCTOBER 31, 2025

It was July 2024 during an England national team camp in the Netherlands, and goalkeeper Khiara Keating was facing a crisis that had nothing to do with her exploits between the sticks.

The 21-year-old had just used the last of her Gummy Wax, the quintessential ingredient to her signature bun when she plays, ensuring every last one of her strands stays in place for the duration of play.

Keating is a Manchester native who plays for City, and on October 25, she became the first Black goalkeeper to represent the Lionesses. She told *The Athletic* that she positions her bun high atop her head to take up more space inside the goal. This is her hair ritual, and in the environment of national team camps in elite sport, routine is paramount.

But without that Gummy Wax, there was no styling to be done—nor did there appear to be any alternatives within reach.

"She was hoping maybe that I brought Gummy Wax to camp," fellow Lioness and Tottenham forward Jessica Naz told *The Athletic*. But Naz, who alternates between braids and a high bun of her own, uses different products for her hair.

"She's like, 'Oh my God. I have none left. How the hell am I gonna slick my bun?'" Naz recalled.

That was how they found themselves on a trek to the closest shop they could find—in a place Naz called "the most dodgy area"—that sold the hair-styling product.

The matter of hair for many Black female footballers in the UK isn't as simple as a ponytail, a finger-swoop of gel and a headband or prewrap. Players such as Keating and Naz, alongside others of African descent, including Bunny Shaw, Kerolin, Lauren James, Sandy Baltimore, Michelle Agyemang, and Deanne Rose, have tapped into the rich heritage of Black hair culture that is their birthright.

By doing so, they've flipped that gaze around—not so much demanding to be seen as refusing to hide or blend in. With box braids, cornrows, extensions, sew-ins, or licked-back buns with intricately laid edges that swirl across the hairline, Black footballers are taking the "look good, play good" mantra to new heights.

It's unclear exactly how many Black footballers are in the Women's Super League. A league spokesperson told The Athletic they "do not hold that information centrally," but the eye test leaves no doubt that they, and players of colour, are in the minority.

That lack of diversity is also apparent at the national team level: of the 28 players called up to that July camp last year, four were Black. When England won the Euros in 2022, there were three Black players out of 23 on the roster. The figure improved to four in their repeat campaign this summer.

The disparity casts an inevitable gaze upon the relatively few Black female footballers who compete in the UK.

Keating's earliest memories of getting her hair done with her younger sisters were traumatic. "My mum's white, so she didn't really understand 'til we got a bit older...our hair used to knot way easier than her hair used to knot," she told The Athletic.

Keating's mum tried to brush through those knots when she encountered them—and it didn't go over well. "She never understood why we were crying, but then the older you get and the longer she keeps doing it, the more she understands."

Keating and her sisters began watching YouTube Black hair tutorials. "When you get into high school and you're around all your friends, you kind of get speaking to them, seeing how they do their hair on FaceTime and stuff," Keating added. (As Keating spoke, she kept her hands busy by twirling a tube of Topicals lip balm, a Black-owned skincare brand.)

As with Keating, Naz's mother was also the first to care for her hair, plaiting her and her sister's into cornrows, a simple style that didn't require young children to sit still for hours like box braids do. Naz, now 25, said back then it was more about looking neat and presentable than styled, necessarily.

With time, Naz said, "You're like, 'Oh, let's add some beads in it. Can I do different colours?' and all of that, so I think it got to a point where it was really exciting."

Long before they sit for a new style, Keating and Naz find joy in the scouting process. Keating and Shaw trade photos of trends on Pinterest and Instagram, and Naz has long drawn inspiration from other Black female footballers, especially when she started playing.

The pool of inspiration was shallower back then; there weren't many Black female footballers around. But now, Naz says: "I'll see someone else have a hairstyle and I'll be like, 'Oh, that's actually quite nice. I'm gonna try that next time.'"

Now that Naz and Keating are responsible for their own hair, they've hired stylists and braiders.

Naz also applies a relaxer to chemically straighten her natural curl pattern (a process her mum taught her) and alternates between pulling it back into a high bun and braids. Keating goes with her slicked-back bun when she's in season and usually saves her braids for longer stretches of time off; for the past three years, she's gone to the best friend of one of her aunties.

The first person to touch Naz's hair after her mum was a high-school friend who had opened up her own salon.

Booking hair appointments as a professional footballer is a complex exercise: braids, twists and extensions can take as long as six hours depending on the techniques employed.

Keating, who got extensions a day before her interview with The Athletic, had to travel to London to achieve the look she wanted. That's three or four hours on the train, plus the time it takes to install them. In those cases, players have to dedicate their full day off to beautification.

But even that is an imprecise science. Naz has lived in London all her life, with access to an array of Black hair stylists, but football is her priority. Any changes to her carefully crafted schedule trickle down.

"There have been times I've had to cancel my appointment, and then when I cancel, all the other slots have been booked," Naz said. Her last resort when this happens is to squeeze it in after training, sitting in the salon chair late into the night. Ideally, she does this when she has the following day off so she can sleep in.

Black hair aesthetics are deeply rooted in precolonial African traditions in countries and cultures across the continent, where adornments such as cowrie shells and braid patterns were imbued with meaning. Black hair can be manipulated into a variety of textures, shapes and lengths, and it can withstand a spectrum of colours.

The ability to embrace so many different looks (and embody the attitudes they carry) is a privilege many Black people embrace with pride. It's also proven difficult at times for other communities to understand or keep up with it—even as many adopt and appropriate those same styles for themselves.

When Keating arrived at City training after her latest hair appointment, "one of the Japanese girls, as soon as I walked in, her eyes were like…" Keating said, her own bulging wide on the screen of our Zoom call.

"'Cause she's never seen my hair down. She looked like she'd just seen a ghost, which was quite funny, but when I used to come in with braids, they all used to say it looked really sick."

Moments like that, Keating said, are due more to surprise at the switch-up than negative feelings about her hair. And with the diversity across the club, she's never the only one causing a stir like that. (In fact, when Brazilian striker Kerolin joined City last year from North Carolina in the NWSL, it was Keating who passed along her hair braider's contact when she sought recommendations.)

Other times, teammates ask questions that make Black hair feel like a spectacle, so the person asking can better distinguish what is "real" from what is not.

"A question I get asked a lot is, 'How long is your natural hair?' Or, 'Oh, does your hair feel heavy?' Because they always see me in extensions," Naz said. "Sometimes people have to be a bit cautious about some of the things they say."

Like Keating, Naz noted the strength in numbers; now that she has Black teammates such as Lenna Gunning-Williams, Drew Spence and Araya Dennis at Tottenham, there's less pressure to speak for the entire Black community.

Naz has also seen the way mainstream culture tends to move toward Black style, gradually normalising that which used to be considered exotic.

"Everyone in the changing rooms is using edge control brushes," she said. "Back then, everyone was asking, like, 'What's that? What would you use it for?' So, I think it's becoming a lot easier.

"People are a lot more cultured now, even wearing bonnets and do-rags and stuff like that."

TAMERRA GRIFFIN is a global women's soccer writer based in Northern California. She has covered the 2023 Women's World Cup in Australia and New Zealand, the Women's African Cup of Nations, and the Women's European Championship, among other international tournaments. She regularly reports on the National Women's Soccer League and the U.S. women's national team. Prior to soccer, she was an international correspondent based in Nairobi, Kenya, where she wrote about presidential elections and political movements, LGBTQ rights, and culture across East and Southern Africa.

A Stranger Shattered Their Lives. At First, They Didn't Know Why.

JULIET MACUR

FROM *The New York Times* • SEPTEMBER 28, 2025

For months after it happened, through sweaty South Carolina days and cooler starlit nights, even when the air eventually grew so chilly that she could see her breath, Katie Lesslie sat curled up in the cushioned porch swing of her white house in the woods, staring past her backyard and into the distance.

Images flashed through her head: her two children, Adah, 9, and Noah, 5, playing over there to her left, climbing on rocks and running wild on ground made soft by fallen pine needles.

Her father-in-law, clad in his doctor's scrubs, playing "Highland Cathedral" on his bagpipes outside his house.

Her mother-in-law, whose motto was "if it's worth doing, it's worth overdoing," in her kitchen cooking family favorites like B's favorite mud pie.

As Katie sat and thought, her husband, Jeff, brought her food. And fuzzy blankets. And boxes of tissues, to wipe away their never-ending tears as they searched for an answer to a question that had none.

Their life in Rock Hill, S.C., had been idyllic, rooted in Christian faith and service, and centered around a 50-acre family compound, a place the Lesslie clan called The Land.

Jeff's parents, Dr. Robert and Barbara Lesslie, bought the property in 2002, hoping that their four children would build houses of their own there.

The plot had been just brambles and loblolly pine trees planted in rows for future harvest. With long, slender trunks, the pines looked like an army of matchstick soldiers so tall that they touched the sky.

Dr. Lesslie had a wondrous vision for his real estate. Three ponds stocked with bass and bream. A stage and a field for music festivals. A little barn for mini-donkeys, mini-horses and goats. An 18-hole Frisbee golf course.

The anchor of it all would be a big brown house for him and his wife, and it would become known as the big house.

And then someone they had never met, someone they had never even heard of, showed up and shattered that bliss, leaving behind a level of pain that could break any family's bond.

'Where Are My Kids?'

Katie, a preschool teacher, was home for spring break on April 7, 2021, her 36th birthday. Recovering from a Covid shot, she was napping while her children were at the big house with their grandparents. Jeff was in town, running his hospice and palliative care business.

Around 4:45 p.m., the hysterical barking of the family labradoodle, Gibson, jolted Katie awake. She then heard police sirens growing louder.

She raced to the big house. A landscaper who had been mowing the lawn stopped her short. He was on a call to 911. Police cars were pulling in.

"Where are my kids?" Katie asked him.

He just said, "I'm sorry. I'm so sorry."

Two heating and air conditioning technicians, both fathers of three, had been shot in the driveway. One, James Lewis, was on the ground, motionless. The other, Robert Shook, had been shot multiple times, but somehow managed to call his boss to tell him what happened. He would later die from his wounds.

A police officer stopped Katie from getting any closer to her in-laws' house. The shooter had not been apprehended. She called Jeff and his sister Amy Kulbok, who also lived on the property.

For what seemed like hours, but was probably just 10 minutes, Katie waited at a cedar tree maybe 100 feet from the front door of the big house. She watched as troops of law enforcement officers swarmed the area.

SWAT teams, state and local police and teams of police dogs. The thump of helicopter blades droned from above, drowning out the chirping cicadas. Again and again, she shouted, "Where's the ambulance?"

As a police officer watched over her, a voice came over his walkie-talkie, too quickly for him to silence it.

"There were four people in the house," it said. "They're all gone."

Katie turned numb.

"I heard screaming and I couldn't figure out where it was coming from," she told me recently, in the family's first interview since the shooting. "And then I realized it was coming from me."

Katie joined Jeff and Amy on the adjacent county road. Jeff asked his sister, "Is it true?" She nodded.

He threw a water bottle at a tree. And then he grabbed another tree with both hands and dug his nails into its thick bark. He thought of the shooter and shouted, "Lord, forgive him!"

Amy, a trauma therapist with a master's degree in Christian counseling, had been standing behind Jeff, with her hand on his shoulder.

"That's how we're going to do this," she said. "That's how we're going to proceed."

The Crime Scene

Living in Rock Hill, known as Football City, U.S.A., the Lesslies were surrounded by the game, and many of them were fans of it.

For years, Dr. Lesslie had season tickets to the University of South Carolina and the Carolina Panthers. Jeff helped Adah memorize the Panthers' theme song.

The town of about 75,000 claims to have churned out more N.F.L. players per capita than any other town, locals say—so many that the Lesslies were not aware of all of them. They didn't know that a former N.F.L. player, Phillip Adams, was living with his parents a quarter-mile down the street.

Adams, a standout high school cornerback who went on to play at South Carolina State, was chosen in the seventh round of the N.F.L. draft and bounced around the league—six teams in all—from 2010 to 2015, before returning to Rock Hill.

After football, he lost his way. He struggled to find a new career. Responsibilities weighed on him. He helped care for his mother, Phyllis Paden-Adams, a teacher who became a paraplegic after a car accident. He also had a child to support.

Friends and family said Adams struggled with memory loss and mental health issues and had shown increasingly aggressive and erratic behavior.

And then on one warm spring day, Adams, 32, left his parents' house and hopped onto his blue four-wheeler, headed toward The Land. He was carrying two submachine guns.

He jumped over a fence, emerged from the woods, walked to the driveway of the big house and opened fire on Mr. Shook and Mr. Lewis, the HVAC workers.

As far as the Lesslie siblings—Jeff, Amy, Lori and Robbie—can surmise based on their mother's wedding rings sitting near the kitchen sink, she had been preparing a meal there, with Adah and Noah watching television behind her, when she looked through the window and saw Adams shoot the men outside.

She ran to lock the front door and rushed the children to the exercise room, where Dr. Lesslie was on his elliptical machine. Adams shot through a window, unlocked the door and followed them.

He shot Barbara Lesslie five times in the back as she tried to protect her grandchildren. He shot Dr. Lesslie seven times. The police later recovered two dozen spent bullet shells and projectiles from the property. Law enforcement officers who saw the crime scene were offered counseling.

Adams dropped his cellphone on his way out, and the police found him at his parents' house. Hours later, after a standoff, he shot himself in the head.

He had left no note, no explanation. He was not one of Dr. Lesslie's patients. Investigators found no connection.

"I think the football messed him up," Alonzo Adams, his father, told a local television station, raising the question of whether the head injuries he sustained during his career played a role in his decision to kill six strangers.

What followed has become something of a rite of passage for the N.F.L.'s deceased. A medical examiner extracted Adams's brain from his skull and shipped it on ice to a lab where neuropathologists would slice it, stain it, scan it and look for clues that might explain the former player's behavior.

Their goal was to find out if he had chronic traumatic encephalopathy, or C.T.E., the degenerative brain disease linked to repeated blows to the head in contact sports like football. Its symptoms include mood disorders, memory problems and impulsive behavior, and it has been found in hundreds of former football players.

'You and Me'

Each day felt endless as the Lesslie family tried to move forward against the swells of grief.

News helicopters circled above. Reporters called and visited, hoping to conduct interviews. Speculation about motives spread on social media.

The script was familiar for a mass shooting. Scrutinize the killer. Examine the victims' past. Await the reaction from the victims' families, be it uncontrollable sorrow or rage, or calls for gun control or retribution.

The Lesslies chose an uncommon path. Their initial public statement said that as followers of Jesus Christ, they were "enveloped by peace that surpasses all understanding."

They wrote: "To that end, our hearts are bent toward forgiveness and peace. Toward love and connectedness. Toward celebration and unity."

They wanted the public to know that they were not angry with Adams. There was no room for hate in their already bursting hearts.

Katie later described their ability to forgive, and forgive so quickly, as an inexplicable gift from God.

Amy said, "I see the preparations of God's handiwork for years and years in advance, kind of leading to where we are."

Growing up in Rock Hill, the Lesslies attended the First Associate Reformed Presbyterian Church each Sunday, and the four siblings said they felt loved, free and sometimes feral—as teens they hosted rowdy house parties with bands when their parents were away—and that it forged an inseparable bond.

Their Scottish clan motto is Grip Fast, and they were so close that they got similar tattoos: a figure that represented their mother, holding out her arms. Each of her children, as stick figures, were hanging from her.

Dr. Lesslie, who was 70, was a respected doctor: He worked in and directed emergency rooms for 25 years, started an urgent care center and opened a hospice service. He also was the author of a popular series of Christian-themed books that were often sold in airports, including one called *Angels in the E.R.*, about inspiring stories he had witnessed on the job.

Barbara Lesslie, 69, was a beloved staple at a place called Camp Joy, a Christian camp in the Blue Ridge Mountains of North Carolina. It serves adults and older teenagers with intellectual and developmental disabilities like autism or Down syndrome, and all the Lesslies, young and old, helped out there every summer.

Dr. Lesslie was known there as Dr. Rob, the camp doctor who would start the day by playing "Amazing Grace" on his bagpipes. Mrs. Lesslie was Ms. B, a Bible teacher, and her animated lessons were fueled by her time in community theater. She had long joked that she wanted her ashes scattered onto a Broadway stage.

Jeff, now the executive director of the nonprofit that runs Camp Joy, met Katie there more than 24 years ago when they were counselors.

"Something changed in me when I first went," Jeff said. "And then the Lord put his hooks in all of us."

After the murders, the Lesslies saw signs from God that comforted them. Lori, whose married name is Lori Alexander, found a note in their mother's Bible, written in their mother's cursive. The words on it were, "How to live in troublesome times," and "God controls our circumstances! God will meet our needs! God is with us!" and she mentioned Romans chapter 8, which promises deliverance despite current suffering.

On their father's night stand, the children found a book called *Suffering* by Paul David Tripp. One passage Dr. Lesslie had marked with a red star recommended that people avoid bitterness because "it erodes your motivation to do the good and constructive things that every sufferer needs to do so as not to lose his way."

One day, Jeff walked the grounds, winding his way through the orchards of apples, figs and pears, crying while pondering the idea that his parents were his past and his children were his future. Thinking about Adah and Noah, he asked God, "Show me, I just need to know they are OK."

He went into his silent house and climbed onto Noah's bed, burying his face in the little bear security blanket to soak in the scent of his son. Then he got on Adah's bed and hugged her green blanket.

Atop her stack of "Harry Potter" books, he found an empty notebook with a piece of paper tucked into it. On it was a song Adah had written called "You and Me."

You and Me…we can love one another. Even through the hardest times. Even through the darkest days, we can love one another. Even in the deepest fog, we will find one another and love each other. When people see us they will see Jesus Christ in You and Me.

It ended with "Ooh" written in big, rounded letters 16 times, and Jeff could hear his daughter singing it.

The Villain

Dr. Ann McKee, a neuropathologist at Boston University and the world's leading expert in C.T.E., has studied thousands of brains for the disease. She runs a C.T.E. brain bank at the V.A. Boston Healthcare System that is filled with them, most from former athletes who competed in contact sports.

Families hope she can find an explanation for their loved one's behavior. Why had that person turned into someone they did not recognize? Why had he become so paranoid and depressed? Why did he kill himself? And why, in a growing number of cases, did he decide to kill others?

To find answers, Dr. McKee and her team examine the brains with microscopes, magnifying glasses and scanners, while family members and other interested parties—like the Lesslies—anxiously wait.

It is an excruciating wait filled with fears and tears. A wait that Katie Lesslie mostly spent on her porch swing.

Eight months after the shooting, Dr. McKee delivered her report at a news conference held by the county coroner, and the Lesslie family gathered in Amy's living room to watch it.

Dr. McKee announced that Adams had stage 2 C.T.E.

She said that Adams's 20 years in football caused the disease, explaining that stage 2 was associated with aggression, impulsivity, explosiveness, depression, paranoia, anxiety, poor executive function and memory loss.

Dr. McKee called Adams's frontal lobe damage unusually severe, similar to that of another former N.F.L. player, Aaron

Hernandez of the New England Patriots, and that it might have contributed to his homicidal behavior. She pointed out, however, that there are usually multiple reasons a person becomes homicidal, and that physical, psychiatric and social factors can come into play.

In 2015, Hernandez was convicted of shooting and killing a man. He was 27 when he killed himself in prison.

"C.T.E. is the villain of this story," Amy decided. "This has to be it. This is the only thing that makes sense."

Two Versions of Grief

The Lesslie family met face-to-face with Adams's parents in August 2023 after many failed attempts to connect.

Rev. Dr. Carlton Brown, the Adamses' former pastor and a chaplain at the sheriff's office during the shooting, had brokered the meeting, hoping it would help both parties heal. Three pastors from three churches attended. All three said they were amazed by what they witnessed.

They gathered in a building across from the New Mt. Olivet A.M.E. Zion Church in Rock Hill, the Adams family's parish, and sat at a table in a large room with empty beige walls and beige vinyl floors. Jeff Lesslie broke the tension with a story.

He told Adams's parents that he had the clearest vision in his head of Adams, Adah and Noah. They are in heaven, and Adams is pushing the kids on a swing. He paused and said, "I am so sorry for your loss." He told them that he was relieved to have forgiven Adams while he was still alive.

Struggling to talk, Ms. Paden-Adams apologized and asked for forgiveness. But the Lesslies stopped her, saying it was not their fault. C.T.E. had turned Adams into someone else, they said. The families hugged and cried and said they had been praying for each other.

"We were living with a whole different set of grief, and theirs is a grief I can't understand," Katie said later. "But I do know what it's like to be a mama who lost her son. That is our level playing field."

Rev. Angela Boyd, the pastor of the New Mt. Olivet Church, said one of her lasting takeaways was that the N.F.L. should take better care of its players.

The N.F.L.

The whole Lesslie family started reading about C.T.E. when Adams's brain was sent to be studied. After years of research, Katie and Jeff wrote to Dr. McKee in the fall of 2024, asking to meet her. They said they wanted to learn about her C.T.E. studies on football players.

Katie went to the meeting in Boston with a list of more than a dozen questions, including: "What steps can be taken to care for players that are showing signs of C.T.E.? What steps can be taken to prevent C.T.E. in the first place?"

They now joke that they earned a Ph.D. in C.T.E. in the two days they spent with Dr. McKee and her team. They donned lab gear and watched her dissect and examine a brain. They listened to presentations about C.T.E. research and the brain bank program, and examined slides and images of Adams's brain.

The Lesslies left believing that football officials at all levels, especially those in the N.F.L. because of the league's extraordinary influence on the sport, had failed to protect Adams. If not for C.T.E., they said, the murders would not have happened.

"The question is, could it have been prevented, yes or no?" Jeff said of the shooting. "If yes, then you have to do something to fix it. And, based on everything we've seen and heard, we believe it was yes."

Adams's parents, through their lawyer who is handling a wrongful death lawsuit against South Carolina State and the N.F.L., declined to comment.

The N.F.L. declined to comment on the Lesslies' criticisms of the league. Instead, in an emailed statement, a spokesman said the league supports "the long-term health and well-being of every player, both on and off the field," including retirees with neurocognitive disorders.

Jeff misses football. But he said he can't watch again until the N.F.L. and football's youth, high school and college organizers do more to make the sport safer.

In particular, he and Katie said, families need to know more about C.T.E. so they can make an informed decision about their children's participation.

In Rock Hill, tackle football starts at age 7.

"Your son, who's 7 now, looks so adorable and real cute in that jersey and huge pants," Katie said. "But you know what could happen? That 7-year-old could turn 32 and walk a quarter of a mile down the road and kill six people. That's the danger of football."

The Land

After the shooting, the Lesslies were drawn to the big house.

Lori, an assistant high school principal who lives in Georgia, had the bullet holes repaired and slept in the bedrooms, determined to preserve it as a happy place. Jeff played his guitar there, singing tunes he used to sing to Adah and Noah at bedtime.

Katie told no one that she was sneaking off in the mornings, before sunrise, to work out on the rowing machine in the big house's exercise room. Its stained and damaged flooring had been replaced.

She would row and row, focusing on Adah, her insatiable reader who had tackled *Little Women* at 7, and Noah, her boisterous butterball of a boy who was always trying to make people laugh with physical comedy.

At times, Jeff and Katie wanted a break from the memories. Their house, especially its two vacant bedrooms, sometimes made Katie physically ill. Jeff had flashbacks whenever he heard bullfrogs croaking. That sound had been so loud the days after the shooting as he walked the well-worn path from his house to Amy's.

But the agony followed them away from home, too, where people often ask them, "Do you have children?" Sometimes they say yes, they have two, and they are waiting for them in heaven. Other times, when they don't want to make someone feel uncomfortable, they do something that feels so wrong. They answer, "No."

Knowing they could not escape their sorrow, they all chose not to move away from the property Dr. Lesslie had officially christened with the name Siochain. In Gaelic, it means peace.

One of Jeff's best friends bought the big house, and Jeff still has the key. He goes there when his friend is out of town to house sit or walk the dog. When inside, he slides his hands along the walls. He lies on the floors.

The Land has a way of absorbing grief, the family said.

Yet the emptiness lingers.

JULIET MACUR has been a reporter at *The New York Times* for more than two decades. After graduating from the Columbia University Graduate School of Journalism in 1997, she was a sports reporter at newspapers in Orlando and Dallas before moving back to the Northeast in 2004. She lives outside of Washington, D.C., with her husband, daughter, and rescued Labrador mix who snoozes under her desk when she writes.

Bucky Irving, Tom Moore and a Unique NFL Player-Coach Relationship

DAN POMPEI

FROM The Athletic • JUNE 26, 2025

TAMPA—It's outer-space silent at 5:30 a.m., except for a few birds chirping at the suggestion of dawn.

Tom Moore, who would be on the Mount Rushmore of NFL assistant coaches if there were one, has been sitting at his desk at One Buc Place for more than two hours. He is going over a stack of plays higher than a seven-layer cake when in walks Bucky Irving, the day's first ray of light.

"I just come to check on my dog, make sure you doing all right," Irving says.

"Just doing my therapy," Moore says, pointing to his work.

Moore and Irving are people of routines, and this routine plays out every morning the Bucs gather. When Moore was a boy, his father, Howard, taught him to leave early enough to change a flat tire and still arrive on time. For decades, the Bucs' senior offensive assistant has been getting to work at 3:15. Irving, a second-year running back whose phone is always set to DND, is in bed by 9:30. He doesn't need an alarm to be up at 4:50. His first stop at work is Moore's office.

Sixty-four years separate them, but seeing them together you'd never know it. Moore, born before a U.S. flag was raised on the beachheads of Normandy, is 86. Irving, who came into the world after the Twin Towers fell, is 22.

Irving inquires about Moore's wife, Emily, and their dogs. Moore tells him about Patsy, a rescue named after Patsy Cline; when people wonder what kind of dog she is, Moore says she is a "Carolina Brown," as fitting a description as any. They thought Patsy was shy, so they gave her a companion, a Sheltie named Reba (as in McEntire).

Moore tells stories about players he's coached. He says that before every game, Barry Sanders ate one green apple. Irving, who has been compared to Sanders by NBC analyst Rodney Harrison and others, says he eats a bowl of Cinnamon Toast Crunch. They look at one another and smile—not like coach and player, maybe more like grandfather and grandson.

Bucs coach Todd Bowles says he understands their connection because he saw the animated movie *Up*. "Their relationship is kind of like the old man and the little Boy Scout kid in that movie," Bowles says. "Somehow, they formed this unlikely bond. I mean, it's coach-player, but they're damn best friends too, and I love it."

Irving and Moore might seem like an odd couple, but if you knew them, you'd understand.

On the back right side of Irving's neck is a tattoo of three crosses. One represents his father, Marcellius Washington, who was killed—shot, and stabbed three times—when Irving was 2. Another signifies his grandmother Darlene Irving, who died at 59 when Bucky was a junior in high school. The third is for his half-brother Jordan Raybon, who was shot and killed when he was 16, when Irving was a freshman at the University of Minnesota.

Irving wonders how it would have been different if his father had lived. He has asked his mother, Latisha Irving, what his father was like, and what he would have thought about him. But he doesn't think of what he's been through as injustice. He thinks of it as incentive. "The things I had to see growing up made me pray to God every day that I could go in a different direction and not get caught up in the things that were going on around me," he says. "I feel everything happened for a reason and God gave me some challenging things to go through so I could get where I am now. I know they are watching over me and really proud."

When he was 5, Irving started playing organized football for the Hazel Crest Mustangs in suburban Chicago and led them to their first championship in about two decades, Latisha says. Bucky was usually the smallest kid in his grade, but he played at a level with kids who were older than him.

At Hillcrest High, he played wide receiver, quarterback, defensive back and kicker in addition to running back. In two seasons, he had 3,264 rushing yards and 587 receiving yards.

After one year at Minnesota, Irving left in search of an offense that was a better fit. He found it at Oregon, where he had 2,238 rushing yards, 712 receiving yards and 21 touchdowns in two seasons.

NFL scouts were skeptical though, partly because he is 5-feet-9, 192 pounds, and partly because his combine performance—4.55 40-yard-dash, 29.5 vertical jump, 9-7 broad jump—wasn't as impressive as his tape. "I'm not really a guy that's into running around in T-shirts and drawers out there," Irving says. "I'm a guy that plays real football."

Five running backs were chosen ahead of him in the 2024 draft, and he wasn't picked until the fourth round. "You know, we're kind of small people, but we've got big hearts," says his mother, who is 4-11. "Sometimes people underestimate you, and that was really stressful to him because it meant so much to him. But I just prayed that he end up where he wanted to be, and he loves it in Tampa."

That became evident during his rookie season when Irving averaged 5.4 yards per attempt, the third highest in NFL history among rookies with at least 200 carries. Of his 1,514 combined yards, 609 came after forcing missed tackles, second most in the NFL last season, according to Next Gen Stats. His 4.03 average in yards after contact per rush led the league, according to The 33rd Team.

"He's blessed," says Moore, who defers to running backs coach Skip Peete when it comes to Irving's technique and fundamentals. "He has great vision, the ability to make people miss and can go the distance."

Irving's production last season was especially impressive considering he started only three games and had fewer carries than 18 running backs. This year, his opportunities are likely to increase substantially. Bowles says he expects greatness, as the game has slowed down for Irving and he's improved his footwork and pass protection. "He got to where he needed to be, but his footwork wasn't always the cleanest last season," Bowles says. "He's cleaned that up."

Irving lights up a room as easily as a scoreboard. His mother, a chef who is changing the name of her catering company to Bucky Soulfood & Catering, says her son always had a warm, welcoming spirit.

"I always try to bring others up, ask how they doing or joke around a little bit," says Bucky, whose idea of a hobby is taking walks. "You never know if somebody's having a hard day."

Bucs receiver Chris Godwin has been taken by Irving's smile. Bowles, Peete and others sometimes see that smile when he pops into their offices after he sees Moore. "He's the most outgoing, gregarious person," Moore says. "He just loves life."

When Irving was at Minnesota, coach P.J. Fleck gave him a figurine of Mr. Incredible, the Pixar superhero with superhuman strength and stamina, because he wanted Irving to play like Mr. Incredible might. Irving fulfilled his coach's wish and still carries the figurine with him to every game, an old soul with an action figure in his backpack.

IRVING IS BEGINNING a journey that Moore has survived better than almost anyone.

Moore was a backup quarterback and kicker at the University of Iowa so long ago that, Bowles teases, he shared a backfield with Moses. In the early 1960s Moore served in the Army, including a period as an officer in Korea, where he was the head coach of the First Cavalry Division football team. It was the only time he was a head coach. He's won four Super Bowl rings as an assistant, coming 42 years apart—two with the Terry Bradshaw–led Steelers, one with Peyton Manning's Colts and one with the Tom Brady Bucs.

In 1975, Moore unknowingly increased his chances of survival in the coaching world by aligning himself with a quarterback from Parkside High in Jackson, Mich. Moore, then the offensive coordinator at the University of Minnesota, successfully recruited him then tamed his wild streak. He later convinced the Steelers to sign him as an undrafted free agent and converted defensive back, then helped him get into coaching and eventually worked alongside him and, later, for him.

Of all the relationships Moore has had with players, that one with Tony Dungy is the most similar to the one he has with Irving, he says. When Moore arrived at work in the small hours, Dungy would sometimes be waiting outside in the cold for him to let him in so they could visit. "He loved football like Bucky," Moore says.

Says Irving: "Every day he gives me advice to keep my head on straight, not to get comfortable and stay humble." On the grease board in Moore's office are six words that Moore believes lead to many downfalls. He and Irving talk about them regularly.

1. GREED. Moore has advised Irving to not confuse contentment with compensation. He told him when he started working for the Steelers, he was one of six assistant coaches on staff, each of whom was paid the same yearly salary: $28,000. All of them were more focused on the next Super Bowl than on the next pay raise.

2. JEALOUSY. Moore has coached players who see others' statistics and become disenchanted. He warns Irving not to be like them. Eighteen NFL running backs had more carries than Irving last season, but he says he was not frustrated. "I've never been the type of guy to go to a coach and ask for more carries," he says. "I want everybody in the room to have success and as long as we get the win, I'm happy."

3. BOREDOM. To Moore, champions don't become champions without rehearsing the same mundane steps repeatedly and without wearing out the rewind button on a remote control. Being invulnerable to boredom, Moore says, enabled Brady to win a Super Bowl with Moore when he was 43. "I don't think Bucky will get bored," Moore says. "No. 3 won't get him." Says Irving, "For real."

4. DEATH BY INCHES. Many start to get comfortable and cut corners, Moore says. Moore remembers the 13 years he coached Manning, saying the quarterback prepared for the last game they were together just as he had for the first. Even though Manning knew shortcuts, he didn't take them. "It's easy to say, 'I know it all, I'll watch three hours of tape instead of five,'" Moore says. "Peyton didn't, and that's why he was great."

5. B—-ING. The 2021 Bucs had a lot to complain about, but they weren't complainers. That's a reason, Moore has told Irving, he believes they won the Super Bowl during the COVID-19 pandemic. "We had every situation possible you could complain about," he says. "We had half the guys dressing in the indoor facility and an outdoor shower for them. It was like a MASH operation. We had a trip from hell when we got to the airport at 1:30 and didn't get to Charlotte until 11 at night. But I never heard one player or coach b—- the entire season."

6. AGENDAS. Moore has seen many assistant coaches become preoccupied with a promotion, or with becoming a head coach. He could have been one of them, having interviewed and been a runner-up for head-coaching jobs with the University of Minnesota and the Detroit Lions.

The closest he came to having an agenda was wanting to coach pro football in 1974. He told Irving about leaving the University of Minnesota to join the New York Stars of the World Football League. But the Stars struggled financially and didn't pay Moore for six months. A $5,000 loan from fellow coach George Perles and an offer to return to the University of Minnesota saved him, and he learned a lesson. Since then, he's been pleased with his role, whatever it has been.

With the Bucs, he takes a macro look at the offense, sharing ideas on pass concepts, the red zone and third-down situations. And he does much more, including contributing to the defense. "When Tom has something to say, you listen because he doesn't speak all the time," Bowles says. "When he sees that I'm agitated, he calms me down."

As long as Moore can share his passion, the light within continues to shine.

"BUCKY.... MY GREAT Grandson."

That's what Irving wrote on the grease board in Moore's office. Beneath it is his phone number.

Moore has two children, two grandchildren, three step-grandchildren, and two great-grandchildren. Irving has had a stepfather since he was 12. His high school coach, Morgan Weaver, also treated him like a son, taking him to visit colleges and sharing life lessons.

But the bond between Moore and Irving, in a league often devoid of sentimentality, is unlike any other.

"I just look at him like the grandfather I always wanted to have, who knows about football and can coach you in football," Irving says.

When players like Irving trust Moore the way he does, it makes his life's work seem worthwhile. "I love the kid," he says.

Before games, Moore stands beneath a goalpost to watch warmups. As Irving talked with Moore in the end zone before one game, a photographer took their picture—Irving with his arm around Moore, one of them with so many yards ahead of him, the other with so many yards behind.

Irving made two copies of the photo. One is in his locker. The other, framed, sits on Moore's cabinet behind his desk. It's the only photo in his office.

DAN POMPEI is a senior writer for The Athletic who has been telling NFL stories for four decades. He is in his 20th year as a voter for the Pro Football Hall of Fame. In 2013, he received the Dick McCann Memorial Award—since renamed the Bill Nunn Award—for long and distinguished contributions to pro football.

Joel Embiid Sees You

DOTUN AKINTOYE

FROM ESPN • JULY 16, 2025

It has taken months to get here. Months of waiting, for Joel Embiid to play, for him not to play, for him to decide what, if anything, he wants to say about a season that once seemed so full of promise.

We're in his piano room. He's leaning back on a couch that seemed spacious until he eased his long body onto it. He's wearing a matching set—pinstriped shorts and a camp collar shirt. His son, Arthur, peeks around corners from the hallway to see what we're up to. His wife, Anne de Paula, is upstairs preparing for her birthday celebration that evening. Decorations are being arranged in his dining room. It's the end of March, nine days before the knee surgery that will likely decide Embiid's basketball fate.

He used to have fun with interviews. Before he ever played a game in the NBA, while he spent two years on the shelf rehabbing from surgeries to his right foot in the summers of 2014 and 2015, he was a media darling, both wry fabulist and helpless confessor.

But not after this past year. These days, he's wary, a little distracted by the Phillies game he's watching on his phone. I wonder if he might politely show me the door. We make small talk for a bit. He looks bored.

He does this with new people—gives little of himself, pretends not to watch while he weighs and measures.

I ask if we can start, on the record. He agrees.

Embiid has many reasons to call this off. He thinks explaining himself will be distorted into defending himself, which will be caricatured as complaining. And look around—his second child, a daughter, is on the way. His parents are taken care of. His family is secure for generations. He's an inspiration in Cameroon.

We're inside his lavish stone colonial, a mansion that sits perched atop a gently sloping hill in the Philadelphia suburbs. The hand towels in at least one of his 11 bathrooms are monogrammed with his initials—what does he have to complain about?

"I care about how I'm going to be remembered when it comes to basketball, but not as a man," Embiid says. "As a man, you can't tell me nothing."

We're a few feet from each other, and I find myself edging forward in my chair to hear him. His voice is so small it seems to emphasize his other dimensions. This is the inward, solitary Joel Embiid, known by very few.

His friends are protective, verging on paranoid. They see Embiid as he sees himself, as someone beset on all sides. Which is to say, they love him on his terms.

"When you have his trust, it's kind of intoxicating," one says. "It's like you just penetrated this force field that nobody gets to be in."

So I ask him right away, "Who do you trust?"

"Hmm," Embiid says, seconds of silence passing by. "I mean, uhh."

He looks at me, a sharpening of his attention seems to ask: *What do you think you know?*

"I've never been the one to have a lot of friends," he says finally. "And even then, with the ones that I consider close, I never try to go deep into anything."

"Why?" I ask.

"A quiet family. Dad, extremely quiet. Mom, quiet too.... From the moment that I was really young, you could never really open up about anything."

He expects me to understand. We're both from the same part of the world, neighboring countries in West and Central Africa. We run through our short diaspora litany together: Beatings. Demanding fathers. Mothers more than their match.

What it is to be loved by such people: "You know they love you.... But it is not all love like, 'Come here and give me a hug.' That's not happening. I never got any of that."

The need to defend them: "The way I was raised is also one of the main reasons why I'm here."

The need to renounce them, too: "The way I was raised is not the way I'm raising my kids."

Maybe it's the background we share. Maybe it's because he started therapy in the fall. Maybe it's the six months he has spent in the basketball void—his fans on the verge of mutiny, his relationship with the 76ers shot through with strife, the late prime of his career interrupted by a lost season at 31 years old, just as he seemed to attain the full flowering of his brilliance—maybe now he needs to talk.

Everyone else is. The Embiid discourse, let's call it; a narrative meant to assign a verdict of blame for why Embiid's transcendent ability has not produced a championship or even a Finals appearance. And there are summary statements bubbling now, too, career obituaries. The Ringer, citing his injuries, recently ranked Embiid—who was league MVP in 2023—as the 84th-best player in the NBA. Bleacher Report has him at 66th all time.

After surgery to repair his meniscus in February 2024, Embiid spent the 2024–25 season either recovering from or playing through pain. He played just 19 games and looked like himself in only a fraction of those. Now, he's in the middle of what he's rightly calling the "most important" offseason of his life, rebuilding his body again, preparing to launch into what he hopes will be, if all goes well, his final chapter as an elite-level player. It's not hysterical to wonder about the end—we might be watching it. And if we are, then what has Joel Embiid been?

He's been misunderstood. He's not blameless in that. He's been dominant, and then hobbled or absent. He's been resented for that.

Even his most painful grief has been thrown in his face. At the start of Embiid's rookie season in 2014, his 13-year-old brother Arthur was hit by a truck and killed. The day Arthur died, Embiid ignored a series of phone calls. When he finally answered, it was terrible news.

Even now, phone calls can send a tremor through him, a quicksilver slice of panic—someone is dead. In fact, he rarely answers texts or calls. His notifications are turned off.

Those who need to reach him do so through his assistant or his wife. His replies can take months.

"I have a reputation of being not a good texter," Embiid tells me, adding that he probably has 10,000 unread messages.

"You're kidding," I say.

He reaches for his phone, taps the screen and leans forward to show me. More than 9,500 unread texts and 875 missed calls. Some of the messages are years old.

"I just can't do it," he says, sitting back.

I ask who this annoys most in his life.

"Everybody," he says.

EMBIID IS GETTING comfortable, stretching his legs. I ask him why some people who adore him have jokingly called him an a--hole.

"I like to troll a lot," he says. "I wouldn't say I'm an a--hole."

He thinks on it for a second, then concedes, "At times, I can be an a--hole."

I first met Embiid in Chicago late last year, after he returned from a seven-game absence due to left knee issues. Loose, jovial talk filled the visitors locker room at United Center, an air of celebration. Sixers veteran guard Kyle Lowry ordered four trays of wings from Chicago's famous Harold's Chicken.

After a cold start against the Bulls, Embiid looked like himself in an eight-point victory. Lithe and destructive, a one-man revolution of hybrid plays who has layered skill on skill for years. Watch him think his way around the court, moving, as he did that afternoon, between low-post bully to midpost spinning fadeaway artist to metronomic rise-up shooter at the elbows and nail. See the film study, the drills, the painstaking work. This is talent working on itself, shaping and reshaping.

He outscored the Bulls by himself in the second quarter.

His offense was a sideshow compared to what he did to then-Bulls guard Zach LaVine late in the second. LaVine attacked Embiid downhill off a screen, swerving left and wrong-footing Embiid. What happened next happened very slowly and very fast all at once. Embiid whirled, turning his back to LaVine for a moment. Against 99% of the NBA, LaVine wins the duel from this position. But Embiid came out of his twirl between LaVine and the rim. They jumped together, Embiid's momentum carrying him backward, a high hand turning what looked like a LaVine dunk into a contested miss.

No coach in the world would teach that. No drill can prepare you for it. At Embiid's best, there's no one to compare him to. Not Nikola Jokić or Luka Dončić or Shai Gilgeous-Alexander, who for all their offensive gifts can't turn the interior of the defense into a black hole. Not Giannis Antetokounmpo or Anthony Davis, who for all their versatility can't ascend into a trance of pure jump shooting.

You could feel it in the locker room; if Embiid were healthy enough to play like that, this team could achieve anything. It was early December, and there was still enough time to hope.

Embiid eyed the Harold's Chicken spread, plucked a wing and walked to his locker. After a wait, he fronted the media scrum.

I asked him how he found a rhythm after starting 0-for-7 from the field. Postgame white noise.

"I just got lucky and started making shots," Embiid said.

Refusing to smarten up, I asked, "Does it really feel like luck?"

"Yeah, it is luck."

I stood directly in front of him. His expression was frozen in an affectation of boredom. He held that for a tense second before a smile started to play at the corners of his mouth.

Everyone cracked up.

This is a perquisite Joel Embiid experience, one where he decides how full of it you are by watching as you try to discern how full of it he is.

During his freshman year at Kansas, Embiid would sometimes pretend his English wasn't good enough to understand what people were saying. He started to tell an exoticizing story in those days, that as a boy in Cameroon, he wandered alone into the jungle and killed a lion as a rite of passage.

"People actually believed him," his college coach, Bill Self, recalls. "There was a lot of things that he would do in fun, but I never knew him to be much of a talker as far as expressing true feelings."

The jokes worked as shelters, places to hide himself. Instead of being known, he subsisted on being known as clever.

Watching him in the locker room in Chicago, I imagined him looking at his college teammates, trying not to smirk at their credulity. A reporter asked how hard he worked to get back for this game.

"Trust the process," Embiid said, referencing the Sixers' 2013–16 tanking strategy from which his nickname derives. His smile is gone.

But stony hostility doesn't suit him. He's sensitive, about to display his wounds. "I got to give short answers, because when I give long answers, they try to twist my words," Embiid said, turning to a couple of teammates.

"Good answer! Good answer!" Tyrese Maxey called out from his locker.

We stood in the aftermath of a galling media cycle. It started in late October when a *Philadelphia Inquirer* writer mentioned Embiid's son and his late brother in a column chastising Embiid's lack of professionalism and inability to stay in shape. The column implied there was a gap between Embiid's conduct and his public statements about playing to honor his brother's memory.

"I've done way too much for this city, putting myself at risk," Embiid responded days later. "I've done way too much for this f---ing city to be treated like this."

When the columnist showed up in the locker room the next day, the two men came face to face. "The next time you bring up my dead brother and my son again, you are going to see what I'm going to do to you," Embiid said. The altercation ended when Embiid shoved the columnist and Sixers staff stepped in between them. The NBA suspended Embiid three games without pay.

Months later, the column still gnaws at him.

"I don't care if the NBA wants to fine me $1 million, $2 million, $5 million, $10 million, I would still do it," Embiid says. "If he walked up to me just like he did, I would push him away again."

Embiid hasn't stopped blaming himself for leaving his brother in Cameroon to play basketball in 2011. Francois Nyam, one of his agents in 2014, called Embiid the night Arthur died. He says the first thing Embiid managed to say after sobbing was, "That's my fault. I'm a piece of s---."

Embiid's family had planned to be together on draft night in 2014, but after Embiid's first foot surgery, doctors told him not to fly. He remained in Los Angeles at his agent's home while Arthur stayed with family friends on the East Coast before returning to Cameroon. The accident happened nearly four months later. The brothers hadn't seen each other in three years.

"It's never going to change," Embiid says, all but whispering. "I still feel it."

WEEKS AFTER THE locker room altercation in November, the Sixers held a closed-door meeting to address the team's calamitous 2–11 start.

Details of the meeting leaked the following day. Maxey, whom Embiid considers one of his best friends, confronted Embiid about being late for team events and dragging the morale of the group down.

Embiid told a reporter, "Whoever leaked that is a real piece of s---." He reportedly vowed to find the source.

"I know who leaked it," Embiid tells me during a late-night phone call after the season ends.

"You do?"

"Yeah, but I'm not going to—the past is the past," Embiid says. "The one thing I'll say is, it's hard being around people that do those sorts of stuff.

"That goes back to the trust thing. Once you cross that—you can't expect me to be part of a team meeting again. That's just not going to happen."

"The way you're talking, it sounds like this person is still around," I say.

"I don't know," he says.

"Come on, Joel, you know who's on your team right now," I say, laughing.

"Free agency just started," he says. "I don't know what's going on."

"So there's a chance this person may not be around next season," I say.

"No," he says. "There's a chance they're still around."

Take a sentimental journey: A young Joel Embiid watches Kobe Bryant win his fourth championship in 2009 and falls in love with basketball. He starts playing seriously at 16. In July 2011, he is discovered at a camp in Yaoundé, Cameroon's capital and Embiid's hometown. He leaves his family behind and moves to the U.S. as a raw but gifted prospect two months later. He improves at a miraculous rate, is recruited by several elite programs and ends up at Kansas after witnessing Late Night in the

Phog in Lawrence. He is the No. 3 pick in the 2014 NBA draft. You know the rest.

It's a fairy tale, one that obscures a period of profound rupture for Embiid. He was first shepherded by then-NBA player and fellow Cameroonian Luc Mbah a Moute and Nyam to Montverde Academy, a prep school west of Orlando, Florida. After struggling for playing time his first year, Embiid was relocated again, this time to The Rock School in Gainesville, Florida.

With the help of his new coach at The Rock, Embiid moved in with a host family. Marcy Hansen's first thought when she saw 18-year-old Joel Embiid was that there was no way he would be able to sleep on her daughter's recently vacated twin mattress.

He was nearing 7 feet tall. His accent was thick, his English halting. If someone asked him what city he lived in, the best he could come up with was "Florida." Hansen noticed quickly that he was struggling. He would lie to his parents on the phone, insisting he was well, then sink into a morose silence.

There has always been something lonely in Embiid, something he can't quite explain. One of his most vivid childhood memories is of visiting France on a family vacation around the age of 12. But while everyone left to go sightseeing, Joel stubbornly holed up in his aunt's apartment, playing video games. His parents left him out of subsequent family trips to France, bringing just his two siblings.

"From then, it never really changed," he says.

Hansen was desperate to cheer him up and connect with him. She made him chocolate chip cookies and brought him Chinese takeout for lunch. She hoped her son would bond with him over basketball, but Joel was too closed off.

"It felt weird for me," Embiid remembers. "I got there, one of the first things that I saw was guns."

Hansen's husband, Ric, is a veteran and an avid hunter. Embiid's father, Thomas, was an officer in Cameroon's military, but Embiid didn't know people lived with so many guns in their homes.

"I don't think anybody understands my point of view," Embiid tells me. "Why I was reserved and why I liked to be in my room, why I tried to lock the door...I was kind of scared."

Basketball was little consolation. Embiid hardly bonded with teammates; they noticed the distance and left him alone. He told his coach he had preferred the dorms at Montverde, where he roomed with another international student who also spoke very little English.

"He was thrown into a totally different world and then thrown into another world, within a year," Hansen says. "He probably didn't let us in as much as I would have liked."

Eventually, Ric Hansen approached Embiid's coach, and they arranged for Joel to move in with one of the team's assistant coaches.

Memories of Embiid from this period are often bright and vivid and totally superficial: He was in the room, he was friendly, tall, he ate something sweet, he didn't seem to be paying attention until he would supply a sharp quip, surprising people. He is beloved, missed, cheered from afar.

Nothing was above Embiid's suspicion, not even evaluations of his talent. "He didn't know that he was going to be a D-I player, which is kind of crazy to me," says Freddy Bitondo, a friend and former Rock teammate. "He would tell me stuff, like, 'If basketball don't work, I'll just go to a school for four years and find a job.' And I'm looking at him, like, 'Yo, you're killing us in practice; what are you talking about, bro?'"

When he arrived at Kansas, Embiid was convinced he would redshirt as a freshman and spend five years in school. "You're going to be the best guy I've ever had," Self told Embiid.

By the end of his freshman season in spring 2014, Embiid was a projected No. 1 pick. He went to Self and confessed he didn't feel ready. He didn't know how to eat healthy. He didn't even know how to drive.

"I actually decided to stay," he says. "In my head, I was like, 'I don't deserve this. I only averaged 11 points.' I didn't know much about basketball. I didn't understand how the whole system worked."

But those closest to him—his father, Mbah a Moute and Nyam—told Embiid it was time to go. He packed his bags and moved to his agent's mansion in Los Angeles.

While there, recovering after his first navicular bone surgery, Embiid remembers returning late one night and realizing he didn't know the security code to get back inside. So, he did what any teenager might do: He jumped the fence, his surgically repaired right foot still in a cast, and set off the intruder alarm.

He was, at the time, less than three years removed from the JV team at Montverde, where he once caught an outlet pass alone under the basket, only to leap cluelessly in the air, past the backboard and out of bounds. His life was being accelerated at a speed he could not comprehend, propelled by a story about himself he did not believe, supplied by people he did not trust.

"I never knew how good I was," Embiid says. "What are these people talking about? What am I going to do about it? Am I going to believe what they say?"

THE MOMENT ADAM Silver announced Embiid as the No. 3 pick in the 2014 NBA draft, ESPN's feed cut to Embiid staring blankly into the camera.

"He seems confused," Bill Simmons, an ESPN columnist at the time, said on the broadcast. "Get Joel some coffee."

Embiid later explained that the tape was delayed, and the broadcast eventually played his actual reaction—he pumped his fists and smiled. But in some ways, he has never fully caught up to that delay.

Embiid and the 76ers waited two years for his foot to heal. Reports at the time claimed that he hadn't been taking his rehab and nutrition seriously. His third year in the league (but first on the court) was cut short by a meniscus tear in the same left knee that troubles him now. A couple of weeks after the 76ers shut him down that season, he jumped on stage at a Meek Mill show, ripped off his shirt and danced to the sound of cheers. The 76ers president of basketball operations at the time, Bryan Colangelo, scolded Embiid publicly. Embiid had "crossed a line, perception-wise," Colangelo said.

The following season, 2017–18, he was recorded eating a burger courtside while having his foot rubbed by a trainer before a game. An early iteration of the Embiid discourse emerged: *Joel's lazy. He doesn't care.*

"I STILL SEE a lot of people bring it up, talking about the silly stuff I used to do as a kid, just my second, my third year in the league," he says. "I started playing basketball at 16. You would not be in this position by being lazy.

"Starting so much later than everybody else, having to learn the game at the rapid rate that I did, coming to a new country, not knowing the language, learning a different culture, adjusting, being by yourself, that would not happen if you weren't focused."

I ask him in what ways he is responsible for being misunderstood.

"Go through all the media narratives," Embiid says. "I haven't been paying attention. So, I don't know what's happened."

He's kidding, of course. I'm expecting him to smile any second now.

But he doesn't. Instead, he repeats himself, his voice more urgent: "Go through the narratives."

Joel makes excuses.

"It's not making excuses. When you're hurt every year and everybody knows it, it's the truth," he says. "Now, do you believe, if he was 100 percent, does he have what it takes to have a chance at winning? I think a lot of people believe that because I've shown it in the regular season when I was healthy."

Now, he's the one leaning forward.

"What if I did this and I was like, 'You know what? I'm just going to chill all season and coast and average 25? Or 20.' And in the playoffs, I go average 30. Would that make me look great?

Probably. If I went from averaging 23 to 30—a playoff riser. Oh, my God. Joel Jordan. Whatever.

"The Brooklyn series two years ago is a perfect example. Double me everywhere. Half court, as soon as I had the ball, that coach was like, 'Go get it.' And guess what? I was fine with it because we kicked the ball out, we made shots, and we won. But guess what it did? It lowered the stats.

"So, if that's the narrative that's out there, I'm OK with that because I know what I'm going through and I know what's going on. And no one is in my body to understand what I'm going through."

"What other narratives?" he asks.

Joel cares too much about individual awards.

"If you are in a position to win an MVP, I don't care who you are, you're going after it because I never believed I would be in this position, first of all. Second of all, when I got in the league, I thought, 'Yeah, maybe I'll have a chance to be a great defensive player.' I never thought I was going to be this good offensively."

His thoughts drift back to the playoffs, irritated: "You're basically saying that he's playing harder in the regular season than he's playing in the playoffs, which doesn't make sense because if you look at the minutes, the minutes rise. And you're playing harder. And you do more on both ends of the floor."

He takes a detour into his postseason plus/minus numbers, which measure up with the greats of the game, then chides himself for sounding like his trainer and confidant, Drew Hanlen, who 13 minutes into a phone call sent me a link to Embiid's playoff stats.

"You want one more?" I ask.

"Yeah, I want it," he says.

Joel is talented but doesn't have the extra intangible stuff it takes to lead.

"No one is a winner until they've done it. I'm fine with that narrative because I haven't done it. Charles Barkley, great player, right? But he never won. [Allen Iverson] never won.... But that doesn't mean they weren't great. They were amazing.

"Everybody leads in his own way. I lead on the court," Embiid continues. "Over the years, you also grow, and you learn a lot. If you ask my teammates now, they'll tell you a way different story than my teammates a couple years ago, because years ago, I was nowhere to be found."

"Why?" I ask.

"I don't know," he says, briefly leaving the battle against his critics to look inward. "I think it goes back to how I was raised. I don't want to say lonely but I came to the States, I was alone. I always taught myself to not trust anybody."

By the summer of 2014, the 76ers were a year into then-GM Sam Hinkie's "Process." At that point, all Hinkie had produced was an injured big man (Nerlens Noel) and a flawed, soon-to-be-traded Rookie of the Year (Michael Carter-Williams) who couldn't shoot.

Embiid arrived in Philadelphia that fall and had already been declared out for the entire 2014–15 season after surgery on the navicular bone of his right foot. He was 20 years old, cast as a redeemer, and a cloud of uncertainty hung over him and the team.

Deflecting the pressure, he instead played the part of the cutup. He loved social media banter, fronting a one-sided Twitter romance with Rihanna and taking a ride with Vice Sports where he sarcastically played up stories that he drank Shirley Temples by the pitcher.

His former coaches in Florida and Kansas barely recognized him. "I didn't know that he had the ability, or wanted to have the ability, to have all eyes on him," Self says. "In my mind, I'm thinking, 'Jo, what are you doing? Would you just keep your mouth shut? Stay off of social media.'"

Behind the scenes, Embiid was in crisis. He was crushed under the grief of his brother's death, living alone at the Ritz-Carlton in downtown Philadelphia, as if he didn't expect to be around for long. He played video games, ate poorly and hardly slept. His foot wasn't healing. He couldn't play basketball. Rumors spread that his weight rose to nearly 300 pounds. He contemplated quitting.

"He was hanging on by a thread," one friend says.

His relationship with the 76ers unraveled. Embiid believed something was wrong with his injury, but the team brushed it off as laziness, several sources told me. Frustrated, he quit showing up to rehab and training and stopped communicating with the team.

"I had to start being an a--hole," Embiid says. "Whatever they asked me to do, I was, like, 'I'm not doing it.'"

The 76ers, unsure what to do, responded by repeatedly fining him. Embiid tells me he stopped keeping track of how much he was fined that year after the amount reached $300,000. "It's worth it," Embiid remembers thinking. "They're not listening to me, and I'm not going to keep putting my body at risk."

Hinkie, meanwhile, raced to modernize the 76ers' health and performance operation with Embiid in mind. At the start of Embiid's tenure with the 76ers, his rehab had been overseen by an intern.

Hinkie hired David Martin, who had been working at the Australian Institute of Sport for 21 years. For the next year, Martin fielded monthly email questions—the most rigorous professional test of his career. One question stood out: *How would you build a team and treatment plan for a 7-footer with a navicular bone injury?*

In one of their first meetings, Hinkie drew a square and then another square inside that one that took up about 90% of the first one's area. The first square was the totality of Martin's time. The second was time spent getting Embiid healthy.

Hinkie emphasized that Embiid's combination of size, skill and talent was extremely rare. Martin had worked with special forces units and a Tour de France champion, but as he listened to Hinkie, Martin thought he had found the culmination of his career.

In June 2015, Hinkie and Martin flew to L.A. to meet with Embiid and Dr. Richard Ferkel, who had operated on Embiid's foot a year before. The news was bad. Embiid's foot had not healed. Embiid sat quietly. Martin was the stranger in the room. He felt Embiid watching him.

"He has a real piercing gaze," Martin says. "You can just see him looking at you in a way. Like, 'Don't feed me any B.S.'"

Embiid remembers feeling disappointed but also vindicated. He was right, and his critics within the organization were wrong. Something had been wrong with his foot. He wasn't imagining pain or making excuses. This was a difficult lesson to unlearn; it is easy to become a prisoner of one's own victories.

A nebulous and contradictory *they* began to form in Embiid's mind: the coaches, front office executives and medical staff who had "cast him out," as one friend puts it. They wanted to save their jobs, he thought. They wanted him to play hurt—to prove themselves right for drafting him, to prove themselves right for not wanting to draft him, to sell tickets, to show that he didn't sell tickets. *They* would be just as happy if his career lasted 18 months or 18 years.

Loyalty became overwhelmingly important to him, and his search for it, his willingness to test it in others, became a way he forged a path within the organization. He remained in a protective bubble, amassing and shedding adherents.

Martin, eager to prove he could be trusted not to abandon the young star, often stayed in Philadelphia with Embiid instead of traveling with the team. One day, he noticed a mess of $20 bills on a table in Embiid's apartment. Martin suggested Embiid put the money away; traffic through Embiid's apartment was frequent—nutritionists, trainers, housekeeping staff.

No, Embiid said, if anyone took anything, he would know.

"Are you planting this?" Martin asked. "Are you trying to see if anyone will steal from you?"

Embiid didn't say anything.

"Maybe you're checking me out," Martin said. "Maybe you want to know if I would take your money."

They both laughed.

"I don't necessarily do it *to* people," Embiid tells me. "I'm just going to leave it, and if something is missing, I'm going to know exactly who took it.

"Because that's happened; I've had money or other things that have gone missing," he says.

"When it did happen, I didn't need to confront anybody. That was just, like, 'OK, all right. I got what I needed.' Now, I know not to talk to these people and never trust them."

AFTER EMBIID'S SECOND surgery in the summer of 2015, Martin assembled a small, protective core of advocates.

Kim Caspare, an experienced physical therapist, quickly became a key member of the group. In what others mistook for laziness in Embiid, she saw fear—this was a young man who didn't trust his body, the advice he was getting or the intentions of those giving it. Embiid needed "a family around him," Caspare remembers thinking. "'I've got to just take care of this guy, because this guy is hurting.'"

Caspare began as a consultant but became such a steadying force for Embiid that the Sixers hired her full time in 2019 as a physical therapist. Her initial stint was supposed to last four weeks, but she went on to work with Embiid for nine years.

By the time Embiid met Caspare, his reputation for flaking was well-established. But Caspare says that was never a problem between them. "Never once did Joel not show up when we said we were going to," she says. "But I've seen over [nine] years that he didn't show up for many people."

Embiid did not bend to the traditional command structure of NBA teams. "It's the NBA. People are wrong and strong all the time," Martin says. "They say it loud and say it with authority and expect people to listen to them—and Joel's not easily manipulated."

Embiid's reputation within the organization was toxic. Everyone was talking: training staff, coaches, massage therapists, reporters, even interns whose main activity was snagging rebounds.

"People whisper in hallways," Martin says.

Embiid was an enigmatic giant, his face shrouded in a hoodie, shuffling slowly and wordlessly, appearing and disappearing, it seemed, on his whim. "He just wouldn't talk to anybody on the team," one person familiar with the situation says. "Literally completely silent."

Things got so bad that Martin drew up a confidential survey for members of the performance department. They were asked to answer multiple-choice questions about several players, including Embiid: *Do you think this guy will ever be an MVP? An All-Star? A starter on a championship team? A rotation player? Do you think he'll end up in Europe?*

The results were dismaying. "Nobody believed in Joel," Martin tells me. "They just weren't into him." Martin was convinced Embiid would never be able to heal in an environment that was so hostile. He decided to go to Hinkie and owner Josh Harris and ask to take Embiid out of the country, to Aspetar, an orthopedic and sports medicine hospital in Doha, Qatar. After some resistance, the team relented.

Desperate to make the trip count, Martin scheduled a series of appointments with experts. Embiid often missed those meetings. When Martin asked him what was wrong, Embiid explained that he wanted to stay on an NBA schedule. Games are played in the evening; players go to bed late and wake up late. That made sense to Martin—one of the goals of the visit was to improve Embiid's sleep. When he switched the consultations to the afternoon, Embiid's absences and tardiness stopped. Embiid liked Aspetar so much that the team sent him twice, once in February 2016 and again for a two-week stint at the end of March that year.

A pattern had emerged. Those loyal to Embiid and invested in his future became an organization within the 76ers organization.

Embiid's allies saw him as wounded and gifted and alone and in need of reinforcing. Martin, trying to understand how to work with Embiid and explain his behavior, started reading in-depth about working with gifted children. They flattered his proclivities (he did not communicate, so they became his go-betweens, covering for his tardiness) to get the most they could out of him, if not always the best.

"I probably should've just been like, 'Get your ass up off the table and get on the floor,'" Caspare says. "But I didn't do that because he would've maybe gotten off the table and walked into the locker room and done nothing. So I couldn't risk that."

I asked Martin if he feels now that he might have coddled Embiid during this critical early period of his career.

"Joel is really unique," Martin says. "When you sit with him for a bit, it feels like you don't need to play by all the rules. There's a lot of weird rules in the NBA, and there's a lot of things that are culturally expected in the NBA, and they're really designed to make owners feel comfortable, and general managers feel powerful, and coaches feel intelligent, and support staff feel respected."

"I don't know if I'm being perceptive," Martin continues. "Or if I'm creating an elaborate justification for him."

Years later, it's difficult for those who surrounded and supported Embiid to parse between damaging him with indulgence and saving his career.

"If you really went back to the past, and you were there in those moments, you would know him being in the league, and becoming an MVP is a miracle," one member of Embiid's circle says. "There are top coaches, there are top league executives who did not believe he would step foot on the court again."

I SAT WITH 76ers head coach Nick Nurse and president of basketball operations Daryl Morey in a sunny conference room at the team's practice facility in Camden, New Jersey. It was a late morning in early April, and players trickled in for practice.

There were only five games left in the season. The Sixers would lose four of them, finishing 24–58, their worst record since 2015–16, the year before Embiid's debut.

Both men have had run-ins with the Sixers fans and media throughout the 2024–25 season. At MIT's Sloan Sports Analytics Conference in March, Morey caused a stir when he said he used AI modeling to help make personnel decisions and angered fans further when he said, "Anger is all that drives Sixers fans as far as I can tell."

For Nurse, it was the aggravation of spending the season as a mix between surgeon general and press secretary, a role he was clearly fed up with. "I'm up there answering medical questions all the time," Nurse tells me, his hands gesticulating. "'Hey, [Embiid's] getting this thing on Tuesday. We'll have more information on Wednesday.' Well, something happens on Tuesday, and this MRI doesn't happen, and now it's Wednesday, and they're like, 'You said you were going to give us an update today. Why didn't you?' Well, the timeline has changed. That's the timeline I had two days ago, but now it's changed.

"Don't be mad at me, I'm just telling you what's happening."

The confusion about when Embiid would play became an ongoing storyline, causing frequent tension among fans, reporters and the organization. In late November, an unexpected Embiid absence turned the Wells Fargo Center into a mass game of Clue. Embiid was scheduled to warm up and then decide about playing, but he never did. One reporter said he wasn't even in the arena. Another said they spotted his knee brace in front of his locker. Another said they saw a cellphone on his usual chair but couldn't confirm whether the phone was Embiid's.

"He's insanely private," one Sixers staffer told me that night.

But not inscrutable. Nurse and Morey only had to look.

His pregame warmups were little operas. Every miss in his routine aggravated him. Missed and looked up at the sky, raised his arms and asked, why? Missed and rolled his eyes in contempt.

Missed and shook his head in exasperation. Missed and bent over to clutch his sweats at the knee, hands balled in tight fists.

There was more, a repertoire of Embiidian gesture and expression: There's the head clutch that means he's irritated with himself or a teammate but can also mean it's so stupid and ridiculous how good I am. There's the one he does when a shot comes off his fingers wrong but goes in anyway, where he tilts his head and does that thing with his mouth that signals he's having a little mock think. A little jut of the lower lip, the "could be worse" face. There's the one where he shoots his arms out from his hips like he's about to flash finger pistols and say let me see your hands. Instead, his fists stay balled, and he swears at himself, viciously or rapturously.

He was waiting for things to go wrong, and they did. He somehow tripped and fell on two separate occasions during warmups. First in Chicago, where no one seemed to notice, and then again on Christmas Day against Boston, where the clip went viral.

When he got to his feet and slid off the black protective mask he had been wearing (weeks before, he had suffered the fifth major facial injury of his career, dating to his Florida AAU team), his face was a particularly Embiidian blend of expressions: He was pissed. Over it—I mean truly, deeply sick of it all. He couldn't believe it, and then, wait, of course he could. He stared at the ground, shaking his head at it like even the parquet court was out to betray him.

He turned Christmas afternoon into a spectacle of exuberant spite. He hates Boston, and Boston hates him. Where better?

He Eurostepped past Jaylen Brown and Payton Pritchard for an and-1 and did the DX chop. He drained a 3 right before halftime and swung his arms into an "up yours" gesture that made the crowd shriek its loathing. He stood near center court yapping at fans, placing his hand over his heart, waving goodbye. He made two late free throws to seal it and walked backward with a diabolical grin on his face.

His moods descend on him and become the weather of a whole game, a whole team, a whole season.

"I THINK PEOPLE forget he had a real injury at Golden State," Nurse says. "But leading up to that point, he was playing the best basketball of his life."

It was some of the best basketball we have ever seen.

The Sixers were 26–7 with Embiid in the lineup before he injured his left knee at Golden State in January 2024. He was averaging 35.3 points in 34 minutes, outpacing Wilt Chamberlain's 1961–62 season and on his way to becoming only the second player in history to score more than a point a minute. He scored at least 30 in 22 consecutive games, the fifth-longest 30-point stretch in NBA history. He tallied 16 straight games with at least 30 points and 10 rebounds, tying Kareem Abdul-Jabbar for the second longest such streak.

In December 2023, the Sixers went 8–1 with Embiid on the floor. He averaged 40.2 points and 12.6 rebounds at a comical 60.6% shooting rate.

There were statement pieces, too. A 51-point, 12-rebound performance in a late December dismantling of the Minnesota Timberwolves. Then, in January, a breezy 70-point, 18-rebound outburst against the Spurs, the old-fashioned way—he made one of his two 3s.

Embiid missed the next two months after the Golden State game, recovering from meniscus surgery on his left knee. He returned late in the season, clearly hobbled, to make a playoff push. The Sixers won their final eight games and qualified for the play-in tournament, where they beat the Miami Heat and moved on to a first-round series against the New York Knicks.

Embiid looked dominant early in Game 1, starting 4-of-5. In the second quarter, he pump-faked, then stepped through and chucked the ball off the backboard, leaping past Mitchell Robinson to dunk the ball over OG Anunoby. It was an incredible, audacious move, an all-time playoff highlight until he landed and his left knee wobbled and he collapsed to the floor.

As he lay on his back, an overhead camera showed him with his hands clasped on top of his head, the left side of his face frozen. He made an improbable return in the second half of Game 1, though the 76ers lost. And after a controversial loss in the final seconds of Game 2, Embiid conducted his postgame interview at his locker with his head bowed and his hand over his brow, trying to hide his facial paralysis.

He was defiant, bristling as one reporter asked him a question in French. "I'm not talking in French," Embiid said, cutting the reporter off. He promised the 76ers would win the series.

But the pressure of his rushed return from injury was starting to tell. He had been diagnosed with Bell's palsy days before the series started, after he began suffering migraines. He was short of fitness because of the injury, visibly limping, worried about the integrity of his grotesquely swollen knee, enduring nearly round-the-clock treatment and forced to play heavy minutes in the most critical games of the season. His vision was blurry, and his head ached. He was hardly sleeping because his left eye wouldn't close.

Caspare began running Embiid through a battery of exercises to help him reorient himself in space, to move his whole head to scan his surroundings because his eye couldn't move in the way he was used to.

"I was sitting next to him in the locker room," his former teammate Nicolas Batum told me. "I saw his knee before every game, after every game."

Batum shook his head. "I saw his knee," he said again. "I have no idea how he could even walk."

Embiid doesn't know how he managed to keep playing. Hanlen would ask him after every game if he was going to keep going. "I was like, 'No. There is no chance,'" Embiid says.

Hardly anyone knew how bad it was. Information about him is at a premium in the best of times; in a crisis, he closes himself off. Embiid was "alone in his agony," Caspare says. "People don't really know what's what. They think it's his knee. But it's not his knee. It's his knee, it's his eye, it's his whole system."

In the middle of late-night treatment sessions, Embiid would look at Caspare, his eyes drained. "I don't know if I can do it again," he would say. "I can't do another minute." But then he'd talk himself back up, "OK, I'm going to do another minute."

Embiid cycled through a wheel of emotions: deflated, worried about his long-term health, overwhelmed by pain, desperate to play, desperate to be saved from himself, afraid of letting the team and the fans down, wary of letting anyone know what condition he was in.

On the morning of April 25, the day of Game 3, Caspare left Embiid's house after another late-night treatment session. She had seen enough. She sent Embiid a long text at 2:29 a.m.

It reads, in part: "Do you have the ability to give yourself some grace and compassion? I'm here to remind you that you are deserving of that. Who cares about what people think about your eye? You are allowed to fail. You're allowed to lose. But you are not allowed to feel shame or feel hopeless. There is no place for such emotions. You have fought. It has been a courageous fight."

She tried to give him an out, worrying his efforts had reached "crushing proportions." She urged him to play under a hard minutes restriction, even though it was the playoffs: "Maybe we discuss it with the team. Joel wants to go out there and give everything he has, but the team has to put a hard minute restriction on you, limit you to 25 minutes."

Regardless of his decision, she promised: "You can do anything. And I am with you no matter what."

She didn't hear from him that morning or afternoon. He showed up at her treatment table in the arena at his usual time. She started getting him ready. She handed him her phone.

"Did you read this?" Caspare asked.

"Yes," Embiid said.

They shared a look—he was going to play. Embiid scored 50 points that night in a must-win Game 3, a playoff career high.

The Sixers lost the series in six games. Embiid averaged 33 points, 10.8 rebounds and 5.7 assists. He had nothing left late in games when the adrenaline wore off and the pain took hold. "I knew I only had about two quarters," he says. "My body just was, like, 'Nope, that's it.' There was nothing I could do. I shot probably, like, 10 percent in the fourth quarter."

Embiid looks back at the series with ambivalence. "In those situations, you wish some of the people upstairs kind of had your back and were like, this is not OK," he says. "You're not playing."

"I've had to stop Joel a couple of times," says Martin, who left the team in 2019. "When he gets into competition mode, it's really difficult to have a meaningful conversation.... And that was before he was super famous."

Embiid worries that too often, he's made the wrong call, allowed himself to be coaxed back to the court too soon, pushed himself because of what type of player and person he wanted to be, taxing his body and leaving him vulnerable to repeat injuries. This is one of the feelings he's been trying to unpack in therapy.

"It's basically damned if you do, damned if you don't. Because if you don't play, then, you know, there's this whole narrative.... I never cared about the 'soft' comments," Embiid tells me on the phone. "All I cared about was the team and my teammates. I never wanted to feel like I was quitting on them. And obviously, that goes back to the whole thing in therapy about not wanting to disappoint people."

"Ultimately, I guess I made those decisions. And then you got to live with it."

Weeks before, at his home, when I brought up the Knicks series, he sounded like he had made a different kind of peace with his choices. I asked him if he was going to take steps to protect himself if others wouldn't.

He looked me in the eye and said, "We can sit here and I'll tell you I'm changing, but I know myself. I don't think that's going to happen.... I always want to play."

GRANT HILL, THE managing director of USA Basketball, watched Embiid toil through the Knicks-Sixers series from courtside as a broadcaster. He admired that Embiid played injured, even if he thought it wasn't "the smartest thing." Hill had spent a year recruiting Embiid for the Paris Games that would begin later that summer.

It started with a visit to Embiid's house in the fall of 2022. Embiid had recently become a citizen of France and the United States. His Olympic allegiance was up for grabs. Hill knew that Team USA needed a big who could contend with the size and physicality of the international game. The 1996 USA team Hill played on had featured Shaquille O'Neal, Hakeem Olajuwon and David Robinson.

"He brought a dimension to our team that we hadn't had in really quite some time," Hill says. "In previous Olympics, you know, we had bigs that were very mobile, bigs that could get out and switch, but weren't necessarily a post presence, with all due respect."

The meeting, which Hill thought might only be 15 minutes, went for nearly two hours and left a strong impression on Embiid. "He just came to get to know me," Embiid says. "I appreciated that."

Hill was equally impressed. "He was very thoughtful, very smart, very engaging," Hill says. "There was just a lot of depth.... I don't know if he's accurately or adequately portrayed."

Embiid gave no indication where he was leaning, and the two men kept in contact for the next 12 months. Hill visited the Sixers in a Boulder, Colorado, hotel on Oct. 4, 2023, sneaking past Sixers beat writers. Reports had surfaced that France wanted an answer from Embiid by Oct. 10. Embiid resented the ultimatum: "I was like, 'Nope, you're not going to do this to me.'"

Hill's phone rang the next morning. Embiid said he was going to play for Team USA. It was Oct. 5, Hill's birthday. "That was the best birthday present I got that day," Hill says.

When Embiid reported to camp for Team USA in early July, he was "not at his best," Hill says. "But we were patient…we knew we needed him." He had been working daily with Hanlen and Caspare by his side in the weeks leading up to the camp. By the time Team USA was in France preparing for its first match of the group stage against Serbia, Hill says Embiid "was the best player on the court."

Embiid was excited to do the little things. He geeked out about setting screens for Steph Curry. But he promptly got sick ("Really sick," Caspare says. "Nobody really knows how sick.") in the rain at the opening ceremonies, traveling from Paris to Lille apart from the rest of the team. He played wanly against Serbia in the first game of the round-robin and sat out the next game on orders from team doctors.

His presence was vital in the medal rounds, though, especially in the semifinal rematch against Serbia. For the first and only time at the Paris Games, Team USA trailed in the fourth quarter before Embiid and Curry led a comeback. Embiid scored seven consecutive points.

"We don't beat Serbia without him," Hill says. "Us being patient with him had paid off."

But nothing with Embiid is ever so simple. "He's pushing his risk of injury in a setting where he's not even gaining anything except riding tails of other all-stars," wrote one veteran Philadelphia commentator before the medal rounds had begun.

Even Embiid's choice to represent Team USA was criticized. On one hand, by those who said Embiid should have tried to qualify with Cameroon, and on the other by members of the French delegation who said Embiid had approached them about playing for France and being fast-tracked to French citizenship for that purpose.

As the Sixers rolled into their season and Embiid's knee did not respond to the ramp-up, his Olympics moment became tarnished. A new appendix was added to the Embiid discourse: *Glory seeking in Paris had cost him his health.*

Embiid and his circle are quick to swat the notion away. "Compare that to the way I was moving against New York," Embiid says. "No, it did not set me back." His responsibilities in Paris were limited, and his playing time was irregular. He says he wasn't 100% but his knee and body felt good.

"He was OK to get his contract, and he was OK to win a gold medal," Caspare says. "We were OK."

THE 76ERS FALTERED while Embiid missed 17 of last season's first 21 games through injury and league suspension. Injuries to Paul George and promising rookie Jared McCain compounded the problem. The public grew hungry for answers. Embiid's old doubts, the sense of spooky doom that accompanied some of his injuries, began to take hold. Postseason after postseason, a broken face, a shattered thumb, an LCL sprain, a hyperextension, meniscus tears, Bell's palsy.

"Every single year, you start asking yourself questions like, 'Why?'" he said to reporters during the Knicks series. He brought it up again in December, saying he struggled not to feel bad about himself.

And next to his bad luck has always been this: "He's so big and he's so mobile," Caspare says. "That's two contradictory things when you jump, and land, and load, and push." Embiid is large, dense and long and yet he has traits one finds in smaller athletes: rhythm, coordination, scary fluidity. Martin compares Embiid to a semi-truck maneuvering like a Ferrari. "That's a lot of inertia," he says. "It only takes a small angulation to be a little bit off and then the joints are going to weather that abuse."

His brilliance sits hand in hand with his risk. We are always witnessing both.

And on top of his risk was this: He had never quite silenced his own doubts. The questions that had persisted in his mind since his days at The Rock when he baffled teammates with the idea he was going to have a normal job or that led him into Self's office wanting to redshirt and then wanting to stay even when he had emerged as the consensus No. 1 pick—those are voices only recently subdued.

Embiid won his first MVP in 2023, but it wasn't until the next season that Hanlen felt Embiid fully stepped into his talent. "There were so many times where I was, like, 'You're better than you think,'" Hanlen says. "Last year [2023–24], was the first year that I thought he had 'f--- it' mode. Where he just knew, like, 'Man, I am good enough to impact the game in whatever way I want to.'"

Embiid says before he injured his left knee against Golden State, he was close to what he considers his final form: 35, 12 and 7 rebounds on 50-40-90. "I'd seen everything. There was nothing you could throw at me that could throw me off," he says. "From me being 16 to 29, and even in those 13 years of playing basketball, I missed about five years' worth of games.... The way I see it, that was a normal progression for someone that started playing basketball that late."

Last year's injury threatened to undo all this work, not just physically but psychologically. "I'm telling you that this confidence, the trust, that's a big factor," Caspare says. "He never really believed in himself until very recently and then he got fricking hurt."

Loved ones started to notice just how badly he was struggling. Eventually, it was Jameer Nelson, a friend and former player and now assistant GM of the 76ers, who approached Embiid in September and recommended a therapist Nelson trusted.

"I was, like, 'There is no chance. I don't believe in none of that,'" Embiid says.

But he trusted Nelson, so he started going—and he's still going.

"To this day, I'm 100 percent committed to it," Embiid says. "But I will not sit here and say that my belief is ever going to be 100 percent in therapy."

The sessions have gifted him a narrative about himself, an explanation he defaults to frequently. "Feeding into the pressure of you got to play, got to go out there, can't let people down and this and that," Embiid tells me. "That's probably one of the reasons why I'm in this position now."

The uncertainty about his knee reignited old tensions between Embiid and the Sixers' front office.

After months of uncertainty, false starts and recurrent swelling, Embiid couldn't take it anymore. In February, before a loss to the Milwaukee Bucks, Embiid told ESPN's Lisa Salters that he would need another surgery, which reportedly surprised the organization. Morey acknowledged that surprise in our meeting.

"If you don't want to listen to me, then I have to find something else, to make sure that I'm going to be listened to," Embiid tells me. "When I told Lisa that, I think it was a cry for help.... It feels like everybody refuses to acknowledge what's actually going on."

NICK NURSE LEFT to run practice as Morey and I lingered in the conference room. We spoke about his job, about being in the middle of Embiid's story when so many talk as if we're at the end, about holding a bunch of possible futures in your head at the same time.

"That's exactly how I think about it," Morey said. "Very few people get that actually."

But the story wants an ending. So I asked.

I asked Morey about a possible future where Embiid's knee doesn't heal, a future where he's never an MVP-level player again.

Morey paused.

In September, he and 76ers owners bet $192.9 million against that future, a three-year extension that will pay nearly $70 million to Embiid at age 34. They bet George's four-year, $212 million contract, too, a deal for a skillful but diminishing player whose value as a premium third option can only be justified if he's the elite supplement to a championship-winning superstar. Embiid is the kind of player you double down on, triple down. You lose your job over him. Disappear. Hinkie did. Hinkie's mentor, Morey, might yet.

"I take it back," Morey said. "I don't think…"

Morey never finished the sentence. Mulling that future sent a current through his body, and through the entire room. His words came apart in a laughing fit. He laughed, and the 76ers' communications rep, who had been sitting in the room, laughed, and I laughed, and I didn't even know why.

Morey stood out of his chair and walked to the door. "I'm going to choose to think of the positive today," he said, and walked out.

I VISIT EMBIID again a week after his surgery in April, enter through the same door, use the same bathroom, slip on the same shoe covers, walk down the same pale hall, sit in the piano room and wait. He's watching baseball on the phone again when he lumbers in, his left knee wrapped in gauze. He's wearing a Team USA T-shirt and Sixers shorts and furry slides. This is his second operation on that knee in 14 months. He's already started rehab.

He has a cold. His voice is scratchy, even quieter this time. He looks exhausted.

I tell him what happened with Morey and then ask Embiid the same question.

He gives me an inscrutable look. "I'm about to stand up and leave, too," he says.

And it happens all over again. He starts wheeze laughing. A member of his team who has been sitting in the room starts laughing, and I start laughing.

When it's over, Embiid is coughing, tears in his eyes.

"It's going to work out," he says after we settle. "I believe in myself, believe in God. It's all about doing the right things. It's going to pay off. So, there's no question of if it doesn't work out."

I asked them both to look into the abyss, a future of salaries they couldn't live up to, careers they couldn't rescue. They both laughed in my face and said, yeah, right.

Earlier, I had asked him a broader version of that question. I asked him to imagine a future where he's finished playing basketball, whatever successes and failures the next few years bring.

He talked about escaping, traveling with his family, enjoying the fruits of his labor. His face was expectant. "The end looks like y'all would never hear from me again," he says. "I can't wait."

THE PIANO ROOM—OCCUPIED by dark oversized ottomans, high curtains, a marble fireplace—looks ripped from a catalogue. Sometimes Embiid and Arthur sit at the piano to bang some keys, but the only people who play are Embiid's sister or Nurse when one of them comes over.

But above the couch where Embiid sits hangs a painting, a portrait of Embiid dressed like an aristocrat. At his chest, he holds a Goldendoodle. I laugh when I first see it.

Embiid tells me he snagged it from the set of a Mountain Dew shoot. A gag gift, hardly worth remarking upon except it's the only thing in the room that looks like a decision made by Embiid.

The Goldendoodle in the painting is Klaus Hinkie De Paula Embiid. De Paula is Embiid's wife's last name. Hinkie is for Sam, the GM who drafted him and was forced out before Embiid played a single NBA game. Klaus is Embiid's favorite character from *The Vampire Diaries*, a TV show he has rewatched maybe 10 times.

All of this sounds funny until Embiid tells me he rewatches his favorite shows to fall asleep at night.

And there's no laughter left in it after I learn his dog Klaus died in October 2020 from internal injuries after an elevator closed on him. Like many of Embiid's jokes, the painting contains shards of his pain.

"I lost my best friend this morning!" Embiid posted on Instagram. "Knowing my background, Dogs in the house was always unheard of and impossible, but having you taught me something different about this world we live in."

"That was my first dog," Embiid later tells me on the phone. "When you have that, and tragedies like my brother, you don't want to forget. You always want to..."

His son, Arthur, who has been floating in and out of the conversation, playing hide and seek, grudgingly leaving to brush his teeth, walks back in, having lost his struggle to avoid being sent to bed.

"Can I get 21 hugs?" Arthur asks.

I listen to them count out their hugs.

"OK, love you," Embiid says.

When Arthur is gone, Embiid continues: "I don't know how people deal with death. But I always felt like I need stuff to kind of remind me of why I'm doing this. The reason why I'm in this position is because I pushed myself because of what happened to my brother.... Same thing with the birth of my son.

"Sometimes when you just walk by and you look at that, it kind of reminds you. But then again, at times, that also has a negative effect. When I go home to Cameroon like I did last year... there's a lot of pictures of my little brother all over the house.

"You see it, you just start crying."

"I HOPE ONE day someone makes a show or, whatever, writes a book about it," Embiid says of his time with the Sixers. "We went from GMs having burner accounts. And then we've had great guys that we drafted, but then again, stuff happened that no one could ever figure it out. The drama, Sam Hinkie being kicked out, bringing in the Colangelos. It's been a lot of things that have happened. And that's what I'm talking about when I'm talking about continuity. It starts at the top."

In so many ways that count, he's at the top. Through three front office regimes, three head coaches, a gallery of failed, too quickly aborted or still emergent costars—Ben Simmons, Jimmy Butler, James Harden, Tyrese Maxey—Embiid has been the 76ers' continuity, and the ways he has learned to carry or shirk that responsibility have shaped the 76ers in his image.

Embiid learned the game in a solitary way. He was an autodidact who would watch Hakeem Olajuwon videos and replicate the moves. He blew Self and his Kansas teammates away with the rapid evolution of his skills. One night, before Kansas played New Mexico, Embiid walked into a teammate's room with his laptop open. Look at this move, he said. I'm doing this tomorrow.

And he did. Embiid caught a botched lob pass on the break, backed down his defender on the low block and left him frozen with a dream shake, finishing with an up-and-under reverse layup. "Ooh! Ooh!" Shouted the color commentator. "Olajuwon!"

When Hanlen and Embiid work on something new, Hanlen will demonstrate the move while Embiid circles him, asking questions and narrating what he's seeing. "Show me again. Show me again. Show me again," Embiid says. Then, "I got it."

But the restless solitude in which he nurtured his talent is no use in leading a team. "I never wanted to be a vocal leader," Embiid tells me. "The way I was going to lead is my action. When I get on the court, whether it's playing hard, carrying the team, doing whatever I have to do to put us in a position to win, that's how I always saw myself as leading."

His first NBA head coach, Brett Brown, tried to steer Embiid toward the example of another quiet-by-nature big man, Tim Duncan. But Duncan had the organization of the Spurs around him. Embiid had the Process, and all its attendant chaos. And he had a Twitter account, where he put on a persona at odds with who teammates and coaches encountered in private.

"You try to find yourself. You don't really know who you are," Embiid tells me, exasperated with how the foibles of his youth have clung to him. "I tried to become a little bit more serious because I felt like that was more me.... The trolling part, which I still do, I couldn't keep up with it because that just wasn't me."

Embiid's season and a half long stint alongside Harden, with whom he grew close, accelerated Embiid's evolution as a leader. Their bond taught Embiid that closeness off the court translated into on-court success. Maxey has been a particular beneficiary of this change. It was Embiid who steered Hanlen and Maxey together. And last summer, when Maxey signed a new deal with the 76ers, he credited Embiid as the first person to vocally support him. In Sixers camp in October, Embiid was the first to single out the promising rookie McCain.

Embiid speaks of Harden with deep affection. He thinks the 76ers gave up too quickly on that iteration of the team. What was required after their Game 7 collapse against Boston in 2023 was tinkering in the margins, not another restart.

"I kept going back to it, the continuity," Embiid says. "When you feel like you have something, instead of building up on it, you just start over. And that's been like that every single year."

LACK OF CONTINUITY is more than just an organizational gripe for Embiid, it has been a feature of his life since he committed himself to basketball as a teenager. And with the 76ers, the departures are partly of his own making.

He refuses to exert himself over personnel decisions, only to later complain about them. The exit of Jimmy Butler is the most obvious example. His reasons for this are rooted in his own personal history.

He wonders what would have happened to him if the 76ers had an established star with the clout to ship him out early in his career.

"I always told myself I will never be responsible for someone losing their job, someone getting traded, someone getting fired," Embiid says. "Don't ask me about if we should sign and if we should trade anybody."

It's a principled stance, but it's also a desire to have something his talent and status will not allow him: innocence. When Embiid plays his latest sports video game obsession, *MLB The Show*, he trades and trades until his team is invulnerable, only then does he play, securing in make believe what he cannot in life—a guarantee against his doubts, his silence, his bad luck, his frailty, his complicity.

"No one knows this, but even James [Harden] is not talking to me," Embiid tells me. "That's the part I don't like about being 'that guy,' because it puts you in the middle of those situations. Because if you ask James, he probably believes I had something to do with him not being here. And I'm just like, 'I won the scoring title. You won the assists title. We had a pick-and-roll that was unstoppable.'"

"It hurts when you feel like you haven't done anything wrong," he continues. "When you think you have a relationship like that with somebody...you lose a lot."

EMBIID INVITED MARCY and Ric Hansen to a Sixers game last fall in Orlando. They waited by the locker rooms after the buzzer, taking pictures with Nurse and a couple of players until Embiid was dressed. Marcy sent me a picture of the three of them from that night. Embiid, wearing a cream sweat suit, stands between her and Rick, arms around them both.

"She's one of my favorite persons," Embiid says of Marcy. "She was great to me."

"We talked about his son," Hansen says of the reunion. "And I know that he's going through stuff. But I feel like he's settled, he's good."

She starts to cry softly.

"I wish I could see him more. And he probably wouldn't even understand that," she says. "I'm a mom. And I gave my heart to him as a mom. And I don't know that he ever received it that way."

Kim Caspare has a 5- and 2-year-old, but friends call Embiid her oldest kid. The first time we speak, she's on her way to relieve the babysitter. When I bring up a picture of her and Embiid hugging after he won his MVP award, she starts sobbing.

"I just know how many hours we put in that were not seen, that nobody knows about...365 days, I think we worked 355 of those days that year," she says. "Finally, he was seen. He held an entire team. The 76ers weren't that great then. He was the guy that got them great. He was that. He was the one."

She and Embiid stopped working together after the Olympics. There was no longer any way to balance working with Embiid with the needs of her family. She's based primarily in her New York offices, where she works with athletes throughout the NBA.

The pressures of spring and summer 2024—the Knicks series and the turnaround to make it to Paris, the worrying about Embiid's health with a major contract extension hanging in the balance—took a toll on their working relationship.

"I felt really helpless sometimes," she says. "I lost my guy. He's not in tune. I don't know. It was weird." He still showed up for her. He still worked hard. But he grew distant.

Embiid knows working with him on his body is an all-consuming job. He understands why Caspare had to break away, but if it were up to him, and her family situation allowed, they would still be working together.

We're on the phone and I hear something in his voice, something guarded, far different from the person who just counted out hugs with his son.

"Can I ask you something personal?" I say, which is ridiculous. Everything we talk about is personal.

A little pause. "Yeah," he says.

"Is that relationship OK?"

"If you want me to be honest," he says. "I'll be honest."

His voice takes on a hard edge: "We all have a job to do and my job, obviously, is to go out on the basketball court and produce."

Then it softens; he's about to show his wounds: "It just wasn't the same anymore. So, I felt like everything kind of changed when things got bad."

And I can hear it now, he thinks he's found another betrayal, another abandonment. He cannot see that maybe this time, the roles are reversed: "You want people to be there when things are going great, and when things are going bad, you want the same people that you trust. And I felt like that wasn't the case."

He and Caspare text every couple of months. When his relationships go sour, they tend to lapse into silence. He retreats into his formidable privacy. Caspare thinks this is the first year she won't be invited to Arthur's birthday party.

"You never know with Joel," she says.

I asked if that was hard for her.

"I gave my entire life to him—nine years," she says. "Yeah, it's kind of hard to fathom that."

WHEN EMBIID AND I speak for the final time in late June, he tells me he's making some changes this offseason.

"We're not going to push anything," he says. "For my whole career, I felt like we never took that approach."

A week before, Morey had said he was hopeful Embiid would be back in time for training camp in September.

"We don't have a timeline," Embiid tells me. "Hopefully, sooner rather than later."

I ask if the organization supports his new, patient approach.

"I don't know how they feel. The only thing I'd say is—this is a business," Embiid tells me. "It's all about the results.... If I come back early enough and I'm still not myself, guess what? You're not winning any games."

Embiid, who says the only "stain" on his career is being ringless, spent the postseason a picture of thwarted desire, too pained to watch any games, too pained not to pore over the box scores. "I wanted nothing to do with the playoffs," he says. Because of rehab, he hasn't stepped on a court. He resorted to texting his friend and Pacers' star Tyrese Haliburton to offer encouragement during Indiana's run to the Finals.

It was Haliburton who coaxed Embiid back toward the game. "He kind of got to me, he kept trying to convince me to watch," Embiid says. He tuned in to see Haliburton close out the Knicks in the Eastern Conference finals.

He ignored the Finals too until the lure of Game 7 proved irresistible.

When Haliburton went down with about five minutes left in the first quarter, his right Achilles torn, Embiid turned the game off in disgust. "Unbelievable," he says. "I kind of shed a tear."

We're talking regret. Still in his high-curtained piano room. By now, it's early evening, the light is starting to dim.

"I wish I had someone that could have told me," Embiid starts to say. "You know, when you're young..."

He stops, swerves into a surprising confession, unsolicited. He showed up late to the arena the night he scored 70. One of basketball's greatest scoring feats was tossed off by a player who had to scramble into his jersey, lace his sneakers in a hurry and skip his warmup. He's half sheepish, half bragging when he says it.

I watch him, try to read his face. I don't believe him at first. "You didn't just casually say you showed up and dropped 70 without warming up, did you?"

He looks at me and says, "I guess."

And for a second, I can't tell, hours into talking to him, months into looking at him, whether this is one of his tests of my credulity. But his smile starts to tell, slow and sly until it cracks into laughter, and I know—he's serious.

He takes me on a sentimental journey, one with familiar steps. First, he fesses up: "That's not the right approach. The right approach would be to come in, get your lift in."

Then manages, just about, to look himself in the eye: "When I was younger, I still took care of myself but not enough."

He takes a breathless step forward, near to the dark heart of it, the narrative that buttresses all the others, *What if Joel did this to himself, what if he's to blame*: "I don't know if that could've played a role in some of the injuries that I've had."

Before retreating into safety, consolation: "How do you stop someone elbowing you in the face," he asks. "How do you stop someone falling on your knee? You can't stop that. And it happened, a meniscus tear, because someone fell on your knee. It doesn't matter what type of preparation you do."

His weaknesses and his misfortune are no truer than his courage, his strength, his sacrifices, his astonishing ascent. He has made and is made of all of it.

"It's not like I didn't prepare myself. I did," he says. Embiid stirs, fists stuffed in the front of his T-shirt, and barely contains the eddying of unreconciled things. He burrows in. There's no place in him safer than this, no narrative more perceptive or elaborately justifying—he's taking his long view. How far he's come, how much it's cost and how much he's done, the miracle of it.

"Because if I didn't prepare myself and I didn't work hard, there's no way you start playing at 16 and you get to this level, it's impossible, I don't care what anybody says, and..."

And you know the rest.

DOTUN AKINTOYE is a staff writer at ESPN. He is a former Nieman Fellow and finalist for the National Magazine Award in profile writing.

For the Gaudreau Family, a Year of Incomprehensible Grief—and Immeasurable Strength

PETER BAUGH

FROM The Athletic • AUGUST 26, 2025

Twenty-five years ago, when building his family's home in Oldmans Township, N.J., Guy Gaudreau crafted the flooring by hand. He drove to Vermont and cut down the white ash trees from his father's wood lot. He oversaw the kiln-drying of the logs, the sawing of the planks, the molding of the panels—every step of the process.

The result is well-polished and smooth, except for a single spot.

Tucked away in the kitchen, the spot once contained a knot, which popped free, leaving behind a hole the size of a quarter. Naturally it became a source of material for Guy's two sons, John and Matty, who enjoyed trying to disrupt his usual even keel. The brothers would jokingly question their dad's choice of wood, talking about how it was cheap, until a riled-up Guy fired back, defending his work.

"That's the way the boys were," Guy says, chuckling.

Full of humor. Full of life.

On Aug. 29, 2024, the eve of their younger sister Katie's scheduled wedding, John and Matty were struck and killed by an alleged drunk driver while riding bicycles near their childhood home. John, a star winger for the Columbus Blue Jackets known to many NHL fans as "Johnny Hockey," was 31. Matty, who reached the second-tier AHL as a player before recently pivoting to coaching at the youth level, was 29.

In the year since, the Gaudreau family has found flickers of light amid the darkness. NHL teams have invited Guy, a retired coach and community rink manager, to join them on the ice for practices, and countless letters from around the world—Canada to Sweden, Germany to Russia—have filled the parents' mailbox. Meredith Gaudreau welcomed her and John's third child in April, four months after Madeline Gaudreau gave birth to her and Matty's first.

Through it all, Guy has been proud of his family's efforts to keep the boys' memories alive. Of course, he adds, "I'd rather have them back."

Voice just above a whisper, he continues, reminding himself of the cruel reality.

"I can't have them back."

No guide exists for processing grief of this magnitude. Each member of the Gaudreau family shares the same two losses, but their experiences are far from uniform. Guy sometimes wakes up in the middle of the night and wanders through the house, wondering how this bad dream came to be. Older sister Kristen posts pictures of the brothers to her Instagram story on a near-daily basis. When Katie traveled to Italy for her delayed honeymoon last month, she felt a sting every time she saw an advertisement for the 2026 Milano Cortina Olympics. John had so badly wanted to play at the tournament.

"Some days you have an OK day, and then halfway through the day something will hit you," says their mother, Jane Gaudreau. "Then some days you wake up and it just feels like someone is sitting on your chest."

Jane has learned to prepare herself for the predictably hard moments, like the boys' birthdays and Mother's Day. But others catch her by surprise. At her job, writing Matty's old jersey number, 21, on a piece of paper. At a family friend's wedding, watching the mother-son dance.

Or at home one day in March. As Jane walked through the kitchen, her foot tripped on the divot in the white ash floor.

It didn't hurt at first. But then she looked down, saw the hole and started to sob.

WITH A GUEST list topping 200, Katie's wedding was scheduled for Aug. 30, 2024, in the Philadelphia area. The day before, John and Matty went golfing with their fellow groomsmen, then returned with everyone to Guy and Jane's home. The Gaudreau brothers hung out in the hot tub by the backyard pool, laughing into the evening.

Sometime around 8 p.m., they hopped on a pair of bikes and rode off to see a friend.

Meredith last saw John that morning, before he left for golf, when he gave goodbye kisses to her and their daughter, Noa, and son, John Jr. He had packed the car "in perfect Tetris fashion," she later wrote in an article for the Players' Tribune, filling it up for John Jr.'s christening, Katie's wedding, and their eventual return to Columbus for the 2024–25 NHL season. It was the four-year anniversary of the day he asked Meredith to marry him.

Meredith was in her first trimester of pregnancy. Madeline was further along, at 23 weeks. Her last interaction with Matty came that evening, while she was at a Philadelphia hotel where visitors were staying for the wedding. They texted about their future baby's name, which they had already decided.

At approximately 8:19 p.m., according to court documents, John and Matty were cycling along the narrow shoulder of Pennsville Auburn Road, around two miles from the family home, when an SUV moved to the center of the two-lane road to pass. From behind, a Jeep Grand Cherokee then sped up to the right of the SUV, fatally striking the brothers from behind. The driver, who is facing charges of aggravated vehicular homicide and involuntary manslaughter, among others, posted a blood alcohol level of 0.087, above the legal limit of 0.08.

In the aftermath, the family converged on Guy and Jane's house. Guy dropped to the floor and bawled. Meredith was unable to stand up, she wrote in the Players' Tribune, at once "awake and having nightmares." It was all too much for Madeline, who caught a ride from a friend to her and Matty's home some 10 minutes away. She went to bed by herself, hoping to wake up and learn it had just been a terribly vivid pregnancy dream.

Both Gaudreau parents were admitted into a local hospital that night: Guy out of concern for elevated heart rate and blood pressure, and Jane because she had entered what family described as a catatonic-like state at the house upon hearing the news, incapable of responding, no matter how loud Katie screamed her name.

Jane and Guy each stayed two nights at the hospital. They were put in separate rooms, but the nursing staff allowed Jane to climb into Guy's bed and sleep there. There was no cure for what they were feeling, but at least they weren't alone.

LESS THAN A week later, Meredith and Madeline visited a funeral home to plan a joint memorial service for their late husbands. At one point that day, the two wives were in a room with Lewis Gross, John and Matty's agent. When the funeral director asked where Meredith and Madeline wanted flowers to be sent, the group began tossing around the idea of accepting donations to a charity.

"Maybe we should start a foundation in the boys' name," Gross suggested.

In setting up the John and Matthew Gaudreau Foundation, the wives focused on areas of passion for its namesakes. In a public letter launching the foundation in March, Meredith and Madeline, who serve as co-presidents, expressed a desire to "expand youth ice hockey opportunities, help hockey families facing tragedies, as well as help families that are unfortunately also affected by drunk driving, like ours."

Now a registered 501(c)(3) non-profit, the foundation maintains an online store selling hoodies and hats—products the brothers would have worn. The wives are planning their first event, likely a golf outing. Someday, Madeline says, they hope to pass the reins on to the next generation of Gaudreaus.

"A lot of times when Matt and John are spoken about, it's with a lot of sadness and heaviness, and rightfully so," Madeline says. "But I want to change the narrative, and rather than talking about the tragic way we lost them and how they should be here, talking about the foundation and what we're doing with it is what I'm trying to do."

The foundation has received ample support from the hockey community. Meredith was amazed to learn that three NHL players even asked for donations to it in lieu of gifts at their respective summer weddings: Blue Jackets defenseman Zach Werenski, who also had Noa Gaudreau serve as flower girl, and the Florida Panthers' Matthew Tkachuk and Sam Bennett, both of whom played with John on the Calgary Flames, his first NHL team.

"I look at it as, 'I have an opportunity to do a lot of good and help people who need help,'" Meredith says. "That's what feels good to me."

Guy and Jane, meanwhile, pursued a separate charitable effort in putting on the Gaudreau Family 5K, which raised money for an adaptive playground at Archbishop Damiano School, a school for students with special needs where both Jane and Kristen work. A family friend came up with the idea, and a group of nearly 20 handled the organizing. Neither parent was ready for such a large undertaking so soon after losing John and Matty.

The race took place in Sewell, New Jersey, on the last day of May. Less than 24 hours before, Jane saw that the weather forecast included rain. She went upstairs to the brothers' childhood room. Aside from trading the two twin beds for an adult-sized one, the family has kept it virtually unchanged over the years. The dresser is still full of the boys' sweats, swimsuits and other clothes they used when visiting home.

Jane plopped onto the bed. She stared up at the sports-themed wallpaper bordering the ceiling.

"Hey guys, I know I haven't heard from you or you haven't given me any signs," she said. "But maybe you could just do me this one favor."

The rain passed by the time of the race.

MADELINE ALWAYS LIKED the idea of having tattoos, but wanted to be certain she would never regret her choice before getting one. Clarity has come over the past year. She now has six, including a "J 13" for John and his jersey number on her left arm, Matty's name below her ring finger, his and their child's initials on her right wrist, and a particularly special one on her left abdomen.

"Love, Your Husband," it reads.

Madeline took those words from a card Matty once gave her. The tattoo is in his handwriting. Others came before it, but this was the most emotionally difficult: Before the process began, the artist had mixed the ink with Matty's ashes.

Both Meredith and Madeline have now gotten multiple tattoos with their husbands' cremated remains, all done by the same New Jersey–based artist. Now, the wives are always carrying John and Matty with them.

They aren't alone. Guy, Jane, Kristen and Katie all wear bracelets with the brothers' jersey numbers on them. At Katie's rescheduled wedding in July, her bouquet featured those same numbers: 13 small roses for John and 21 large ones for Matty.

"I tried really hard to just keep saying their name," she says.

There are public tributes everywhere, too. At Hollydell Ice Arena, the rink where Guy worked as hockey director until 2020 and taught the brothers to skate, an ice sheet for younger players now bears a new name: the Gaudreau Rink. At Gloucester

Catholic, where John and Matty played high school hockey before leaving for the junior level in the USHL, a banner honoring them stands outside the gym across from a trophy case of photos, as well as a No. 13 Flames jersey autographed by John.

Multiple memorials have sprung up on the side of Pennsville Auburn Road. A cross with the boys' names rises from the ground, surrounded by artificial flowers. Two bikes, both painted white, are chained to a post, their wheels intertwined with weeds. It's part of a lush country area, surrounded by soybean fields, farming equipment and big skies.

Prior to the crash, Guy would frequently jog and bike down that stretch; now he refuses to go by it and isn't sure he ever will again. Madeline won't drive past the site either, unless absolutely necessary. She knows the memorials are well-intentioned. But to her, the white bikes represent how the brothers died—not how they lived.

For this reason, whenever Katie passes it while leaving her nearby house, the youngest Gaudreau sibling instead tries to imagine how happy her brothers must have been before the crash.

"They were the two closest people I've ever met in my life," she says. "I try to think about how they were probably joking with each other and laughing and being together."

THE BROTHERS ARE everywhere at Guy and Jane's house. The Hobey Baker Trophy that John won as college hockey's top player with Boston College in 2013–14 sits atop the dining room table. Matty's locker tag from a run with BC to the NCAA Frozen Four leans against a cabinet. A digital frame cycles through photos of the brothers on a kitchen counter, right above the quarter-sized hole in the floor.

Nearby, at the top of the refrigerator, a magnet of John and Matty's jersey numbers keeps a picture in place. It was taken one long-ago Halloween, before Katie was born. John and Matty are both toddlers in it, dressed as clowns. Jane is holding Matty, and Kristen carries John, a decade his senior. White face paint covers the boys' faces, as Guy stands between them wearing a pirate's outfit complete with an eyepatch.

Staring at her brothers on a recent summer day, Kristen sees their children.

"Look at that face," she says, gesturing to little John and then to a picture of Noa further down on the fridge. "It's the same face."

Like Noa, Carter Michael Gaudreau takes after his dad: He was born at 8 pounds, 3 ounces and 20½ inches—the exact same measurements as John. With big cheeks and a round face, middle child John Jr. follows John more in personality than looks—observant and a bit on the quiet side. Now 2, Noa is the only one old enough to have memories of her dad but doesn't quite understand what happened.

"I tell her you're in heaven and that we can look at photos and videos," Meredith wrote in her Players' Tribune article, formatted as a letter to John. "It crushes me every time."

Matty used to tell his wife he was born to be a dad. Now his son, Tripp Matthew Gaudreau, resembles him in his mouth and chin, Madeline says. Guy adds that Tripp is lanky—just like Guy's dad and just like Matty. His favorite toy is a hockey stick. Soon, as hard as she knows it will be, Madeline will bring him to a rink. Matty was so looking forward to that.

To Madeline and Meredith, the children offer purpose. After Tripp's birth in December, despite the cold temperature outside, Madeline noticed a blue butterfly by her hospital window. It stayed there until she was discharged. When she came home with Tripp, another blue butterfly greeted her at the door.

But life away from those sources of light is more difficult.

"I feel like I have two personalities now," Madeline says. "I have one when I'm with Tripp and I'm present and I feel happy.

"Then the other part, when he goes to bed, I just feel kind of like a shell of a human."

For Madeline, it's important to experience the sadness, often alone. Sometimes she walks outside and talks to Matty. Others she spends in silence, feeling his presence. In the days after the crash, someone gifted her a journal titled "Letters to my husband." She keeps it next to her bed and writes in it every night.

"Who I was is not anymore," she says. "I haven't quite figured out where to go from that."

On Friday, Meredith and Madeline plan to spend the anniversary of John and Matty's deaths together, with their children, on the Jersey Shore. The fact that it's the one-year mark, Madeline says, holds no significance to her. Every day without her Matty is painful. She doesn't want to give any added power to this one.

Through the pain, the wives are creating happy memories. Meredith brought Noa and John Jr. to pregame ceremonies honoring John in Columbus and Calgary last season. In June, when Meredith went to Los Angeles and announced the Blue Jackets' first-round pick in the NHL Draft, Noa watched on TV, clapping her hands and grinning.

"Go, Mommy, go!" she chanted.

On her first Mother's Day with Tripp, Madeline knew Matty would want her to do something for herself. Instead, she felt better doing something for him. Taking care of their two-acre property used to always fall to Matty, who never minded the yard work. Guy and Jane had even given him a riding mower as a housewarming gift.

After Matty's death, a neighbor took care of the landscaping. But that day, Madeline felt the urge to do it herself. She looked up a YouTube tutorial on using the mower, put on a pair of Matty's brown boots, climbed into the seat and turned the key.

In the year since the loss of his sons, Guy isn't sure that the grief has gotten easier to manage. He knows he's not as fun as he used to be, and he worries that friends only see him out of pity. For a time, he struggled to talk about John and Matty's accomplishments or look at pictures of them without crying or feeling anger at all his family has lost.

"I start getting jealous of other people that have their kids, and I don't have mine," he says. "Not that I want anything bad to happen to anyone. It just makes me feel like I got [robbed]."

The sleepless nights haven't gone away, either. Sometimes, drifting through the house, he turns on the TV for a distraction. Or he calls his brother Eddy and cries through the phone. Recently, though, he believes he's started turning a corner in at least one regard: Reminiscing about his late sons is easier.

Standing in the kitchen, Guy smiles as he recounts John's first NHL goal, scored in his Flames debut wearing a No. 53 jersey now kept in the dining room. He raves about Matty's growth at Boston College, developing from a freshman who barely played to the team's leading scorer as a senior. He laughs about preparing steaks, cheese omelets and milkshakes for the boys' breakfasts, trying to help them add weight to their skinny frames.

"Good kids," he says. "Good boys. It's hard to get up every day without 'em."

After taking September off from work, Jane returned in October to her job as a finance associate at Archbishop Damiano. The job is part-remote, and she carpools with Kristen on the days she goes in. Jane doesn't like driving alone. The quiet makes her think of John and Matty, and if she turns on the radio, sad songs do the same.

The stream of letters arriving at the house helps. In one, a mother wrote about how Matty, while playing for the USHL's Omaha Lancers as a teenager, took her son, a nervous newcomer to the team, under his wing. In another, the author wished that Jane would give talks on how to keep a family close. Katie thinks she should write a book.

"We might not have had as much time as we wanted, but the time we had was better than a lot of people have with their families in an entire lifetime," Jane says. "And I would rather have that and have that closeness and be together than not have that."

Though retired, Guy stays busy. He runs, mows the grass, cleans the backyard pool and takes trips to see his mom in

Vermont, where he taps trees to make syrup. In addition to serving as a guest coach at practices with the Blue Jackets, Flames, Philadelphia Flyers and Vegas Golden Knights, Guy took the ice with Team USA at February's 4 Nations Face-Off, where he learned that general manager Bill Guerin had originally pencilled John in for the national team at the upcoming Olympics.

But all Guy could really do when on the ice with the NHLers was push pucks around and chitchat. At that point, the former coach wasn't mentally ready to run drills again.

The pain lessens when he's with his grandkids, who call him Pop-Pop. He notices it when leading Kristen's 10-year-old daughter Kamryn through pushups and other basic exercises in the living room—as he did with John and Matty and as he will likely do someday with their kids. He notices it on days when he babysits Tripp and hopes that the boy inherits Matty's athletic prowess.

"When I'm holding him, I don't have such a big hole in my heart," he says.

Before their deaths, John and Matty told Guy that they wanted him to come out of retirement to teach their kids hockey. Guy hopes he can find the strength to do that and prays that all four of John and Matty's kids want to play the sport that their fathers loved.

This summer, he helped a friend coach a two-week camp in Pennsauken, N.J., a 30-mile drive from the Gaudreau family house. He spent seven hours a day on the ice with children ages 6 to 12, split into two sessions each day, leading drills and power skating sessions and scrimmages. His brain, he says, needed to start working again.

Guy describes himself as a demanding coach, unafraid to yell. This style didn't fully come out at the camp, but he "started feeling a little bit like my old self," he says. Watching the kids improve, he continues, "I kind of felt like I accomplished something."

Getting up at 6:45 a.m. every morning proved a struggle, and Guy returned home exhausted at each day's end. But he enjoyed the experience. He slept better those nights.

PETER BAUGH is a staff writer at The Athletic focused on covering hockey and writing features. Now living in Brooklyn, he is originally from St. Louis and attended the University of Missouri. He is the author of *Force of Nature: How the Colorado Avalanche Built a Stanley Cup Winner*. The Athletic's Alex Prewitt was his editor on this story.

Notable Sports Writing of 2025

ANDREA ADELSON
"Inside FSU softball coach Lonni Alameda's cancer experience." ESPN. May 21, 2025.

SHIREEN AHMED
"Canadian national soccer player Ali Ahmed one of many athletes thriving during Ramadan fast." CBC Sports. March 25, 2025.

ROBERTO JOSÉ ANDRADE FRANCO
"Crawford, Álvarez and the decline of the superfight." ESPN. September 18, 2025.

KEVIN ARMSTRONG
"Born to Run." NJ.com. November 13, 2025.

NATE ATKINS
"Rams' Byron Young started out at Dollar General. Now he's on the verge of NFL stardom." The Athletic. November 14, 2025.

FATMA ELZAHRAA BADWY
"Inside Fatma Mahrous' journey to becoming Egypt's Paralympic weightlifting star." *The New Arab*. January 1, 2025.

ABE BEAME
"Why the Liberty Is the Best Sports Franchise in New York Right Now." BK Mag. September 4, 2025.

JOSEPH BIEN-KAHN
"Island Time." *The Believer*. December 18, 2025.

SAM BLUM
"Accused of giving away his team's pitches, Derek Bender reckons with the world's mistrust." The Athletic. February 27, 2025.

DOUG BOCK CLARK

"30 Hours in a Hurricane, on a Race With No Course." *The New York Times Magazine*. March 12, 2025.

ROB DAVIS

"Nike Says Its Factory Workers Earn Nearly Double the Minimum Wage. At This Cambodian Factory, 1% Made That Much." ProPublica/*The Oregonian*. April 25, 2025.

MICHAEL-SHAWN DUGAR

"Marquette King was one of the NFL's best punters, then he was gone: 'I'm definitely blackballed.'" The Athletic. November 21, 2025.

BRUCE FELDMAN

"Raising Arch: How Cooper and Ellen prepared Texas' QB for the Manning family spotlight." The Athletic. June 25, 2025.

NATHAN FENNO

"Seattle athletes were terrorized in a spree of burglaries. 'They feel unsafe in their homes.'" The Athletic. October 15, 2025.

NATE FILE

"After one of its most beloved players suddenly died, the 'Dadball' pickup basketball group is fighting to save the gym where they play." *Philadelphia Inquirer*. June 5, 2025.

LEE V. GAINES AND GEOFF STELLFOX

"How 3 Muslim sisters helped change the rules of American women's wrestling." NPR. July 12, 2025.

BRITTANY GHIROLI

"How did Mike Trout, the best baseball player of his generation, fade away?" The Athletic. November 5, 2025.

YANG-YI GOH

"Shai Gilgeous-Alexander on His NBA Rivals, Fashion Secrets, and Why He Wants to Retire Young." *GQ*. October 13, 2025.

IRA GORAWARA

"When sorority influencers meet Alabama football, game days turn into a campus-wide catwalk." The Athletic. November 9, 2025.

SEAN GREGORY
"A'ja Wilson Is *TIME*'s 2025 Athlete of the Year." *TIME.* December 11, 2025.

ANDREW GREIF
"An NBA star's family fought for years to help their brother. Now they want to help others." NBC News. October 10, 2025.

MATT GUZMAN
"'The Mustang': Now Longest-Tenured Spur, Keldon Johnson Ready to Ride Again." *Sports Illustrated.* October 22, 2025.

DAN HAJDUCKY
"Inside the shift in evaluating MLB draft catching prospects." ESPN. July 8, 2025.

DOUG HALLER
"Clayton Kershaw, Max Scherzer and a rookie-year meeting for the history books." The Athletic. August 6, 2025.

KATIE HEINDL
"Bury your monuments," Basketball Feelings. March 30, 2025.

ADAM HIMMELSBACH
"The Making of AJ Dybantsa, the most exciting basketball prospect in Massachusetts history." February 26, 2025. *Boston Globe Magazine.*

RYAN HOCKENSMITH
"'I found your dad': The mystery of a missing climber." ESPN. April 17, 2025.

MITCHELL S. JACKSON
Shedeur Sanders Didn't Fall Down the NFL Draft Board, He Was Pushed. But Why?" *Esquire.* April 30, 2025.

CHLOÉ COOPER JONES
"Drag City." *Victory Journal.* August 28, 2025.

JAY CASPIAN KANG
"Heir Ball: How the Cost of Youth Sports Is Changing the N.B.A." *The New Yorker.* June 23, 2025.

LULU KESIN
"Dawn Staley's home is with South Carolina women's basketball but she's forever Philadelphia." *Greenville News.* June 5, 2025.

JULIE KLIEGMAN

"What Does A Great Trans Athlete Deserve?" Defector. November 15, 2025.

LEA KONCZAL

"The (Mostly) True Story of Galveston's Legendary Deaf Lifeguard. *Texas Monthly*. August 31, 2025.

AISHWARYA KUMAR

"Inside NASA astronaut Sunita Williams' journey through space." ESPN. March 18, 2025.

EDEN LAASE

"For Harvard's Harmoni Turner, There's a Time to Play, and a Time to Heal." Hoops HQ. March 14, 2025.

KIESE LAYMON

"The Worst Shot Ever Taken." *The Believer*. December 18, 2025.

EMILY LEIKER

"Justin Jefferson is finding he fits in the fashion world." *Minnesota Star Tribune*. December 19, 2025.

KEVIN MERIDA

"LeBron James: A sense of where he is." *The Washington Post*. January 15, 2025.

EVAN MOORE

"Justice Batted Last: The Untold Struggles of Black Chicago Baseball Players." Chicago Defender. March 3, 2025.

JASON QUICK

"George Karl, Hall of Fame coach, wonders: Does his voice still matter to the NBA?" The Athletic. May 7, 2025.

DANIEL ROBERTS

"Polymarket and Kalshi Are Shitposting Their Way to Legitimacy." Front Office Sports. November 29, 2025.

ALYSSA ROENIGK

"At Jackie Robinson's high school, Altadena rebuilds after fire." ESPN. June 20, 2025.

MICHAEL ROSENBERG AND PAT FORDE

"Inside the Gambling Ring Allegedly Linked to Point Shaving Across Pro and College Basketball." *Sports Illustrated*. February 25, 2025.

CHIP SCOGGINS
"'Healing is possible': After his son was convicted of murder, Mike Tate felt a stronger calling to mentor Minneapolis youth." *Minnesota Star Tribune*. October 8, 2025.

SUSAN SLUSSER
Giants' Matt Chapman on his life with Tourette syndrome: 'You can still accomplish anything.'" *San Francisco Chronicle*. September 3, 2025.

ANDRÉS SOTO
"How Diana Taurasi's fiery competitive streak ignited a women's basketball revolution." *The Los Angeles Times*. March 2, 2025.

ALEX SQUADRON
"John Fanta Has All the Fun." Hoops HQ. January 27, 2025.

ROMAN STUBBS
"A beloved skier, an audacious jump and the complex grief left behind." *The Washington Post*. April 5, 2025.

JAYLON THOMPSON
"Scouts raved about Jac Caglianone for 1 reason. Then he gave them more to consider." *Kansas City Star*. May 12, 2025.

MARCUS THOMPSON II
"Luka Dončić's Dallas return reminds us that some things are bigger than titles." The Athletic. April 18, 2025.

WRIGHT THOMPSON
"The Boston Celtics and the price of history." ESPN. May 15, 2025.

LAURA VAN DEN BERG
"Rule-Breakers." *The Believer*. December 18, 2025.

DAN WETZEL
"The predatory web of sextortion increasingly ensnares young athletes." ESPN. August 10, 2025.

JACOB WHITEHEAD
"Suleiman Obeid—Answering Mohamed Salah's questions about the death of the 'Palestinian Pele.'" The Athletic. August 16, 2025.